From Tom R

7

MICHIANA
POTTERS

MATERIAL
VERNACULARS

Jason Baird Jackson, *editor*

The

MICHIANA POTTERS

Art, Community, and Collaboration in the Midwest

MEREDITH A. E. McGRIFF

INDIANA UNIVERSITY PRESS

This book is a publication of

Indiana University Press
Office of Scholarly Publishing
Herman B Wells Library 350
1320 East 10th Street
Bloomington, Indiana 47405 USA

iupress.indiana.edu

*Manufactured in the
United States of America*

Cataloging information is available
from the Library of Congress.

ISBN 978-0-253-04964-3 (hardback)
ISBN 978-0-253-04965-0 (paperback)
ISBN 978-0-253-05240-7 (ebook)

1 2 3 4 5 25 24 23 22 21 20

Cover image: Pottery from the author's collection. All of the pieces pictured were made by potters who have exhibited at the Michiana Pottery Tour and/or participated in Michiana wood firings.

Top shelf (left to right): Jennifer Beachy, Parker Hunt, Dick Lehman, David Gamber, Mark Goertzen, Stephanie Galli, Todd Leach.

Second shelf (l to r): Justin Rothshank, Unzicker Bros. Pottery (Tom and Jeff Unzicker), Chad Hartwig, Brandon "Fuzzy" Schwartz, Bill Hunt, Dick Lehman, Todd Pletcher.

Third shelf (l to r): Irina Gladun, Eric Strader, Samantha Hostert, Mark Goertzen, Eric Botbyl, Brandon "Fuzzy" Schwartz, Mark Goertzen.

Fourth shelf (l to r): Marvin Bartel, Sadie Misiuk, Keith Hershberger, Fred Driver, Troy Bungart, Mark Nafziger, Zach Tate.

Bottom shelf (l to r): Moey Hart, Troy Bungart, Unzicker Bros. Pottery (Tom and Jeff Unzicker), Justin Rothshank, Todd Pletcher, Cindy Cooper, Dick Lehman.

FOR THOMAS, MILES, AND RILEY

CONTENTS

ACKNOWLEDGMENTS

As with any extensive project, I could not have completed my research and writing without the help of numerous others. First, my unending gratitude to my husband, Thomas DeCarlo, who has been my friend, my partner, and my sounding board for every idea that I have pursued in our years together. His enthusiasm for my research, his eye for all things artistic, and his insightful questions and comments have guided my work in more ways than I can count, and his love and assistance both at home and in the field are appreciated beyond words. I am also eternally grateful to my parents, Gary and Lori McGriff, who provided me with the education and encouragement that initially set me on the path to becoming an artist and scholar. Without their unwavering support, and that of my extended family, I would not have been able to complete this book.

I am grateful also to my children—both of whom arrived during the course of my researching and writing—for the inspiration, light, and love they have brought into my life. It is beyond wonderful to be able to learn from them and in turn to introduce them to the worlds of folkloristics and ceramics. And, of course, an extra thanks to all their grandparents for their support, particularly the childcare that allows Thomas and me time to work on our respective projects!

Throughout the process of researching and writing, I have also been fortunate to have wonderful, supportive friends, many of whom are close enough to call family. Jesse, Kristina, Shannon, Michelle, Suzanne, Kelley, Emily, Meg, Jeremy, Tiffany, Shelly, Jess—you have all kept me going through the good times and the bad, and I am forever grateful to have each of you in my life.

I must also thank the faculty of Indiana University's Department of Folklore and Ethnomusicology; you welcomed me with open arms, taught me to be a folklorist, and provided incredible guidance as I began to pursue this new career. In particular, I would like to thank Pravina Shukla for her unwavering enthusiasm for my research and many words of wisdom along the way. She was the first person to show me that becoming a folklorist and studying material culture was a feasible path and went on to provide me with tremendous educational and professional opportunities over the years; I will remain forever grateful for her continued support. Likewise, Jason Jackson welcomed me into the Mathers Museum and, along with the rest of the staff there, helped me to navigate curating an exhibit for the first time. Thanks also go to Michael Foster and Diane Goldstein for their insightful advice on earlier versions of this text, and for their confidence in my ability to complete this research. I must also thank Henry Glassie for his scholarship, interest in my research, and many words of encouragement over the years; without *The Potter's Art*, I might never have found my way to folkloristics.

Many thanks also go to the rest of the faculty and staff of the Folklore Department for their friendship (to the staff in particular for their ever-cheerful guidance on administrative matters). They have been fantastic colleagues during my time at Indiana University and the American Folklore Society. Brandon Barker deserves thanks for spurring my interest in embodiment, and providing guidance as I initially delved into that research. Similarly, Julie Van Voorhis in the art history department provided vital feedback on early drafts of chapter 4. Additionally, my heartfelt appreciation to Jon Kay of Traditional Arts Indiana and Judy Stubbs of the Indiana University Art Museum, who both provided me with not only job opportunities but also invaluable advice on tackling the writing process; their mentorship went above and beyond work-related matters.

Similarly, many thanks to the board, staff, and other leaders of the American Folklore Society who welcomed me into my role there and encouraged my endeavors, both professional and scholarly. To my AFS coworkers, past and present—Tim, Lorraine, Jessica, Jesse, Roz, Evangeline, Alex—you have provided me with a wonderful place to work, and I'm ever grateful for your moral support on projects, like this one, that I have taken on outside of work. A special note of appreciation goes to Tim Lloyd; with research interests closely aligned to my own, he has been a marvelous mentor in recent years and also, unknowingly, gave me inspiration for the structure of this text during a guest lecture, long before we ever worked together.

I also thank the staff of Indiana University Press who have supported the production of this book. In particular, my thanks to Jason Jackson and Janice Frisch for their editorial expertise and encouragement in bringing this book into the Material Vernacular series, and to Allison Chaplin for her assistance in keeping the project moving. My genuine thanks, also, to the two anonymous reviewers who provided encouraging feedback and suggestions for improvements to this manuscript.

Above all, my deepest gratitude to the potters who informed this text. I first learned to make pots from Gloria May, Gary Paschal, Mike Thiedeman, Linda Arndt, Vance Bell, and Ted Neal, and I'm ever grateful for their training. And I could not have written a single paragraph without the insights the Michiana potters kindly shared about their lives and work. In many ways, this book ought to list innumerable coauthors, and I have tried to include their own words in this manuscript as often as possible. In particular, my thanks go to Dick Lehman, Mark Goertzen, Justin Rothshank, Todd Pletcher, Marvin Bartel, Bill Kremer, Zach Tate, Troy Bungart, Moey Hart, Brandon "Fuzzy" Schwartz, and Stephanie Galli for their encouragement, hospitality, and eagerness to engage in numerous conversations about their work. Many thanks, also, to the partners and family members who have been likewise welcoming and kind, particularly Jo Lehman, Suzanne Ehst, Brooke Rothshank, and Anna Corona. And a special note of appreciation to Scott Lehman for his friendship many years ago, which I am pleased to have renewed in recent years.

Those who are most centrally involved in the Michiana pottery community, or who spend a greater portion of their days balanced between clay and fire, are included in the following pages as much as possible by name and with photographs. Yet there are dozens of others who engage with this tradition, who flow in and out of the broader movement, which is urged ever onward by a collective passion for handmade pottery. I am grateful to each and every person who has contributed to the vibrant Michiana pottery tradition; it is an honor to know and learn from you all.

The
MICHIANA
POTTERS

ONE

MICHIANA CONNECTIONS: AN INTRODUCTION

I once heard serendipity described as "the joy of hitting a target you didn't know you were aiming for"—hopefully one day someone will point me to the source of this apt description. Certainly it is one I can relate to, as my research has had many such moments over the years. I did not set out to study the potters who make wood-fired pottery, nor did I plan to focus my research on the American Midwest. However, I was born and raised in Indiana and enjoyed playing with clay as a child, and I believe my background allowed several chance meetings and unexpectedly helpful connections to lead me to this area of research and, ultimately, the completion of this book. I'll begin with my journey in order to give readers some background on my own positionality within the worlds of ceramics and folklore, particularly regarding how I found my way to the potters of Michiana.

I first learned of Dick Lehman's work in clay around twenty years ago, when I was preparing to travel to Japan as a high school exchange student. By that point in my life I had a little experience with ceramics and certainly some enthusiasm for making art, but my knowledge of the big names in American pottery was essentially nonexistent. Dick's son Scott Lehman was also participating on that trip to Japan, and Scott and I became good friends through the course of our travels; we even stayed in touch for a few years afterward. I can vaguely recall meeting Dick at one of the orientation meetings in preparation for the trip, and I remember learning that he was a potter and had connections to Japanese potters. I had recently spent some time with clay and greatly enjoyed it, so I was intrigued to learn of his profession. The memory of that encounter stayed with me, even as I eventually lost touch with Scott and our journey to Japan became a more distant—yet very fond—memory. I subsequently heard Dick Lehman's name at various points throughout the years, from my teachers in ceramics, other potters at art fairs, and so on, but it was not until much later that I would realize the serendipitous connection we had made.

In the intervening years between high school and graduate school, I became more and more enthusiastic about pottery. I learned to fire pots in both the Japanese and American styles of raku and completed a BFA in ceramics and a BA in Japanese language and culture. I toyed with the idea of becoming a full-time artist and participated in art fairs and occasional juried shows. About a year after graduating from Ball State University, I spent a month in Japan making pots at the Shigaraki Ceramic Cultural Park, called *Togei no Mori* in Japanese (fig. 1.1). This was a further bit of serendipity; I would later learn that one of Dick's good friends is a wood-firing potter in the town of Shigaraki, and Dick has visited him there. In addition, Merrill Krabill, Goshen College's current ceramics professor, worked as an artist-in-residence at Shigaraki around the same time I was there (although our stays did not overlap); when I interviewed Merrill in the course of my research into the Michiana pottery community, we reminisced about our mutual experiences at Shigaraki.

While I had an enthusiastic beginning to my ceramics career in my twenties, and I still make and sell pottery and sculpture on occasion, these days I find my interest in ceramics is more of an academic one. I entered graduate school intending to analyze the cross-cultural contexts of raku, since it had been for many years my own focus within the world of ceramics. When I finally began the project of interviewing Indiana potters in early 2012, I was working on my MA in folkloristics at Indiana University, and I (like many beginning ethnographers before me) had little idea where such a project could lead. But fate took its course, and I soon reconnected with Scott and Dick Lehman, beginning new friendships after so many years and unknowingly starting down a path that eventually led to the book that lies before you now (fig. 1.2).

The bulk of my research for this book was conducted in collaboration with Traditional Arts Indiana (TAI), an organization committed

Fig. 1.1. Part of the Shigaraki Ceramic Cultural Park (*Togei no Mori*) facility in Japan. (*Photo by author*)

to "expanding public awareness of Indiana's traditional practices and nurturing a sense of pride among Indiana's traditional artists. It calls attention to neglected aesthetic forms that firmly ground and deeply connect individuals to their communities," a goal they accomplish through documentation, archival work, and public programming (Traditional Arts Indiana, n.d.). My role as a fieldworker for TAI was predominantly on the Indiana Potters Survey, a project I developed in 2012 that entailed surveying professional potters and pottery ateliers around the state of Indiana. The project began as a practicum, developed after conversations with director Jon Kay about my desire to possibly work in public folklore and my existing knowledge of ceramics. He thus suggested I might find some way to work with current potters in the state.

Little did I know what an extensive and rewarding endeavor that would turn out to be. Between early 2012 and 2016, my fieldwork and documentation for the Indiana Potters Survey involved recording audio interviews as well as photographing the artists, studio spaces, processes used, and completed artwork. My focus in the survey was on production potters, by which I mean potters who create functional pottery in large

Fig. 1.2. Scott and Dick Lehman, just after unloading Mark Goertzen's kiln in July 2013. (*Photo by author*)

Map 1.1. Map showing towns and counties in Indiana and Michigan that may be included in the Michiana designation. *(Map created by the author)*

quantities, who usually work full-time making ceramic wares, and who are generally creating items that are thrown on the wheel and glazed and fired in such a way as to be useful in everyday life.

To date, I have sat down for formal interviews with about twenty potters around the state of Indiana, many of whom live in Michiana. For outsiders, *Michiana* is often an unfamiliar word; bringing together the names of two states, it describes an informal regional designation centered around the border of northern Indiana and southern Michigan.[1] The extent of the region is ambiguous, but the main towns where the potters featured here have lived and worked include Elkhart, Goshen, Middlebury, and South Bend in Indiana as well as Cassopolis, Three Rivers, and Constantine in Michigan (see map 1.1). However, it is also important to note that while their addresses may indicate these cities or towns, most of the potters choose more rural properties that lie on the outskirts rather than in the town proper. For those familiar with the landscape of the American Midwest, the scenery encountered while driving through Michiana is easily recognizable: flat plains and gently rolling hills, large plots of farmland dotted with old farmhouses and gambrel-roofed barns, and occasional densely wooded areas (crucial for providing the wood for wood firing, which will be discussed in more detail in chap. 3).[2] Rivers and small lakes are also in abundance in certain parts of the landscape, and both summer homes and full-time residences often line these little waters. Fishing, canoeing, and other watersports are popular pastimes with many residents, including the potters, many of whom are avid fishermen or sailors in their spare time.

My first introduction to the potters of Michiana came early in my fieldwork, when I interviewed Tom Unzicker—a former resident of Goshen and graduate of both Goshen College and Indiana University—for the Potters Survey. At the time of our interview in April 2012, Tom and his brother Jeff were the proprietors of Unzicker Bros. Pottery in Thornton, Indiana, where they made and sold large wood-fired vessels along with some smaller wood-fired tableware and serving dishes. During our interview, Tom mentioned having worked with Dick Lehman and Dick's former apprentice Mark Goertzen in Goshen, Indiana. Hearing Dick's familiar name, I decided I could not pass up the opportunity to reconnect with old friends, so I contacted Dick, Scott, and Mark (who now owns and runs Dick's former studio in Goshen) to arrange a visit. In August 2012, I travelled to Goshen to interview both Dick and Mark for the TAI project; both welcomed me graciously into their studios and spoke quite enthusiastically about their work in clay. As it turned out, my visit was timed quite serendipitously; the very first Michiana Pottery Tour would be held the following month, and I learned about it just in time to plan a return trip. Both Mark and Dick had a hand in planning the tour, and both strongly recommended that I come back at the end of September to experience it. Upon my return I spent a wonderful day visiting the many potters who were participating in the tour, and I soon began to realize the extent of the pottery community within this region. On the tour's eight stops, I encountered potter after potter creating beautiful wood-fired pottery (and many who worked with other techniques as well). Afterward, it occurred to me that there were an astonishing number of potters working full-time in this area, and yet, in my experience, so few people outside of the world of contemporary American pottery—and indeed, few within it—seemed to realize that such a cohesive group existed in northern Indiana; as a longtime resident of Indiana and a ceramic artist myself, I was astonished I had never heard mention of the extent of the ceramic work being done in that region. I was intrigued, to say the least, and thus returned time and again to Michiana to interview more of the potters, to learn about their stories and their art. Admittedly,

Fig. 1.3. Pottery studio from the 2014 exhibit "Melted Ash: Michiana Wood-Fired Pottery" at the Mathers Museum of World Cultures. *(Photo by author)*

I began to neglect my larger survey of Indiana potters in favor of learning more about those in this specific region.

My return trips to Michiana over the course of the next year culminated in my curation of an exhibit at the Mathers Museum of World Cultures in Bloomington, Indiana, called "Melted Ash: Michiana Wood-Fired Pottery." This exhibit opened in August and closed in December 2013 and featured a hands-on mock potter's studio that illustrated pottery-making processes (fig. 1.3), a full-scale model of the front portion of a wood-fired kiln (fig. 1.4), written and pictorial descriptions of the wood-firing process, and a display of pottery from four of the full-time production potters in Michiana—Dick Lehman, Mark Goertzen, Todd Pletcher, and Justin Rothshank—whom I had identified as being central to the wood-firing tradition and who were, fortunately, able to participate. An additional and rather unique aspect of the exhibit was the inclusion of an area where visitors were given the opportunity to physically pick up and engage with handmade functional pots. The tangible exhibit at the Mathers Museum was accompanied by a corresponding online exhibit through the Traditional Arts Indiana digital archive, titled "Beyond Melted Ash," which also focused on the Michiana wood-firing tradition.

Fig. 1.4. Model of the front of a wood kiln from the 2014 exhibit "Melted Ash: Michi-ana Wood-Fired Pottery" at the Mathers Museum of World Cultures. *(Photo by author)*

In conjunction with these two exhibits, I also organized "Stoking the Fire: A Contemporary Pottery Symposium," a one-day event in November 2013 that brought together potters, students, and scholars from around the Midwest to engage in conversations about clay as a medium, the wood-firing process, and the significant human connections that are made through creating pots. I was pleased that many Michiana potters were able to participate, and while I originally envisioned the symposium would appeal primarily to Indiana potters and/or those within a relatively short driving distance from Bloomington, I was surprised and pleased to receive a panel proposal that included Keith Ekstam, professor of art and design at Missouri State University; Dale Huffman, professor of art and chair of the Art Department at Carlow University in Pittsburgh, Pennsylvania; and two potters (Dick Lehman and Zach Tate) from the Michiana area. Both Keith and Dale are close friends with potters in Michiana and have collaborated with them on numerous wood firings over the years, and each of them brought a group of students to attend the symposium. Todd Pletcher and Bill Kremer were also able to travel from Michiana to be part of the symposium. A wide range of topics was covered, including personal commentaries about experiences making pottery, international encounters, experiences with different kinds of ceramics-oriented communities, the collaborative nature of wood firing, and overviews of a few regional pottery traditions outside of Michiana. As the primary organizer of the event as well as the exhibit curator, I was happy to have the opportunity to bring together so many pottery enthusiasts from around the Midwest. Overall, the experience fueled my desire to continue my research in the Michiana area and to further explore the sense of community developed among potters.

The following pages concern my research with these Michiana potters, which began in 2012, continued in earnest through 2016, and is still ongoing (though not as intense as it once was) as I finish writing this book in 2018—I imagine my connection with the people of this area will be a lifelong one. Throughout this time, I have been engaged in tracing the development of a thriving regional group of artisans and what Mark Goertzen has designated the Michiana Aesthetic, a set of ideal characteristics sought by many of the Michiana potters. Considering wood-firing results, the Michiana Aesthetic generally refers to a preference for heavy natural-wood-ash deposits and glossy glaze surfaces and a tendency toward cooler rather than warmer colors. However, as I will explain in later chapters, additional aesthetic elements also tend to show up even in ceramic work that is not wood-fired, including dripping or layered glazes, and forms and decorative effects the potters have borrowed from one another through working together.

Going beyond the visual, the term Michiana Aesthetic also functions as a signifier of community; the desire to seek similar visual elements in their pottery is a bonding point around which potters can (and often do) gather. This is particularly clear when they come together to fire a wood kiln that contains pieces made by many potters, sharing in the work of firing while working toward similar wood-fired effects on all their pots. While Mark, Dick, and others in the group have primarily used the Michiana Aesthetic as an indicator of these effects found on their pottery, I have expanded the term to encompass much broader aesthetic values, including ways of living, preferences in modes of display, and shared values and dispositions in their everyday lives.

In this aesthetic movement in Michiana, process and community are inextricably linked, as each supports the other. The presence of strong mentors (in the local schools, ateliers, and clay guild) instills an enthusiasm for pottery and allows for the training of new generations of potters; at the same time, the availability of energetic apprentices allows production potters to make and sell more work, and passionate students make teachers' jobs more enjoyable. Successful wood firing is dependent upon a dedicated group of potters to care for the kiln, and when coming together around the kiln, friendships are often strengthened, resulting in the mutual desire to fire again, to have another opportunity to enjoy the company of other potters and together improve upon the process. On and on, each circumstance begets the other, and the shared philosophies of work and similar aesthetic preferences discussed in this book can be in large part understood as the result of these interactions, some intentionally sought and some more serendipitous, like my own.

PRESENCE IN MICHIANA

Much of the premise of this book lies in the fact that presence still matters. While globalizing tendencies such as the online availability of information and social networking, as well as the ability to travel far, wide, and often, are prevalent in contemporary society, it is also true that local places, personalized spaces, and face-to-face interactions are still crucial in the experience of everyday life. My focus is on the development of a regionally specific tradition, a group of potters and artists who find the support of one another to be a major reason for pursuing their craft in a certain place. A strong occupational group and a corresponding sense of community are found where there are people who do similar work, share similar values, take pleasure in the same activities, and find frustration in similar aspects of life, and where they are in dialogue with one another about these values and goals. That is not to say that facets such as social media and mobility, which contribute to the accessibility of a very broad exchange of ideas in the world, are any less influential in the lives of contemporary makers; the potters I discuss here have a multitude of resources that they turn to, including broad networks of artists around the country whom they are familiar with and whose work they respect, as well as networks of friends and family who live in other cities or states, and clients and collectors from near and far who purchase their work. Yet when it comes to sharing physical resources such as materials and equipment, when it is a matter of building and firing kilns together, when one appreciates sharing a meal or a hobby or a meaningful conversation—in these crucial situations, the other artists who are consistently present and easily accessible in the same region are the most prevalent and are often the most important source of community feeling that an artist can have.

As folklorist Henry Glassie has said, "History is not the past. It is a story told about the past that is useful in the present. To tell the story of art, we project our values upon the past and gather out of it the works that are useful to us, works that talk to us about our interest(s)" (1999a, 218). I embarked on this project by asking potters to tell me their own histories, to reflect on moments of importance and people of great influence in their lives. In Michiana, their stories converged; they told me of mentors who have had an impact on the lives of many, of their shared enthusiasm for wood firing, and of Mennonite values acquired through heritage or faith. While broader networks also influence their work, it is quite clear that presence still matters. The landscape that provides the trees and thereby the wood for firing, the prevalence of the Mennonite heritage and faith that provides a community of people with shared values, the cost-effectiveness and appeal of small-town living, the development of a strong network of art teachers and spaces where art is valued and artistic growth can be pursued—all have been crucial to the development of the pottery community that can be found in Michiana today. In many ways, this pottery tradition stands apart from others that have been studied by folklorists in the United States; here, the community did not grow out of an abundance of good clay, as we see in the ceramics communities in North Carolina, for example, but instead out of an abundance of like-minded people with similar lifestyles and goals.

Understanding the act of making pottery and the social connections informing that act requires firsthand observation and conversations with those who do that work (i.e., ethnographic fieldwork). Most of the descriptions, observations, and analyses provided in this book rely heavily on the descriptions, observations, and analyses others have provided to me, particularly those individuals who live and work in Michiana and whose lived experience is deeper, more comprehensive, and more fluid than mine. Folklorists in recent decades have been closely attuned to the critical role of individual artists in making creative choices and taking most of the responsibility for the creation of individual works of art; my research, similarly, focuses on individuals, but it has also been focused on the means by which these individuals come together to support one another within their occupation and to create a shared sense of community. Some scholars have found it quite useful to study just one individual and their artistic creations, often focusing on the informant's life history as a way to frame those creative outputs. Several folklorists, particularly those attending to material culture and folk arts, have followed this model.[3] Although I agree that concentrating on one individual can lend great depth to an ethnography, it can have the limitation of foregrounding just one person's experiences of a society or group. Instead, by collecting insights from a number of individuals, I have attempted to merge their perspectives in order to develop a picture of the broader group (while still maintaining clear attributions in my writing when individual ideas are expressed).

Other folklorists taking this approach have provided a substantial influence on my writing. I note in particular the documentation of long-standing pottery traditions in the south and eastern United States, books such as those by John Burrison (2008 and 2010), Nancy Sweezy (1994), and Charles Zug (1986), or *The Living Tradition: North Carolina Potters Speak* (Mecham 2009), as well as C. Kurt Dewhurst and Marsha Mac-Dowell's work on pottery in Grand Ledge, Michigan (Dewhurst 1986; Dewhurst and MacDowell 1987).[4] These models have been a constant consideration during my fieldwork in Michiana; with these examples in mind, I have attempted to gather enough information to allow me, in the text that follows, to highlight multiple individuals who play a variety of roles within the Michiana pottery community.

The Michiana tradition of pottery is a relatively recent establishment that can be traced back to Marvin Bartel's teaching at Goshen College beginning in the 1970s; his former students now comprise a substantial portion of the group, many of whom have also been Dick Lehman's apprentices (and, in later years, Mark Goertzen's or Justin Rothshank's assistants or interns).[5] In my previous writings and presentations about the Michiana potters and their work, I have often called this an "emerging tradition," and by using such a term I am pointing to the recent development of this distinct group. While many of the Michiana potters have looked to similar influences from the global history of ceramics, in our conversations they have primarily defined themselves as a group in reference to local developments between the 1980s and 2010s. This stands in contrast to other locales where groups (often families) of potters are consciously choosing to work with many of the same materials, methods, and aesthetics as the many generations of masters who came before them.[6]

While the Michiana tradition has roots in different locations and historical moments, it has a relatively new sense of stability for its participants. Given that the number of potters in the area has grown so quickly over the last few decades, I feel confident in identifying this as a new locus of pottery production as well as a cohesive and vibrant ceramic movement. This is further demonstrated by the establishment and subsequent growth of the Michiana Pottery Tour; since 2012, it has become an annual tradition and an important aspect of the Michiana potters' yearly cycle of pottery production and sales. At one point in the course of my research, I counted seven studio potters in the Michiana region working full-time and supporting themselves through the sales of pottery. This figure tends to fluctuate; some leave full-time status when they need to supplement their pottery income with other jobs, some who have worked part-time later make the move to full-time, and some move away while new artists come to the area and establish new pottery businesses. Nevertheless, I believe there were between five and eight full-time potters in the Michiana group at any given time during the early 2010s.

In addition to these career potters, there are many more I have called "pottery-adjacent full-time"—three who teach ceramics at the college level and another who is retired from that profession, at least three who teach high school art with a focus on ceramics, the owner of a ceramics supply company established in the mid-2010s, and a potter who also makes and sells custom brushes made of natural materials and wooden pottery tools—all of whom I will introduce in the following chapters. Adding the dozen or more residents who routinely work in clay as a part-time job or who count it as a primary hobby, one finds there is a dense network of thirty or more people who call themselves potters or ceramic artists in Michiana. My focus has primarily been on production potters; as previously noted, this distinction includes those who create functional ceramics in large quantities and who are generally creating wares that are thrown on the wheel and glazed and fired in such a way as to be useful in the serving, consuming, or preservation of food. Items such as vases, garden wares, and decorative tiles also fit into this category. But my research has by no means excluded those who make other types of objects; many are represented in this book. In vernacular terms, I find potters often describe their work as being either "functional" or "nonfunctional" (sometimes "sculptural" or "decorative"), and yet this is a fuzzy distinction, one that potters do not see as an insurmountable boundary. Indeed, most contemporary potters tend to produce works that fit into both categories, though the balance of types of work varies from person to person. They may call themselves potters, ceramists, ceramic artists, or simply artists; whatever the chosen title, they make up a distinct occupational group, and it is their shared work in clay and sense of themselves as a cohesive community that drew my interest and is now the focus of this book.

THE MICHIANA POTTERY TOUR

The inaugural Michiana Pottery Tour took place on a crisp, clear Saturday, the twenty-ninth of September 2012. Established on the model of other tours around the country, this event encouraged visitors to travel, by car and of their own accord, to any of eight locations in the region where potters hosted open house events at their studios, where their work would be on display and for sale (fig. 1.5). The locations for the first tour were comprised of a variety of spaces including home studios, the Goshen Clay Artists Guild, and the Goshen College Ceramics department. A map of the sites, including approximate driving distances and lists of exhibiting artists, was prepared and provided both online and in print at the various locations (see appendix I, map 1.1).

Initially growing out of conversations between Dick Lehman, Mark Goertzen, and Justin Rothshank—particularly, they recount, in acknowledgment that more and more potters were becoming established in the Michiana area—the tour provided an opportunity to draw in both old and new customers and to demonstrate the broad scope of pottery available in the area. Additionally, visits to the potters' individual studios (often situated at their homes) have a very personal feel and allow potential customers to interact with the potter in a more intimate setting than would be available at, for instance, a large group gallery show (fig. 1.6).

In 2012, the idea of a studio tour was not new to the world of contemporary American potters; around the country, a number of dense regional groups of potters support one another and join together to organize events that will support their community and their work. Most of the Michiana potters note that at least part of the Michiana inspiration drew from the tour in St. Croix, Minnesota, which was influenced by renowned potter Warren McKenzie. Well established and well attended, a variety of tours, trails, and kiln openings around the United States doubtless served as inspirations and models as the new Michiana Pottery Tour developed. When I spoke with Mark Goertzen a few weeks before the initial 2012 tour, he was cautiously optimistic about the possibilities

Fig. 1.5. Each year, these bright orange signs for the pottery tour help guide visitors as they drive from location to location. Some of the pottery that lines Mark Goertzen's driveway can also be seen near the sign. *(Photo by author)*

Fig. 1.6. Chad Hartwig (*left*), exhibiting at the studio of Notre Dame professor Bill Kremer in Cassopolis, Michigan during the 2013 tour, discusses his pottery with a potential customer. (*Photo by author*)

for this new endeavor: "Hopefully it will grow enough where we have cause to be open more than one day," he said at the time. Prior to the establishment of the tour, Mark routinely held a fall kiln opening at his home studio, so he knew he would be able to draw a crowd, though the size of the crowd for the entirety of the tour (and their propensity for buying work from other potters) was uncertain. Before the start of the first tour, there was talk of committing to at least two years—not giving up even if the first year was slow. However, business was not lacking on that first day; cars lined Mark's long, wooded driveway and spilled into nearby streets, and most locations saw a substantial number of visitors; as I moved from place to place, I saw potters in near-constant interaction with their guests, happily discussing their work and wrapping up customers' purchases. By the end of the day, the future of the tour began to sound more certain; a significant number of attendees and sales during the day encouraged the potters to continue the event.

The second tour was expanded to two days, which allowed visitors more time to browse the pottery available at all of the locations. This was

Fig. 1.7. A visitor takes a leisurely look at the displays set up on Mark Goertzen's property during the 2013 tour. Each year, low shelves filled with pottery line the path between his kiln shed and his house. *(Photo by author)*

a huge improvement for those attendees who had felt they only had time to visit a few locations in the course of one day, or, alternatively, found themselves quickly rushing through each location without much time to meet the potters or fully appreciate their extensive displays of pottery (fig. 1.7). Propitiously, the addition of a second day did not require too much extra physical labor on the part of the potters; displays were already prepared and were, for the most part, simply left up overnight with only minimal adjustments to ensure the safety of the pottery. Once again, the second tour had substantial crowds and strong sales, and the potters decided to continue the two-day version of the tour for a third year (and then again, and again, with the tour still going strong for a seventh year in 2018).

With each subsequent year there have been slight modifications in the number of locations and the individual potters participating. For example, potters such as Todd Pletcher and Dick Lehman, who participated but did not have their personal studios included in the initial tour, both added their own more recently established studios to the list

Fig. 1.8. A small portion of the numerous displays set up by invited potters at Northern Indiana Pottery Supply during the 2015 Michiana Pottery Tour. *(Photo by author)*

of locations. Meanwhile, some others who previously participated have left the tour due to changes in personal circumstances. Eric Strader, for instance, is in the process of moving his studio farther north, near Kalamazoo, Michigan, and no longer has his own studio location included on the tour; instead, some years he has set up a booth on another potter's property. Additionally, many of the potters began to invite more and more participants from farther away to exhibit at their studios during the tour; for example, Justin Rothshank has hosted up to six additional potters over the years, and Moey Hart of Northern Indiana Pottery Supply included six to eight invited artists in 2014, 2015, and 2016 (see fig. 1.8).[7] While those invited may not be considered Michiana potters, they are often connected in some way; friends and former students or apprentices sometimes travel from states away to participate, while others who live nearby but not quite within Michiana make shorter trips to take part in the tour.

At the time of this writing, it is possible to say that the Michiana Pottery Tour has quickly become very well established; visitors have remained numerous over the years, and sales have been high enough to make the opportunity worthwhile for most Michiana potters to participate year after year. Why, one might ask, has this tour been so successful so quickly? One could say it seems almost a karmic reward for the potters' steady dedication to their craft. Other reasons may appeal to those with less romantic tendencies, yet even with a more grounded explanation, dedication has doubtlessly played a part; those who were well established in their various productions had steady customers to invite to the newly established tour. And, as the oft-repeated phrase goes, there is the importance of location, location, location! All of the sites on the tour are reasonably spaced for a day or two of travelling; perhaps more importantly, the tour locations are mostly located around Goshen, which is within a short distance from larger towns such as Elkhart, Indiana (which is only ten miles down the road); South Bend, Indiana (approximately twenty-five miles away); Fort Wayne, Indiana (fifty miles); and Kalamazoo, Michigan (sixty miles). A number of other larger towns and cities are also within a two-hour drive or less, including places such as Indianapolis, Indiana, and Ann Arbor, Lansing, and Grand Rapids, Michigan. Even the larger metropolis of Chicago, Illinois, is easily within reach. This creates a circumstance in which aficionados from a broader area can easily drive into and around the area for a day, or even stay overnight and continue their adventure for a second day. With this knowledge, the potters have chosen many of the cities listed above for advertising the tour via radio and newspaper ads, especially in later years as they attempt to grow their clientele.

Each year of the tour has included at least two or three sites that feature wood-fired kilns. As mentioned above, Mark Goertzen has long held a kiln opening in the fall, and Justin Rothshank, who also has a wood kiln on his property, has also participated in every year of the tour. Furthermore, Bill Kremer participated for the first two years, and his studio has the distinction of housing the largest wood kiln in the region. Later, Todd Pletcher also built a wood-fired kiln on his own property, and his participation in the 2015 tour included unloading a recent firing of his kiln. The kiln opening events that Mark (with help from the potters who joined him in the firing) and Todd have held during the tour provide an important educational opportunity for those who are not familiar with wood firing: typically, a kiln opening in Michiana involves one potter climbing inside the kiln to pull out pots while one or more potters stay

Fig. 1.9. Dick Lehman (sitting in the kiln and wearing a red shirt) explains the wood-firing process as he helps to unload Mark Goertzen's kiln in September 2013. *(Photo by author)*

outside of the kiln, receiving the pots that are handed out and offering explanations to the crowd that gathers around (fig. 1.9). This process contrasts with some other potters' kiln openings in the US, which are less performative and more like special sales events; instead of unloading the kiln for an audience, some potters prefer to unload the kiln, clean up and price the pots, and carefully set the work out on display prior to the arrival of visitors. In Michiana, the potters are often seeing their finished work for the first time, and the crowd is afforded the opportunity to see their initial reactions and assessments. Often, if a particularly large or fragile piece needs to be unloaded, the potter who made the piece will be called on to pull it out of the kiln, thus taking responsibility for both its safety and its presentation to onlookers.

As the kiln is slowly unloaded in this manner (often at intervals, spread out at advertised times during the tour), the potters give thorough explanations of the effects that are achieved through this firing method. Their excitement is visible when a particularly attractive or unusual piece

Fig. 1.10. Mark Goertzen (*center*) and Todd Pletcher (*right*) discuss some of their recently fired pots with a visitor during the 2012 Michiana Pottery Tour. (*Photo by author*)

is unloaded, and their explanations as to how the effect was achieved and why it is desirable or unusual serves to teach the uninitiated audience members how to appreciate and understand the aesthetics of wood firing. As the pots are unloaded, they are often spread out on the ground near the kiln, and when the unloading is over, the potters gather with their customers to inspect the results and discuss the pieces they are particularly excited about (fig. 1.10). Furthermore, much of the education that takes place is in regard to the hard work that goes into wood firing, the impressive chemical processes that turn wood ash into glaze, and the unpredictability of results and the potter's lack of direct control over the final decorative patterns found on the pieces; these aspects of the process, and more, are elaborated on in depth in chapter 3. This knowledge is not commonplace among those who are not potters; in fact, many potters who have not participated in wood firing may have little knowledge about these processes. Through their enthusiasm and engaging efforts at education, the Michiana potters begin to instill their own sense of wood-fired aesthetics in a broader community of potential clients and hopefully thereby increase sales of the wood-fired pottery that they so love to produce. On the part of the well-informed consumer, then, an appreciation for wood-fired pottery often signals a respect for the materials and the earth, for the look and feel of the handmade, and for the skills of people rather than machines.

While the Michiana Pottery Tour provides a small overview of the pottery available in Michiana (and indeed, over the years, has served as such an introduction for many) there is a much larger story to be told about the development of the pottery movement in this region. For a proper introduction to the bourgeoning Michiana pottery tradition, we must take a few steps back in history: when Marvin Bartel began teaching ceramics and art education at Goshen College over forty years ago, there were no production potters established in the Michiana region, yet a new pottery movement would soon arise.

THE BEGINNINGS OF A MICHIANA TRADITION

The person most easily credited with the establishment of a ceramic tradition in Michiana is potter and professor Marvin Bartel, especially given that there were no production potters remembered to be working in the Goshen area when he arrived.[8] Marvin grew up, attended college, and began his teaching career in Kansas, and by the time he came to Goshen College in 1970, he had obtained an MA and a PhD in arts education and had a good number of years of experience teaching art in various mediums at both the high school and college levels. He stayed at Goshen College for over thirty years and, in that time, taught dozens of students who would go on to become successful artists and teachers in the Michiana area and beyond. Though he has retired, Marvin is ever the art teacher; he continues to teach for the local Boys & Girls Club, and I've observed his gentle education of those who come to his studio during the Michiana Pottery Tour. He gravitates to curiosity, always ready to explain his designs, tools, processes, and creations to interested visitors (fig. 1.11).

Marvin attributes much of his success as a teacher to the structure of the coursework he offered at Goshen College: "My reasoning is, you can learn to make a pinch pot in a day. If you're going to learn to throw, it takes years. So you have to start throwing right away, because it takes the longest to learn. I could work all the hand building in along the way, and they could learn everything. By the end of the first semester, [my students] knew so much of what they didn't know yet, they had to take another semester! It really grew the department." He continues, "[Students] don't even know they want to throw, except once the word gets out. Then they come and watch their friends, and 'Oh, wow, can I try this?' [I would respond], 'Well, take the class.' So that's the way, if you're a teacher, you'll make yourself indispensable really quickly." Marvin also explained the results of this enticing teaching method, which he observed after students had finished their coursework: when he meets former students and asks what they have been doing, they often respond, "Well, I've been making pots." Marvin believes this is "because they know how to learn—so why should they stop? They don't need me anymore. That's what makes me feel the best." Indeed, by my count over half of the participants in both the 2012 and 2013 Michiana Pottery Tours (and nearly a third in 2014) had been Marvin's students—an impressive tribute to his influence in the area's pottery community.[9]

In the mid-1970s, one of Marvin Bartel's ceramics students, Bob Smoker, introduced his friend Dick Lehman (who, at the time, was

Fig. 1.11. Marvin Bartel demonstrates some of his decorative techniques to children visiting his studio during the 2014 Michiana Pottery Tour. *(Photo by author)*

studying religion, not art) to the joy of throwing pottery. Dick recalls the occasion with fondness, saying, "I just loved it from the beginning. It was so responsive, and you had something to show for your efforts. Much of what I was doing was academic and there was no substantial product at the end of it, so I think that is one of the things that attracted me." After this initial experience, Dick went on to learn from Marvin before eventually deciding to set out on his own. Dick established a successful production pottery studio in Goshen, and many full-time potters in the Michiana area now have been Marvin's students or Dick's apprentices or both; experience working in the production pottery studio that Dick established has played a strong part in the education of many production potters, including many who now live outside of Michiana (fig. 1.12).[10]

As for his own beginnings as a potter, Dick vacillated between religious work and pottery, eventually finding that his enthusiasm for clay was worthwhile to pursue full-time. He describes the rather tedious process by which he was making pots in the meantime: going to Goshen College to rent their clay mixer, taking the clay home and into the basement to make the pots, bringing the pots up to the garage to bisque and back to the basement to glaze, borrowing a van to take the pots to the kiln site for the final firing, and so on. "It struck me, at a point, that it was both ridiculous and maybe profound at the same time because it indicated to me that I was wanting to do this badly enough ... that I would be willing to do all that." Finally, in the spring of 1981, Dick began to work with clay full-time. Initially, he rented space for his studio from a friend and local furniture maker, Larion Swartzendruber. A few years later, when that initial space was no longer available, the two decided to continue their collaboration and moved into the Old Bag Factory together, along with a number of other artists and craftsmen.[11] Dick made and sold pottery out of that studio for close to thirty years. His production line included many functional items such as dinnerware, serving ware, teapots, vases, and much more. Large runs of these items would be glazed in similar ways to create matching sets; often pieces would be glazed in a single color, with brushwork details painted on in contrasting colors (see fig. 1.13 for an example of Dick's early production work). Over the years, Dick also experimented with alternative types of firing such as raku, saggar, and wood firing; wrote articles about his work for popular ceramics trade

Fig. 1.12. Dick Lehman explains his process to visitors at his new studio during the 2015 Michiana Pottery Tour. *(Photo by author)*

Fig. 1.13. An example of work made by Dick Lehman during his years working in the Old Bag Factory studio. Tea set, cone 10 reduction firing. *(Photo courtesy of Dick Lehman)*

magazines; and became a very successful and nationally renowned potter, serving as a mentor and an inspiration for many.

Mark Goertzen arrived in 1989 intending to work with Dick for a year. Having studied ceramics at Bethel College in Newton, Kansas, Mark wanted to find a place where he could make functional, vessel-oriented pots, an opportunity most ceramics graduate programs would not provide for him. However, Mark found the opportunity he wanted when his professor, Paul Friesen, introduced him to Dick at a National Council on Education for the Ceramic Arts (NCECA) conference, at a point when Dick was fortuitously looking for an apprentice. It is worthwhile to note that this connection to Kansas, where Marvin Bartel also hails from, is no coincidence; both areas have significant Mennonite populations, and a number of potters have moved between the two areas, noting that they are happy to find like-minded people in their new hometowns. Fred Driver, the current director of the Goshen Clay Artists Guild, also studied under Paul Friesen in Kansas before transferring to Goshen College and studying with Marvin Bartel. Merrill Krabill taught

Fig. 1.14. Mark Goertzen stands in his studio in August 2012, holding one of his favorite wood-fired pots. *(Photo by author)*

at Bethel College in Newton, Kansas, before coming to teach at Goshen College. Additionally, in 2013 Tom Unzicker moved from Indiana to Kansas, where he set up a new studio and built a new wood kiln (his brother, Jeff, remained in Indiana).

In 2012, over twenty years after he first came to Goshen, Mark discussed his professional history in an interview with me and reflected on the initial decision to move to Michiana, saying, "I didn't envision this being long term up here, but it has turned into my home" (fig. 1.14). Mark has since become a mainstay in the Michiana pottery community in terms of both his studio work and his wood firings; Mark eventually built a wood kiln on his property in Constantine, Michigan, and his annual fall kiln opening event served as the basis for the establishment of the Michiana Pottery Tour. Also, in 2011, Mark purchased the Old Bag Factory pottery studio from Dick Lehman, and he has taken on Dick's role there as a mentor to new apprentices—a story I will explain further in chapter 2.

OF POTTERS AND FOLKLORISTS

Ostensibly, this book is about the working lives of Michiana potters, and in the following chapters, I will elaborate on the influence that potters such as Marvin, Dick, Mark, and others have had on the development of a distinct tradition of pottery-making in Michiana. My fascination with the local and personal—specifically my focus on local places, personalized spaces, and face-to-face interactions mentioned above—in large part comes from my training as a folklorist, a profession that I have come to realize is not familiar to many potters (or others who operate in the world of ceramics or art more broadly). I include the following explanations and definitions for the sake of clarity, knowing readers of this book may come from a variety of professional or educational backgrounds. I particularly hope that readers from outside folkloristics will find that this book provides insights into the social nature of art-making and the value that folklore studies can offer in terms of understanding the social lives of individual artists. My ethnographic project has always been translational, in the sense that I have positioned myself between two groups that possess different kinds of knowledge about the world: folklorists (and other academics who do related work in the social sciences and humanities) on the one hand, and potters and artists on the other. I also hope this book will assist in "translating" the experience of making pottery in that I will attempt to explain an embodied experience to those readers who have not had such an experience.

The study of pottery can be a powerful means for understanding regions and groups, as it can demonstrate the aesthetic ideals, functional needs, technological capabilities, and resources prevalent or available in a community. The thoughts of the potter are, in a way, inscribed in the form and surface of the pot, and yet there is a necessity to bring these features into text in order to make the pot relevant to the academic world. Furthermore, much dialogue and activity occurs around the creation of the pot; this is, in many ways, more my concern than the objects themselves. Folklorists Ray Cashman, Tom Mould, and Pravina Shukla note in the introduction to *The Individual and Tradition* that "in a very real sense the song does not exist without the singer and the singing" (2011, 4). My approach to studying pottery mirrors their approach to traditions and the individuals who drive those traditions forward; a pot does not exist without the potter and the potting (or throwing, or turning, or building, or firing, or burning, or pot-making, however you wish to term the various activities involved). But unlike a song, pottery itself has an inherent physical permanence. It is one of the most durable materials in the world, and because of this it has been of primary interest in the archaeological record. Pots are often prominent in museum collections, and they have been written about extensively by art historians, collectors, and potters, in trade magazines, in books, and, increasingly, in online formats. The value of writing about pottery, then, is not necessarily in giving it more permanence or a place in historical records; written works can, however, assist in giving the act of making pottery and the traditions of ceramic artists a broader relevance to the discipline of folkloristics and similar areas of scholarship that are concerned with traditions of craftsmanship.

What does it mean to study tradition or for an artist to be "traditional," to participate in or be influenced by a tradition? For example, it is a curious iniquity of the American fine art world that artists are simultaneously encouraged to seek out international experiences—as many of the Michiana potters have done in travelling to Japan for ceramics-related opportunities—and yet those same artists can be criticized for engaging too much with the foreign tradition they have experienced, for not being unique enough when they incorporate inspirations from those experiences into their work.[12] Once we accept that one cannot make artwork without utilizing one's experiences of the world, we must also accept that international influences will likely be present in that artwork. For those participating in the novelty-focused contemporary art world, the trick, of course, is to incorporate those influences in a noticeably unique way—to bring together different elements to create a style of one's own and not be seen to directly copy the work of others. And yet, how many artists truly set out to copy the work of others? From my observations over the years, I would say it is very few. Even if it were the case that a potter was attempting to directly copy the work of another, they would be doing so in different circumstances: their own studio, equipment, training, materials, resources, and so on, which will almost always lead to differing results. As Dick Lehman has so eloquently stated, "Is not tradition really the succession of solutions which, over eons, are accumulated and handed down to the next generations and not something static and final? Is not tradition as much our responsibility as our inheritance? If we each take the best of what has been passed down to us and apply it, with a healthy dose of curiosity and innovation, to the problems and limitations of our own lives, we all will be extending that tradition in the best possible ways" (1999, 21). This articulate statement so closely parallels a key definition used in folkloristics: "tradition is the creation of the future out of the past" (Glassie 1995b, 395). To say an artist or a potter is traditional is no insult; nor is it an indication that their work lacks individuality or creativity. It is simply an acknowledgment that they have learned of what has come before them, and they have made conscious choices about which aspects they wish to carry forth in their own work.

Further regarding professions, readers should note that I have intentionally chosen to use the term *potter* (or, less often, *artist*) at most points in this text. It is an indication of subject matter—professionals engaged in making pottery—as well as a conscious shift away from the fine art world's use of the term *ceramic artist*. That is not because *ceramic artist* isn't applicable or because it lacks merit as a professional label. However, my research is less concerned with the prestige of an individual artist and much more concerned with a group who share an occupation, a topic taken up more often by folklorists than it is by art critics and art historians. To find scholarship similar to my own, one is better off searching for texts about pots and potters; yet if one wishes to find more objects and artists of the kind and caliber that are discussed here, it would still be entirely correct to include ceramic art and ceramic artists in such a search. Readers should also note that I do not call these potters *folk artists*, though this text is written from the perspective of a folklorist; this requires an understanding of the nature of contemporary scholarship in folkloristics as well as some explanation of the history of the term *folk art*.

The most relevant and succinct definition of folklore I can offer to those who are unfamiliar with the scholarly use of the term is this: "folklore is artistic communication in small groups" (Ben-Amos 1971, 13). In very broad strokes, then, folkloristics is the study of these groups and their communications, and indeed, it has been defined as "the study of communicative behavior with an esthetic, expressive, or stylistic dimension" (Hymes 1974, 133). During the time of my own graduate training, most of the folklorists I encountered and learned from were engaged in the study of aspects of cultural knowledge that are traditional, vernacular, unofficial, and noninstitutionalized and that are typically shared verbally or taught (intentionally or unintentionally) through behavioral examples. Furthermore, my analysis of the Michiana group is based extensively in the narratives the potters share about their lives, and my analysis involves a close consideration of the words they choose to describe both their artwork and the social connections that support and sustain them. I could not make this analysis without the subtle influences that come from my familiarity with the work of folklorists whose research focuses on narrative and other verbal arts. But, whether we are studying what people say, do, believe, know, or make, it is true that across the discipline most contemporary folklorists are engaged with questions about expression, identity, belief, value, meaning, and human connection. And while the term *folklore* may in vernacular usage evoke a sense of the old, rural, naïve, or even untrue, such descriptors are not reflective of the subject matter of contemporary folkloristic inquiry.

This brings us to a related term, *folk art*, that unfortunately was for many decades closely tied to now outdated understandings of "the folk."

I have found that this term and its complex history often lead to challenges when I introduce myself as a folklorist, particularly to artists, art historians, or others who are not familiar with contemporary folklore studies. This is no fault of theirs, as folk art has indeed been historically used to imply a naïve or uneducated artist, one operating outside of the Western fine art world (whose participants were typically of European descent, white, wealthy, and upper class). Often the descriptor folk art indicated that the artist was somehow *other*, particularly by race or class, and conceptions of the "folk," in general, have often been tied up in nationalistic ideas.[13] Scholarship must move forward, and to do so we often must recognize that the work done by scholars of the past was insufficient. Many changes in theoretical perspectives have been necessary to contemporary folkloristics so that we may now treat justly the topics we study and the people we collaborate with in the course of those studies. Thus the conception of folk art as naïve, classist, and racist has been firmly put to rest by many contemporary scholars.

For example, Glassie critiques various means of delineating fine and folk art, noting that when some people say "folk art," they mean art made by someone who is uneducated; and yet education can happen in both formal and informal settings and often occurs within families, between neighbors, or in ateliers as equally as it may happen in schools or universities (as I will demonstrate in chap. 2). Furthermore, when some people say "naïve art," they may mean to indicate "immature fine art," or art made by someone who has not reached a high level of competence within the tradition they are emulating. Glassie demonstrates that neither style nor social class defines fine or folk art and states "all art is an individual's expression of a culture. Cultures differ, so art looks different" (1995a, 210). Ultimately, Glassie concludes, "The difference between folk and fine art is more a matter of academic convention, of differences in scholarly traditions of discourse and approach, than it is difference in phenomena.... If scholars could strip away their prejudices and learn to approach all art in the same mood of disciplined compassion, they would learn that it is all competent, that it all blends the individualistic and the traditional, the sensual and the conceptual" (1995a, 228). The potters in the Michiana tradition all move within the worlds one might define as fine or folk or even craft; in many ways, these distinctions are not useful because there is no doubt in my mind that what they make is all artful.

Therefore, my approach to the terms *folk* and *art* are as follows. I study "folk" in the sense that I take a folkloristic approach, understanding the *folk* in folklore to refer to everyday people. It follows, then, that a folk group is "any group of people whatsoever who share at least one common factor. It does not matter what the linking factor is—it could be a common occupation, language, or religion—but what is important is that a group formed for whatever reason will have some traditions which it calls its own" (Dundes 1965, 2). The Michiana potters clearly constitute a folk group. *Art*, then, I take in the broadest sense to mean creative expression. I am interested in the social lives and aesthetic creations of those who call themselves artists, potters, ceramists, or ceramic artists, and I view their work as a creative expression with recognizable similarities and individual variations, occurring among a group of people who acknowledge one another and exist within a particular time and place. In this book, I present a detailed representation of the Michiana potters as an occupational folk group that is engaged in making art. My representation is focused on the collaborative nature of some of their work, particularly wood firing, and the ways that having a strong occupational group present in the area furthers creativity in these artists' lives.

MATERIAL CULTURE, OCCUPATIONAL FOLKLIFE, ART WORLDS, AND NETWORKS

When I began this study, I intended to do so primarily using the tools available to me through work done by folklorists in the realm of material culture studies, particularly the methods set out by Henry Glassie. His model recommends a combination of approaches to the study of objects as a means of understanding the human beings who make and utilize them. He proposes following an object through its various contexts: primarily creation, communication, and consumption, which "cumulatively recapitulate the life history of the artifact" (1999a, 48). His approach is a thorough means of following one type of object through a culture, leading one to understand, among many things, how and why an object is made in certain ways, using certain materials and technologies;

what the object is intended to communicate, how, and whether it is successful in doing so to its audience; how the object is sold or exchanged; and how it is then utilized in everyday life or incorporated as part of a collection. History, geography, commerce, social connections, and personal narratives all have their places in this conception of the study of material culture, and all of these aspects have played roles in my research and writing.

This being said, however, I found myself stuck in one particular context: that of creation. I had an affinity for the creators of pottery and a specific interest in their educations and social lives rather than the social lives of the objects they were creating. When I inquired into how they were selling their work and what they were trying to communicate and to whom, I found that the most interesting conversations on these topics were already happening among the potters themselves, much more prevalently than with any external audiences. Furthermore, they often seemed to find the most value in the input they could receive from others who shared their profession, others who faced similar challenges in the production and sales of their work, and in the philosophies that lie behind that work. I therefore turned to the study of occupational folklore, as I realized that the contribution my collaboration with contemporary potters could make was much more about the study of an occupational group and less about the study of the pottery (which is already rather well documented through the writing, photographing, and exhibiting done by the potters themselves).

Many studies of occupational folklore or folklife have begun with a group of people who identify as workers in a specific arena and have focused on the expressions of identity, often narrative or song, shared between existing members of that group. In many cases, those identities are expressed in relation to outside forces, including natural, social, economic, and political powers that affect the work or the lives of the workers.[14] For example, Timothy Tangherlini has written about the traditions of storytelling among paramedics; part of his scholarship demonstrates how stories can function as a means to express frustration with either difficult patients or other professionals with whom they must coordinate such as firefighters, police, and hospital personnel (1998). Furthermore, C. Kurt Dewhurst provides numerous examples of the art created by workers in varying industries in Michigan: ceramic figures made for personal use by workers in an industrial tile factory; murals painted by workers in automobile factories and comparable painting done by an employee in a water and light facility; jewelry made from paint drippings by workers in a plant that produces automobile (or similar) parts; drawings, jokes, and related expressions made in chalk on the rubber conveyor belt by workers on an assembly line (1984). All of these are examples of creative expressions made in contrast to and outside of the required work of the job.

What happens, however, when the work done by a group is itself the main form of creative expression? Potters are rather different from the groups addressed by earlier studies of occupational folklore and folklife, many of whom were not artists or craftsmen but instead coal miners, factory workers, and so on. In contrast, the potters' connections do not come from showing up for work at the same factory every day or even from all working consistently in the same space together. Their connection does not come from being together in a major labor-oriented political movement (though many of them do share similar political beliefs and are politically and civically active). They are bound, primarily, by the shared challenges and joys found in their work, and they are further bound by their shared values and similar lifestyles, and much of their cohesiveness as a group comes from the fact that they choose to come together outside of the essential context of the work that they do.

Many of the social aspects of artistic work that I wished to inquire into are encompassed by Howard Becker's notion of "art worlds," which I have relied on heavily in thinking through the work of the Michiana group. Becker considers art as activity, treats "art as not so very different from other kinds of work, and . . . people defined as artists as not so very different from other kinds of workers." Furthermore, Becker acknowledges that all art involves the cooperative activity of a number of people and that the artwork produced is necessarily affected (and thus will show signs of) those relationships. In his definition, an "art world" denotes "the network of people whose cooperative activity, organized via their joint knowledge of conventional means of doing things, produces the kind of art works that art world is known for" ([1982] 2008, xxiii–xxiv). While Becker's conception of an art world is meant to include not just those who are considered artists but others such as suppliers of materials, art dealers, consumers, and critics, I found great appeal in the aspects of his approach that focus on interactions between artists who are situated within the same art world. Becker's conceptualization is not so different from Glassie's; both impress upon us that we must consider all of the people and connections involved in the creation and consumption of art in order to achieve a full picture of the society within which the art exists.

Furthermore, the ways the Michiana potters have described their own work and social circles to me, which will be explored in detail in the following chapters, are reflected in Becker's acknowledgement that an art world is without specific bounds and best conceptualized as a network:

> Art worlds do not have boundaries around them, so that we can say that these people belong to a particular art world while those people do not. I am not concerned with drawing a line separating an art world from other parts of a society. Instead, we look for groups of people who cooperate to produce things that they, at least, call art; having found them, we look for other people who are also necessary to that production, gradually building up as complete a picture as we can of the entire cooperating network that radiates out from the work in question. The world exists in the cooperative activity of those people, not as a structure or organization, and we use words like these only as a shorthand for the notion of networks of people cooperating. ([1982] 2008, 35)

This kind of approach allows me to acknowledge Michiana as a regional tradition but also as an art world that is broadly connected to other artists and movements through history and contemporarily around the world. Furthermore, in elaborating upon his concept of art worlds, Becker offers many useful concepts regarding the development of integrated professionals, the necessity of cooperative links between people (artists and others), and the benefits of cohesive aesthetics within an art world—all ideas that will be explored in detail in later chapters.

Becker's conception of an art world as a network is helpful, but how does this term, *network*, interface with similar terms such as *folk group* and *community*? All of my main collaborators in Michiana have described a distinctly felt "sense of community," both as a group of potters and, in a broader sense, as residents of Goshen and/or the Michiana region with shared artistic and lifestyle preferences. Yet *community* is an ambiguous word, and I turn to Dorothy Noyes's consideration of the concepts of group and network to clarify what is meant by community: "At bottom, folklorists have been interested in the group as the locus of culture and as the focus of identity. Our difficulties with such concepts as 'folk,' 'nation,' 'race,' and so on, may be seen as resulting from the confusion of the two ... I will propose that we distinguish between the empirical network of interactions in which culture is created and moves, and the community of the social imaginary that occasionally emerges in performance. Our everyday word group might best serve as shorthand for the dialogue between the two" (1995, 452).

Accordingly, the sense of community felt and described by this group of potters is brought into being through their ongoing interactions. Noyes clarifies, "The community is in no way independent of the network. The performance that constructs the community ideologically and emotionally also strengthens or changes the shape of networks by promoting interaction. . . . The community exists as the project of a network or some of its members. Networks exist insofar as their ties are continually recreated and revitalized in interaction" (1995, 471–72).

Conceptualizing the Michiana pottery tradition as a social network—that is, an egocentric network of individuals—is therefore in many ways the most fitting approach. First, it allows for the exploration of many interpersonal connections of different kinds, primarily between the most active professional potters in the area, but it also acknowledges the important links they have with family, friends, suppliers, clients, mentors, students, and more. As an occupational network, it is dense at its center, where a tight-knit group of professional potters share the most connections, and looser around the periphery, where part-time and hobby potters still participate in some of the same community-building activities (fig. 1.15). It is also, then, an easy step to perceive the participants in the Michiana tradition together as one cluster within the broader network of contemporary American potters; similarly, a network approach acknowledges that, while this is mostly a regionally-defined group, there are many broader connections that are also quite crucial to each individual potter and to the group as a whole, even if those connections are less often physically present in their everyday lives.

Fig. 1.15. The potters who participated in firing Mark Goertzen's kiln in summer 2013 pose inside the kiln for fun after it has been unloaded. *Clockwise from top left*: Mark Goertzen, Todd Pletcher, Scott Lehman, Todd Leech, Anna Corona (*bottom right*), Stephanie Craig, Bill Hunt, Dick Lehman, Royce Hildebrand. *(Photo by author)*

THE STUDY OF SOCIAL CONNECTIONS IN A
WORLD OF INDIVIDUAL ARTISTS

Individual artists rely on numerous social connections: through history, religion, and region, through education and informally learned habits of body and mind, through collaborative process and liminal space, through the objects they hold dear. Each of the following chapters illuminates a particular kind of social connection that is of benefit to these artists and suggests approaches for the ethnographic study of contemporary artists. I would also suggest that the approaches I have used to understand the Michiana community could be used in the study of historical groups of artists; however, this may prove challenging when records are scarce and artists are no longer present to comment on these topics. With living potters to learn from, I have been able to develop an understanding of this occupational group: how it has evolved, what aspects of social life play the largest part in sustaining its existence, and how each of the potters who are part of this group benefit from the occupational connections they maintain in this region.

Chapter 2 builds on the brief introductions above to Marvin Bartel, Dick Lehman, and Mark Goertzen, elaborating on ways that people are brought into the occupation of pottery in Michiana. While family traditions are prevalent in literature on folk art, for contemporary potters becoming part of this occupation is often not a family matter but rather a personal career choice that involves selecting the kind of work environment and people one wishes to be surrounded with. As such, the personalities and work environments that potters encounter in school or early career experiences can have a strong impact on their identity and the places and ways they later choose to work. Chapter 2 therefore focuses on ways that various educational spaces and ideals impact the process of identity development occurring in Michiana.

While educational influences are crucial, it is also important to acknowledge that in their professional lives potters tend to spend most of their time working individually; most of them spend many hours working alone in their studios, creating pots. Therefore, it is necessary to look for the special settings and occasional events that bring them together and afford them the time to build close bonds with one another. It became clear to me quite early in my fieldwork experiences in Michiana that wood firing was central to the identity and social cohesion of this group. Chapter 3, therefore, is dedicated to examining the development of this process within the Michiana region and the benefits of having multiple artists striving for similar aesthetic results within a collaborative process. Furthermore, this chapter analyzes wood firing through the lens of liminal space, exploring the ways that this intense and uncertain process helps to develop a sense of empathy, community, and creativity among the participating potters.

Chapters 3 and 4 are concerned with aesthetics, particularly how shared processes, moments of creativity and uncertainty, and encounters with the work of others can lead to recognizable aesthetic elements among a group of artists, each of whom still has their own unique style. Chapter 3 begins this discussion by defining the Michiana Aesthetic and illuminating the ways that the collaborative wood-firing process has influenced the development of this aesthetic—elements of which are, notably, present in more than just the wood-fired work produced by these potters. Then, in chapter 4, I evaluate the presence of influence via collected objects; artists are often prolific collectors, and their collections offer ways for them to build social, professional, and aesthetic connections. This chapter also broadens the scope of this study to see how a wider network of artistic connections can remain present in an artist's life through the objects that he or she possesses and utilizes.

Chapter 5 then takes a broader view of the potter's social life, first looking at the history and demographics of the Michiana region to illuminate the development of art-oriented connections there, specifically in the central town of Goshen, Indiana. As I will explain, much of the appeal of this place lies in the people who live in Michiana; having shared religious and/or secular philosophies of life, a similar approach to business and economics, and the ability to build deep connections with those who live in the same area are all key reasons that these artists choose to live and work in the area. This chapter then goes on to look at resources and people who are outside of Michiana or the pottery community, elaborating on social connections and resources that are of benefit to the Michiana potters on a less-frequent basis, yet their presence is significant in making Michiana a viable place to pursue this profession.

Finally, the concluding chapter acknowledges some of the shifts and changes that can take place in a community over time—due to the coming and going of various individuals as well as the economic, health-related, personal, and social challenges that can arise in an artist's professional life—and it looks toward the future to consider what may be on the horizon for the Michiana group. The conclusion also draws together and elaborates on ethnographic approaches to studying occupational groups of professional artists and revisits the importance of terms such as community, network, and art world, which are commensurate with a thorough understanding of the Michiana pottery tradition and those who work within it.

There is no question, in the contemporary fine art world, that an artist can achieve tremendous recognition and artistic success as an individual; my question is, what does a group of artists achieve through the myriad connections with other artistic professionals who are present in their lives? For many potters in Michiana, the answer is success and satisfaction in one's work, the ability to pursue results that would not be possible without the help of others, and a life that is pleasing in regard to not just occupation but family, friends, philosophy, and much more. It is my hope that my integration into this community, with numerous visits and ongoing conversations, both in person and at a distance through various forms of technology, has afforded me a deep enough understanding of the complex social relationships of the mentors and mentees, colleagues, and friends within this group that I will be able to represent them with accuracy in this text. I can certainly thank my own background as a potter and the wonderful teachers and mentors I have had over the years for my easy entry into this group; my knowledge of ceramic techniques and technologies was a major boon and allowed me to orient myself to the work of the Michiana potters quite quickly. Still, while I place high value on my own experiences as a potter and I would recommend that others doing fieldwork cultivate a firsthand understanding of the processes they are attempting to write about, I also want to make clear that I am not personally in the business of making

Michiana pottery. With my hands out of the clay and away from the fire, I can do the work of a folklorist, busying myself with camera, audio recorder, and notebook, attempting to learn enough that I can feel confident in representing this group of artists. In that regard, I am deeply grateful to all of the potters who have sat with me through long hours of interviews and observations, who have graciously invited me to join them at their studios, their homes, and around their kilns, and who have provided input at many stages of my writing.

"Where use meets beauty, where nature transforms into culture and individual and social goals are accomplished, where the human and numinous come into fusion, where objects are richest in value—there is the center of art," says Henry Glassie, regarding the study of pottery (1999b, 34). Following the path set by many folklorists who came before me, I strive now to tell the story of this bourgeoning pottery movement, one that is centered in the heart of the American Midwest at the turn of the twenty-first century, yet reaches broadly to trace influences throughout many other places and times.

NOTES

1. While border studies have been quite important to folklorists over the years, the significance of a state border is limited; those who are, for instance, living in one state and working in another might have to navigate a more complex process of paying state taxes. However, the potters say that any differences between the two states tend to play a very minimal role in their lives.

2. Barns with gambrel roofs are recognizable through the symmetrical dual slope on each side of the roof, the lower slope with a steeper pitch than the upper slope. Construction and interiors can vary significantly. For further information on the history, distribution, and differentiation of barns, John Fitchen's work provides a useful overview of barn scholarship and the differentiation of various barn types (2001).

3. See, for example, Chittenden (1995), Evans (1998), Herman (2016), Jones (1989), Kitchener (1994), Kim (1995), Glassie (2010), and Vlatch (1992), all of whom have profiled individual artists and have provided great insights into the value of the art to both the individual and to that person's community.

4. There are numerous examples outside of pottery as well, and while I cannot list them all here, I will point to Pravina Shukla's *The Grace of Four Moons: Dress, Adornment, and the Art of the Body in Modern India* as a text that had a strong impact on my own approach of highlighting multiple individuals who are involved in an art form.

5. My choice to use the term *apprentice* in this text is also a gloss for similar terms, such as *assistant* or *intern*, that are also utilized often in Michiana. All of these are used to indicate a hierarchical working relationship that allows for a less-experienced worker

to gain practical experience and to learn from a more-experienced worker. See chapter 2 for further discussion of apprentice-type relationships in Michiana.

6. In the United States, North Carolina and Georgia provide many prime examples of this, likely familiar to readers coming from a background in either folkloristics or ceramics (see Burrison 2008 and 2010; Sweezy 1994; Zug 1986; Mecham 2009).

7. Readers interested in the specific changes over the first five years of the tour will benefit from viewing Appendix I—Michiana Pottery Tour Maps.

8. It is worth noting that the pottery tradition in Grand Ledge, Michigan, was nearby and in existence for some time before the current Michiana tradition emerged (Dewhurst 1986; Dewhurst and MacDowell 1987). However, the Michiana potters I have worked with have not mentioned any engagement with the Grand Ledge community.

9. See Appendix I—Michiana Pottery Tour Maps for lists of tour participants from 2012 through 2016.

10. See Appendix II for a list of those who worked for significant periods of time at the studio with Dick and who have since stayed in the field of ceramics.

11. The Old Bag Factory was a factory space in Goshen that has undergone a contemporary renewal as a place for artists and small local shops; see p. 200–1 for more details.

12. I will not give specific examples as I do not have permission to recount the conversations that this analysis comes from; suffice to say, it is the kind of conversation I have had multiple times with ceramic artists (particularly professors) working within university settings.

13. For those interested in the history of the relationship between folk art and race, particularly blackness, I suggest Eugene W. Metcalf's article "Black Art, Folk Art, and Social Control" (1983) as well as *Fever Within: The Art of Ronald Lockett* edited by Bernard L. Herman (2016). For a more in-depth discussion of the problematic historical relationship between folklore and nationalism, see "Herder, Folklore, and Romantic Nationalism" (Wilson 2006).

14. For foundational scholarship on occupational folklore/folklife, see the seminal issue of *Western Folklore* titled "Working Americans: Contemporary Approaches to Occupational Folklife" (1978). In particular, see included articles by Robert H. Byington (185–98), Archie Green (213–44), and Robert S. McCarl, Jr. (145–60).

TWO

EDUCATION, IDENTITY, AND VOCATIONAL HABITUS

IDENTITY DEVELOPMENT THROUGH OCCUPATIONAL EDUCATION

When I was an undergraduate student, I once overheard a ceramics professor sharing an anecdote about a former student, a young woman with a great deal of pride in her long fingernails. As I recall, the professor said he had encouraged her to cut her nails so she could better learn to throw pots on the wheel, insisting that she could not manipulate the clay properly without being able to directly press the tips of her fingers to the clay. The young woman declined, insisting that she was quite adept at altering her actions to accommodate her long nails, and she was thus certain she could manage to throw pots by figuring out the necessary adjustments. Yet in the professor's telling, she was never able to learn to throw with the long nails, and in fact, due to these self-inflicted struggles she was barely able to pass the class. Although this anecdote was not incorporated into a formal lecture, the professor's audience consisted primarily of new undergraduate ceramics students who happened to be working in the studio at that moment; the underlying point of this cautionary tale was clearly to encourage current students to trim their fingernails appropriately—and to adhere to other bodily practices recommended by experienced ceramic artists—if they wished to learn proper methods of throwing and thereby succeed in their ceramics classes.

Folklorists have long acknowledged the importance of beliefs related to one's line of work, and they have often studied the verbal means through which these beliefs are shared. However, most studies of occupational folklore or folklife begin with a group of people who identify as workers and focus on the expressions of identity shared between existing members of that group, often in relation to outside forces (natural, social, economic, political, and so on). There has, however, been little critical analysis within folkloristics as to the means by which new workers are brought into a particular occupational group and how those new members acquire their occupational identity. Furthermore, while the process of training for a craft is usually addressed within material culture studies, often too little attention is paid to how one attains those shared beliefs and aspects of identity that are critical to inclusion within the occupational group. Certainly this tendency is related to a documentary trend in both material culture studies and the study of occupational folklife; Gertraud Koch, discussing in particular the work of Benjamin Botkin, refers to this as the aspiration to "make the expertise, independence, or achievements of certain occupational groups visible" (2012, 158). Documenting where and from whom technical expertise is acquired, along with documentation of the technical expertise itself, is certainly a valuable goal when no other acknowledgment or public record is likely to exist. In the case of ceramics, however, contemporary technical knowledge is well documented and easily found in books, trade magazine articles, videos, and, increasingly, a variety of online sources. It is not my purpose in this book to teach readers how to become potters; my goal is to explore how a sense of community and shared identity is developed among those in the same artistic vocation, and one crucial aspect of that development lies in the educative experiences shared by members of this group.

Informal lessons—such as the one previously recounted regarding fingernails—are not only prevalent in training for specific areas of work, they are crucial to one's identity development when joining a particular occupation. This is clearly demonstrated by Colley et al. in their 2003 study of vocational education and training (VET) courses in the United Kingdom. They argue that "learning is a process of becoming," and they offer the term *vocational habitus* to encompass aspects of vocational education that go beyond the acquisition of technical skills and knowledge (Colley et al. 2003, 471). In their definition, "Vocational habitus proposes that the learner aspires to a certain combination of dispositions demanded by the vocational culture. It operates in disciplinary ways to dictate how one should properly feel, look and act, as well as the values, attitudes and beliefs that one should espouse" (488). This framework draws on Bourdieu's concept of habitus and field ([1972] 1997, 1990). For the purposes of the following discussion, *habitus* can be understood as habits of mind and body, or the structures of beliefs and behaviors that are taken for granted and (usually) not critically analyzed by those who hold or participate in them. A field, then, is the social space in which those habits are developed and enacted. A field is therefore akin to the "small group" in the definition of folklore or, colloquially, a community.[1]

The concept of vocational habitus is therefore appropriate for analyzing the pottery learning spaces available in Michiana and the sense of identity development that occurs among the potters who work in those spaces. To be clear, I do not wish to claim that all potters will necessarily identify with all of the values characterized on the following pages; this is a localized group, and the vocational habitus they share is often related to broader trends in the Michiana region as well as the specific places where they have learned and people who have taught them. In other words, their vocational habitus exists within a specific field, which in this case is specifically used to refer to "a concept for expressing the sets of social relations characteristic of particular learning sites, educational institutions, occupational workplaces, and their associated practices" (Colley et al. 2003, 477). Thus the potters' presence in one another's lives is a continuing influence and helps to reinforce their shared identity; while it is certainly possible to be a potter alone, if you are a part of this group, it is clear you do not wish to be isolated. The Michiana potters also frequently connect much more broadly with potters nationally and internationally, yet these connections are unlikely to have the same sense of immediacy nor exert the same kinds of influence.[2] One could also understand this process as the development of a group of what Howard Becker calls integrated professionals, "because they know, understand, and habitually use the conventions on which their art world runs, they fit easily into all its standard activities," and all have the necessary technical, conceptual, and social skills to navigate within their given world ([1982] 2008, 228–29).

The following pages include numerous examples of the creativity, collaboration, sense of space, frugality, and service that are all crucial shared values among the Michiana potters; while relatively few of the examples I will provide could be included under the rubric of technical knowledge, the prevalence of these themes in my conversations with these potters does clearly point to particular shared dispositions and values that allow for the cohesiveness and sense of community found within this group. My intentions for this chapter are somewhat more complex, however, and my intention is not just to analyze vocational habitus among a group of integrated professionals. Ostensibly, the next three sections provide readers with an introduction to many of the potters who have been primary collaborators in my research, some of whom were already mentioned, at least briefly, in chapter 1. They are often brought in by means of their own initiations into the world of ceramics, which leads to the secondary purpose of this chapter (and also explains its thematic organization): developing a comparison of the many different learning environments available in Michiana, from which the participating artists continually benefit. Building on this comparison, then, the primary analytical aim of this chapter is to explore the relationship between learning environments and the development of a vocational habitus, which correlates to a sense of community felt among those working in the same artistic medium; the analysis at the end of the chapter pulls together the threads presented in the potter's narratives of their initiation into the work of pottery.

For contemporary potters, becoming part of this occupation is often not a family matter, as it may have been in other pottery traditions; rather, it is a matter of choosing an area of study or a career. And, while folklorists are by and large interested in the informal and the vernacular rather than the kinds of formalized teaching offered in a collegiate setting, this approach can lead us to overlook the important informal learning that does occur within institutional settings, not to mention the additional learning and identity development that occurs outside of, but parallel to, institutional education. I will begin with a discussion of college programs, since this is where many of the current Michiana potters say that either their main introduction to ceramics or their decision to seriously pursue ceramics occurred.

COLLEGE CERAMICS EDUCATION IN MICHIANA

As I explained in chapter 1, Marvin Bartel's arrival at Goshen College in 1970 signaled the beginning of a new regional tradition of

pottery-making, and the Goshen College ceramics program continues
to be a primary source of ceramics education in the region today. As a
Mennonite college, Goshen College pulls in many students who are of
that faith, which further reinforces the underlying Mennonite sensibili-
ties—for example, commitment to community, peace, justice, and service; and the incorporation of those values into one's vocation—in the
Michiana tradition of ceramics. (Goshen's Bethany High School, where
potter Eric Kauffman teaches art and has inspired a number of potential
future potters, is also a Mennonite school.) Marvin moved to Goshen
having come from another strongly Mennonite region in Kansas, and he
did so knowing that he would be able to find like-minded people in the
area; he is not the only potter to do so. Many members of the Michiana
pottery community have friends and family in Kansas; it is not uncommon for one of them to travel there, and many have moved back and forth
between the two areas. As I mentioned in chapter 1, Kansas potter Paul
Friesen taught both Mark Goertzen and Fred Driver before Mark and
Fred moved to Michiana, and in 2013 Tom Unzicker moved from Indiana to Kansas, where he set up a new studio and built a new wood kiln.
Merrill Krabill also taught at Bethel College in Newton, Kansas, before
coming to teach at Goshen College; he now runs the ceramics program
that Marvin established.

In reminiscing about his many years of teaching experience, Marvin always speaks of a lifelong passion for instructing his students in
how to be creative—a value he has successfully instilled in others as
well. "What they really need is the ability to think, and know how to ask
questions, and how to come up with ideas, and how to persist, and how
to hang in there when the going is tough," he says. Marvin's approach
to accomplishing this is multifaceted and includes a critiquing practice
that helps his students learn to evolve ideas out of their own work rather
than imitating others, as well as a calculated structure of coursework
that leaves students curious and eager to take more courses after the first
semester. As an active artist in multiple mediums throughout his life,
including metals, painting, drawing, clay, and woodworking, Marvin
also stresses the importance of creating his own artwork while teaching
(fig. 2.1). "I've never thought I could be a good art teacher if I wasn't an
artist," he explains. The discoveries he made about creativity in his own

Fig. 2.1. Marvin Bartel poses for a photo in the sunny upstairs of his studio in fall 2015. He makes many large pieces such as the ones shown here; notably, both the pedestal sink and the toilet shown in this image would be functional if installed. (*Photo by author*)

life undoubtedly led to the influential teaching methods that others in the Michiana pottery community continue to remark about.

Marvin often states that an important element of his approach to teaching creativity lies in the method he employs for critiques: he always asks students to make at least two or more items, which can then be compared. "Now that we've got two of them, we don't have to say anything bad about anything," he says, touting a constructive, comparative approach.[3] Rather than pointing out negative aspects of the work, he will note aspects of one piece that are *better than* the other, maintaining a positive perspective. Students will be successful, he believes, "if you can teach them how to develop ideas, and realize, mindfully realize that they've developed them themselves—the teacher may be there sort of egging it on," he says with a laugh. "And actually a lot of times, it's very hard to find the good thing happening, and you have to really look for it to affirm it. But that's my role, when I'm doing my job right. That's what I'm trying to do as a teacher, is to look for the smallest little good thing that happened, so I can give some affirmation." It seems that Marvin's positive, encouraging approach has indeed been fruitful; many of the current potters working in the Michiana region have been his students, and they have demonstrated that they are not afraid to experiment with new processes.

In reflecting upon their time as students, a number of the Michiana potters have also commented on the importance of Marvin's "try it and see" philosophy in teaching. Dick Lehman explains that his own personal desire and willingness to experiment with many aspects of the pottery process go back to his days as a student: "There has always been a 'what if' component [in my work], and I would say that goes back to Marvin Bartel," he says. "Many students have said, and it was my experience too, that as beginning students we'd go to Marvin and say, 'What do you think would happen if we tried this?' And he would say, 'Try it and see.'" This phrase of Marvin's has become iconic. Dick continues, "I know now, from this perspective, that he was learning from us, and that we did things that he already knew wouldn't work. Because he had been around, [he knew] there are certain things you just don't do. You don't put this much flux in a glaze, you don't put that much colorant. Well, we didn't know any better and we did [those kinds of things], and some of those things were marvelous," he emphasizes. "So we learned, he learned, and the most important learning was that it's okay to try something new." After over thirty years as a potter, Dick's work is still constantly evolving as he enthusiastically experiments with new ideas for forms, textures, and glazes.

Marvin also likes to share the following story to illustrate his support for experimentation among his students. Describing Jeff Unzicker's early days as a student of ceramics at Goshen College, Marvin says, "I came down [to the studio] one day and he was sitting at the wheel and he had this . . . he had decided to try [making a pot] where you throw and coil them, in order to make it bigger. And he had it about, I don't know, three feet tall or something. I said, 'Jeff, this is great!'" Marvin pauses here, for dramatic effect. "Have you measured the kiln?!" He laughs heartily, recounting this moment, and then continues. "Jeff said, 'Oh, I don't care if I can fire it, I don't care, I just wanted to see if I can make it.' I said, 'Oh, that's great, just do it, see how big you can make it.'"

Marvin recounts that at first Jeff made a pot so wide it would not fit through the studio doorway. After that, Jeff made a pot that was still quite large but slightly narrower. It could be moved through the doorway yet was still too big for the kiln. Marvin remembers, "He made this really tall thing, you know, and that thing was sitting around there for weeks. And then one day he came and said, 'What if I would dig this real deep hole out here in the yard, would there be a way I could fire this tall pot in there?' And . . . there are different ways you could answer that question. I said, 'As far as I know, it's never been done, but I'd sure like to see you try.' And so he went right to it." Eventually, Marvin and Jeff worked together and successfully fired the pot in an experimental kiln consisting of a gas burner, a large hole in the ground, some fire bricks, and the lid of an electric kiln. Today, Jeff Unzicker is still making monumental pots, although these days he typically fires in more conventional kilns; he is well known for the impressive two- to three-foot-tall wood-fired pots that he and his brother Tom have sold at art fairs around the Midwest (fig. 2.2).

Following Marvin's retirement, Merrill Krabill was hired at Goshen College to teach ceramics as well as a variety of other art classes, and he is now the chair of the art department (fig. 2.3). Merrill began his own artistic career as a student at Goshen College, where he remembers beginning ceramics by throwing on the wheel. He appreciated starting with a technical challenge such as this, and he says that beginning with a focus

Fig. 2.2. A collection of tall pots stands impressively outside the Unzicker Bros. Pottery studio in April 2012. The studio has since closed, and each of the brothers now work elsewhere. *(Photo by author)*

Fig. 2.3. Students at work in the Goshen College ceramics studio in November 2015. *(Photo by author)*

on process can help lead one into addressing aesthetic questions—for him, this was better than being faced with a "blank canvas," needing to come up with expressive ideas without first developing an understanding of the potential of the medium. When I interviewed Merrill, he had been overseeing the ceramics students at the school for nearly fifteen years, and he still attributed some of the teaching approaches at Goshen to Marvin's influence, particularly techniques for instilling an appreciation for creativity. He describes this as an approach that focuses not on following directions and copying others, but instead on learning to develop one's own ideas. He also prefers to make sure that all students are included in the entire process of making, a method that Merrill says also began with Marvin. "It's important to know how kilns work, how clay is mixed," he says, noting that these are practical skills students will need to have once they are on their own after college. No aspect of the process should remain a mystery while in school, he believes, because the student would then be unprepared to carry on their work independently afterward.

Students' future aspirations are also taken into consideration in the structure of the current art program at Goshen College, which features two tracks that students can choose from—the studio track prepares students for graduate school (including more focus on writing about one's artwork) while the entrepreneurship program does more to prepare students to run a small arts business. There is also a strong visual arts education program at Goshen College that produces a number of future K–12 art teachers, many of whom choose ceramics as part of their studio art training. Merrill notes that the ceramics facilities are rather small— Goshen College is not a large school, and the ceramics program is likewise small, often with only five or six students enrolled in the advanced ceramics class—but the fact that their studio does not have excessive resources or all-new technology is not a problem for Merrill because he knows it helps his students be better prepared to figure out how to make artwork with whatever materials and equipment they have available, however minimal. This is a benefit both to students who will someday teach and to those who follow the entrepreneurship path, since they are likely to be in situations after college where they have few resources to work with. Building a full studio and gathering the necessary equipment can be very expensive and potentially not attainable, particularly for arts educators who have to teach multiple media, so it helps to learn to "make do with what you've got." He also states that "ethically, it feels nice to recycle and reuse," noting that they do things such as mixing their own clay, which allows for the reincorporation of used but unfired clay (potters refer to this as "reclaim"). While enrolled at Goshen College, Merrill's students often connect, as Marvin's did previously, with the local pottery network in order to find part-time work, apprenticeships, or wood-firing experiences that augment their collegiate training in ceramics; the extent and impact of such opportunities will be addressed in the following sections of this chapter.

SOURCES AND RESULTS OF APPRENTICESHIP IN MICHIANA POTTERIES

During or after college—or sometimes without a college ceramics experience at all—many who desire to become production potters find that their best path is to arrange an apprenticeship, assistantship, or internship in the studio of a working potter. This trend is not limited to Michiana, and the benefits of just such a path are discussed often in texts aimed toward a ceramics-student audience; for example, in the early 2010s, potter and professor Julia Galloway was hosting an extensive website called Field Guide for Ceramic Artists, and her recommendations for post-graduation included a substantial section on apprenticeships, alongside other sections on artist-in-residence opportunities, workshops, grants, and further college experiences via a master's program or a post-baccalaureate (often called a "postbac," this would be undertaken after one finishes an undergraduate degree). She cited many potters who have written on the topic of apprenticeship, including Silvie Granatelli, Val Cushing, Mark Hewitt, John Glick, and Gary Hatcher, and concluded that "apprenticeships can provide a nice bridge between university education and practical, real world concerns for ceramic artists. . . . Apprenticeships offer a unique opportunity to gain insight into the life you plan to live and will undoubtedly provide real world experience that may help you become successful in the field" (Galloway 2015). Most of the articles she cited and suggestions she personally added on the site focused on the importance of knowing exactly what the apprenticeship will entail and ensuring it is a good fit for both the student and the mentor. Many of the comments on apprenticeship found in these articles pertain to the benefit of acquiring the personal attributes needed to run a pottery studio, most of which fall outside the technical skills needed for simply producing work in clay; this clearly reflects the concept of developing vocational habitus, as proposed by Colley et al. (2003).

Folklorists with a focus on craftsmanship have often acknowledged the role of apprenticeship in the development of a craftsperson's identity. For example, Marjorie Hunt devotes a chapter to the learning process in her exploration of the stone carvers of the Washington National Cathedral. Hunt focuses on the rigorous teaching of technical skills and knowledge about tools, as well as the hierarchy of roles and the process of ascending from apprentice to master. She also gives substantial attention to the apprentices' process of learning to adhere to standards of workmanship and aesthetic principles that are exemplified and touted by those more experienced in the trade (Hunt 1999). Similarly, this section gives concrete examples of the links between mentors and their former or current apprentices in the Michiana community, particularly those that lie beyond simple technical knowledge and illuminate the kinds of influences these educative relationships can have on the future work of an apprentice.

My use of the term *apprentice* throughout this book indicates a particular type of situated learning in Michiana—specifically, a hierarchical working relationship that allows for a less-experienced worker to gain practical experience and to learn from a more-experienced worker while sharing a workspace and coordinating on the creation of objects. However, similar terms such as *assistant* or *intern* are also utilized often in Michiana; their vernacular usage has a more modern feel while *apprenticeship* can, for some, seem to be an outdated term. Furthermore, *assistant* is often used to indicated a paid position (although it ostensibly drops the implication that the subordinate worker intends to become a master in their own right eventually), and *intern* often indicates an unpaid position (while clearly indicating that this is a step toward mastery). The use of apprenticeship, for the purposes of my writing, includes the possibility of both paid and unpaid work, maintains the implication that the subordinate is working toward becoming a skilled master of pottery-making, and provides a link to theoretical work on apprenticeship that has helped me to frame my understanding of these relationships, such as that done by Jean Lave (2011).

As Lave has demonstrated, doing ethnography can also be a kind of apprenticeship, not only in the sense that I personally have a background in ceramics and have approached this work as a type of "learning about the doing" of ceramics, but also in that ethnography entails living in an ongoing state of "learning to do what we are already doing" (Lave 2011, 156). When I began my fieldwork I was early in my years of studying folkloristics, and I had relatively little experience doing fieldwork and knew little about the potters living and working in Michiana. With each successive visit to Michiana—each new conversation with and observation of Michiana potters—I learned more about my research topic and began to formulate new questions to ask, and new ways to describe and theorize about the observations I was making. For this chapter in particular—and similarly to Lave's work—I was engaged in both "research *on* learning (through apprenticeship) and research *as* learning (through critical ethnographic practice)" (2).

One of the main sources of ceramic apprenticeship in the Goshen area for many years was Dick Lehman and his studio in the Old Bag Factory (fig. 2.4). Although Dick did not complete a college degree in

Fig. 2.4. The Old Bag Factory in Goshen, Indiana, is no longer used as a factory. Instead the building serves a new role as a home for several small local businesses, including Dick Lehman's former pottery studio, now owned and run by Mark Goertzen. *(Photo by author)*

ceramics (nor was he an apprentice himself), he did get his introduction to ceramics via the college environment, taking courses with Marvin Bartel. As I recounted in chapter 1, Dick vacillated between religious work and work in clay for a while during and after college before eventually deciding in the spring of 1981 that his passion for pottery was worth pursuing full-time. Initially, Dick set up his studio in space that he rented from his friend, local furniture maker Larion Swartzendruber, but it was not long before the two moved into the Old Bag Factory together, where they maintained shops alongside other local artists and craftsmen.[4] Jokingly, Dick recounts his early sales strategies as he set up his shop: "The savvy of my marketing approach was, okay, my customers, they walk into this building and to get to my studio they have to walk through the furniture showroom, and they see a $3000 roll-top desk and a $300 chair, and they get to my studio and see a $30 casserole, and they say 'Okay, I'll take two!'" he laughs. There is clearly truth to the usefulness of this approach, because the same studio space still sits in the Old Bag Factory, accessed via a walkway that leads visitors directly through the middle of a furniture store. Prices, of course, have changed over time, and a large casserole dish might cost closer to $80 today, but it is still not as expensive as the Amish wood furniture next door.[5] Dick also acknowledges that there was a learning process involved, and his sales acumen developed over the years: "Starting a business, you either do learn the things you need to do or you fail, and I obviously figured out a way to do it." After over thirty years of pottery-making, having exhibited his work internationally and published many insightful articles in trade magazines, it is safe to say Dick has figured out quite a lot about the business of being a potter.

The production line that Dick developed at the Old Bag Factory was almost entirely wheel-thrown, though some thrown pieces were modified from their original round shape, and other pieces, such as certain lines of plates and other dinnerware, were made with slam-molds.[6] He utilized a gas kiln for his production work and fired to cone ten in a reduction atmosphere. Dick often utilized brushwork decorations on his production work, applying "an intensely colored glaze over less intensely colored glaze." Though Dick says he never properly learned how to draw, he considered learning to use a brush to be an engaging challenge. Images I have seen of Dick's work from this time period often show pieces glazed in a single color, often white or pastel, with little color variation within the glaze; there might be some slight iron spots speckling the surface, or slight translucency showing the mostly smooth texture of the pot, or perhaps a few faint marks where the glaze has dripped. Over this single, solid color, there are often brushed-on decoration in one or two additional colors that contrast with (but also complement) the main color of the piece. These decorations are usually reminiscent of leaves or flowers or involve graceful serpentine lines (fig. 2.5).

In its heyday, Dick's studio incorporated three or even four employees, often including students from Goshen College who would come to work part-time, at first mixing clay or glaze and later throwing pieces for the production line once they were more experienced. "Each of us worked on every pot, whether it was loading or unloading or waxing or glazing or, in my case, I decorated everything," he says, referring to the fact that he did almost all the brushwork on his pots himself. Dick acknowledged that his employees were also aspiring potters, and he tried

Fig. 2.5. An example of work made by Dick Lehman during his years at the Old Bag Factory studio. Canister set, cone ten reduction firing. *(Photo courtesy of Dick Lehman)*

to encourage their own development as individual potters while they were also working in service of his studio. "I think probably the hardest thing in production pottery is to be an employee of someone else, and to spend four days a week making that person's aesthetic using that person's glazes." To nurture the development of his apprentices, Dick says he "asked them for thirty-five hours a week, and to get that done in the first four days. And then, they would have three days to make their own work." Additionally, employees were able to use studio materials for this individual work and paid a nominal price, set by Dick: "I lost money on every pound [of clay] I sold because I thought it ought to be a fringe benefit, but it ought not to be totally free; there needed to be some ownership and responsibility so that they would be making things that they really wanted to make," he recalls. Dick also instituted the "Thursday Night Challenge," an hour-long weekly occasion where the studio employees would work individually to tackle a problem in clay, then come together to share ideas and try new strategies.[7]

Employees of the studio were also invited to take part in designing new items to be produced by the studio.[8] Dick recounts his philosophy in occasionally introducing new designs, saying "I think part of the job of the production potter is not only to make good things that work well and are aesthetically pleasing and that people enjoy having around them, but also keep the maker's interest. So that does mean some change." When it was time to design a new product, Dick would sometimes offer the opportunity to his employees, to see if anyone else wished to work on the design; this approach, he says, "has moved the aesthetic along—it's no longer just mine, it's a collaborative venture, and I think it's better work than I could make alone." He also believes there is an important state of mind necessary when undertaking this kind of collaborative work: "It takes a mature person to participate in that . . . to participate in the design of a production piece. If they're feeling too much propriety about their work, then they can't do it. If they see this as something we're doing together . . ." It is then, he believes, the venture will be successful. Dick is now well known among potters nationally (if not internationally) for his beautiful, gestural forms as well as his experiments with extremely long wood firings and a variety of glazes. Within Michiana, too, he is well known and recognized as an important mentor and leader in the community.

Mark Goertzen arrived in 1989, intending to work with Dick Lehman for a year. As I noted in chapter 1, Mark pursued this opportunity instead of going to graduate school for ceramics because he wanted to focus on making functional, vessel-oriented pots, rather than the nonfunctional, sculptural ceramic art that most graduate programs were emphasizing (fig. 2.6). Although he did not intend to stay long-term, Michiana has become home. In recounting this experience, Mark noted that although he was not particularly fond of the Goshen weather, the environment he found at Dick's studio encouraged him to stay: "I came here and everything at the studio looked almost exactly how I imagined my own [studio] being. I became friends with Dick as well as his employee . . . I didn't intend to stay here, but I did." What began as an apprenticeship became a long-standing partnership in pottery as well as a strong friendship that persists outside of work, too.

In 2010, Dick was dealing with a life-threatening illness and made the difficult decision to sell the Old Bag Factory studio and to do his pottery work at home in Elkhart, to the extent he would be able. Within

Fig. 2.6. Mark Goertzen throwing on the wheel in the Old Bag Factory studio in 2012. *(Photo by author)*

a few years Dick was, fortunately, in much better health, and began the process of expanding his ceramic work once again. He and his wife, Jo, moved closer to Goshen and built a new home as well as a substantial studio building for Dick, which was added as a location on the Michiana

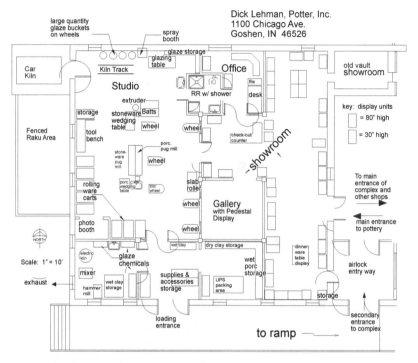

Fig. 2.7. This document (no longer to scale) shows the layout used at the Old Bag Factory, as designed and implemented by Dick Lehman. With minor changes, it remains much the same under Mark Goertzen's ownership. (*Image courtesy of Dick Lehman*)

pottery tour in 2015. However, back in 2010, Mark Goertzen purchased the Old Bag Factory studio from Dick. The space remained much the same in the following years, though it was renamed Goertzen Pottery (fig. 2.7). One of the features of the studio layout that Dick in particular has touted is the arrangement he prefers to use for his glazes. When visiting a friend and fellow potter whose studio was located in an old grain silo—meaning it had only curved walls—Dick was impressed by the convenience of having the glazes in a curved arrangement around central shelves that contained the pottery. By keeping his glaze buckets on wheels, Dick finds he is able to mimic this arrangement in his own studio on days when he has a lot of glazing to do; he can wheel the glaze buckets into a semicircular arrangement and then easily move them back out of the way when he is done glazing. Dick first implemented this arrangement at the Old Bag Factory and has since reused the idea in setting up his new home studio.

Another more permanent feature of the Old Bag Factory space—and one that is more noticeable to visiting customers—is the openness between the production area and the display area of the studio. If you were to visit Mark today, you would notice there is a large, open archway between the showroom and the studio workspace, through which you can almost always see one of the potters working at the wheel. This setup has remained much unchanged since Dick owned the studio; the wheels, at which the potters spend much of their time throwing and trimming, are centrally located, allowing the potters to have a view of customers entering the store. This arrangement is also inviting to customers because they can easily step over and observe how the pottery is made. Other items in the studio that are used less frequently—the large gas kiln, various clay and glaze materials, drying racks, glazing space, and so on—are located on the periphery, along the exterior walls of the studio space, allowing the potters to spend more of their time within view of the sales floor while producing the work they sell.

While Mark and his employees continued producing very similar pots over the years and have maintained some of the same styles that originated with Dick's ownership of the studio, many of the pots in the production line now show more influence from the aesthetic choices Mark has made after Dick left the studio (fig. 2.8). By the time I began visiting the Old Bag Factory in 2012, the pottery on display featured many darker, richer colors of glaze, and while some of the shift to darker colors may have come from the days when Dick was still at the studio, there are also other changes that are clearly reflective of Mark's preferences.

More often than not, pots in Mark's production line are glazed with two contrasting or complementary colors; for example, a turquoise glaze might be paired with a reddish glaze, or a cobalt blue with black (fig. 2.9), or a lighter green or tan glaze might be paired with a darker chocolate brown glaze. Mark also utilizes many ash glazes—a type of glaze that contains wood or soda ash—which tend to run down the pot slightly in the firing, creating texture on the surface of the pot and interesting patterns where one glaze color drips down into a different glaze color (fig. 2.10).

Fig. 2.8. Shelves of pottery on display at Goertzen Pottery in 2013 show influences from both Dick Lehman and Mark Goertzen. The pitchers in the top left corner are clearly reminiscent of the lighter colored glazes and brushwork patterns Dick used in his early days at the studio while other pieces show the two-glaze combinations and use of ash glazes that became more prevalent under Mark's direction. *(Photo by author)*

Fig. 2.9. Pitchers made by Mark Goertzen as part of his production line. Blue ash and black glaze. *(Photo courtesy of Mark Goertzen)*

Discussing the shift, Mark says, "My aesthetic has never been a lot of brushwork. I like glazes that do some running and dripping. I like some of the sense of 'not controlled.'" But this attempt to let go of control can be a challenge. "Sometimes pots come out better than you were hoping for . . . and sometimes they come out worse," he says. Though he has kept some of the same forms and glazes from Dick's designs, which appeals to customers who have long collected work from the studio, Mark has also begun pursuing new additions to their selection of glazes. "It has added a nice freshness to our studio and actually also made me think of making new forms," he says of the changes he's been trying out. "The [glazes] I'm interested in are sort of runny glazes and now I can start making forms for taking advantage of that. I think that's also been nice about this studio." Mark pauses, thinking. "There's always been a sense of play here. Not just cranking out work, it's important to crank out

Fig. 2.10. A large pot on display in Goertzen Pottery in 2012 features some of the dripping glaze effect that Mark likes to pursue in his production line. *(Photo by author)*

some work, but there's also encouragement to explore, play a little bit, in hopes that aesthetics grow and keep growing. And so, I think that's maybe why it has been an attractive place for young people for a little bit as a layover," he says, his comments echoing Dick's. Mark also describes the studio as, ideally, a three-person endeavor; the workflow seems to be best when there are three pairs of hands to work on the various aspects of production.

In the last few years, Mark has preferred to keep at least one or two apprentices or assistants working for him as well as minimal additional staff to help with the sales floor. Moshe Hodges, also a potter, was a long-time employee of the studio through around 2014. Mark's wife, Suzanne Ehst, a professor of education at Goshen College, engages with Mark's work regularly, whether it's helping him to fire the wood kiln or assisting with the promotional writing and online sales. Mark has also hired a local woman who comes in on occasion to help clean and dust the numerous display shelves in the shop. Like many production potteries, the shop has busier times of year, particularly around Christmas, and some much slower times: "The first four months of the year are very slow here," Mark says, "so that'll be the time when we develop glazes and such . . . actually, it's kind of a nice rhythm, if you know you have enough in your checking account, because that's the time when we can a little more purposefully experiment on form, rather than just doing a little bit here and there." Mark does indeed offer a broad selection of forms. The catalog portion of his website divides items into three categories—kitchenware, living-ware, and ovenware—and some of the more unusual items on offer include yarn bowls (to hold balls of yarn while knitting or crocheting, with special cutouts for the yarn to come through), shaving mugs, oil lamps, pâté dishes, brie bakers, honey pots, French butter keepers, and more. Under Mark's guidance, production at the Old Bag Factory continues to move into the future with a steady combination of new inspirations and past successes—a balance first struck by Dick Lehman and later instilled in the many apprentices who have been educated within its walls.

The legacy of the Old Bag Factory studio space, first incorporated as Dick Lehman, Potter, and now named Goertzen Pottery, is also evinced by the number of former apprentices now running their own pottery studios in the Michiana region. Among these are Justin Rothshank and

Todd Pletcher; both Justin and Todd were students of Marvin Bartel, though Marvin retired soon after Todd started classes at Goshen College. Todd still has a strong connection via his apprenticeship with Dick Lehman at the Old Bag Factory, where he also worked side by side with Mark Goertzen. Unlike Todd and Justin, Eric Strader did not attend the Goshen College ceramics program—instead, his main pottery training came from working under Dick Lehman. Like all of the Michiana potters, their personal styles are distinctively different, but Justin, Todd, and Eric all provide examples of the new ateliers established within the flourishing Michiana pottery tradition.[9]

Growing up in Goshen, Indiana, Justin Rothshank (fig. 2.11) connected with clay during his early school years. "I came into high school being interested in clay because of my middle school teacher," he says. During his later years at Goshen High School, Justin studied under Cindy Cooper. When I met her in the early 2010s, Cindy was still teaching high school students and was an active member of the local Clay Artists Guild. She introduced Justin to Jeff Unzicker, who was just a few years older, and Jeff first introduced Justin to wood firing. During his senior year of high school, Justin enrolled in a clay class at Goshen College with Marvin Bartel, and he continued his studies there after high school as well. "There was a really good community of clay folks there at the college," he recalls. After graduating, Justin went to Pittsburg, Pennsylvania to complete a year of service and was apprenticed to a cabinetmaker. During that time, he stayed engaged with clay, even setting up a studio in his basement; he says it was at that point that he really began pursuing clay. In the midst of his year of service, Justin "connected with other folks who were raised Mennonite, committed to arts, faith, and community development," and decided to start a nonprofit that came to be called the Union Project. Located in a large, repurposed, one-hundred-year old church building, the organization functioned as a community center and included a full clay studio, a sanctuary for worship, a venue for performances, a coffee shop, and office spaces available for small businesses to lease. Justin was a founder of the organization as well as the first staff member hired, and he spent about eight years working for the Union Project, running their clay studio and developing a line of production pottery.[10]

Fig. 2.11. Justin Rothshank, along with some of his wood-fired and decal ware, outside of his studio during the 2013 Michiana Pottery Tour. *(Photo by author)*

Fig. 2.12. A selection of Justin's work on display in his studio during the Michiana Pottery Tour in 2015. The top row features a portion of his series of wares with decal images of the presidents of the United States while the lower shelf includes examples of other political figures, pop culture icons, and bright red poppy decals he often applies. *(Photo by author)*

In 2009, Justin and his wife, Brooke, who is also an artist, decided to return to Goshen. They built a home on family property just west of Goshen and built an outbuilding with a walk-out basement studio space for Justin to continue his production pottery line (fig. 2.12). A later renovation added a display and sales area on the main floor of the building and studio space for Brooke on the upper floor, leaving Justin's original studio workspace in the walk-out basement. The two also share a website and often exhibit their work together (fig. 2.13) or travel together to teach workshops. For example, they have travelled with their family and lived temporarily at places such as the Penland School of Craft, where they were both employed to teach residential classes that lasted a few weeks. Brooke's work is usually two-dimensional, and her focus is on creating miniature drawings or paintings, most of which are only an inch or two in diameter. In addition to the many art exhibitions the two participate in together, the local sales they generate through special events at their

Fig. 2.13. This image is from "KNOW JUSTICE," a joint show by Justin and Brooke Rothshank at the Ferrin Contemporary gallery in 2016. The table is set with forty-four place settings, each with two plates, a bowl, and a mug adorned with decals of each of the United States presidents. Brooke's miniature watercolor portraits were displayed on a wall at the end of the table. *(Photo courtesy of Justin Rothshank)*

studio, and sales through their shared Etsy shop, Justin also sells his ceramic work wholesale in galleries around the country, and he is well known for the unique decals (often bright red poppies, political figures, or pop culture images) that he adds to his pots.

Justin's work has a heavily layered look, often involving the layering of two colors of glaze, plus multiple decal images applied over those glazes. His process involves first glaze firing his work, then refiring at successively lower temperatures to adhere the decal images; Justin sometimes fires a piece upward of four times in order to layer on all of the glazes and decals. He is well known for his technique, which he often shares when he teaches workshops both locally and around the country. As a result, many potters in the Michiana area have begun to incorporate some amount of decal decoration into their own work. Locally, Justin is involved in the Clay Artists Guild in Goshen, where he has often taught clay classes. He also provides internships at his own studio, providing some materials and space to work in return for help with his production line or with other tasks around the studio.[11] He also built a wood-fired kiln on his property soon after moving to Goshen, and he connects with many local potters through the two to three annual firings of his kiln (an aspect of the community that will be discussed further in chap. 3).

In some ways, Todd Pletcher (fig. 2.14) was a later addition to the Michiana pottery community, though he has a long history in the area; although he grew up in Goshen, Todd spent many years working in Chicago after graduating from college and returned to live in the outskirts of Goshen in fall of 2012 with his partner, Anna Corona. The two met in Chicago while she was taking evening adult ceramics classes and he was teaching classes for the same organization. Todd's story is similar to Justin's—he began making pottery in high school and then worked at the Old Bag Factory pottery studio with Dick Lehman and Mark Goertzen while attending Goshen College (he was enrolled there during the transition between Marvin Bartel and Merrill Krabill). However, after graduating, Todd spent a number of years working in another field before realizing he wanted to return to clay. "When I was up in Chicago, I was learning a lot about what I didn't want to do with my life," he says. Around 2007, Todd began to shift back to pottery, teaching ceramics classes at different locations in the city and selling some of his own work.

Fig. 2.14. Todd Pletcher shows off a wood-fired pot in the studio he set up in the barn on his property. Photo taken in May 2013. *(Photo by author)*

Todd explains that he finds pottery much more engaging while working for himself than he did toward the end of his time as an apprentice: "When I was making my own designs, as opposed to making someone else's design, I didn't mind sitting down and spending a day making coffee mugs," he says, though he also mentions the tedium that many production potters can face when making large runs of the same item over and over. To develop his own production line, Todd says he often looks back to lessons learned as an apprentice. "I picked up enough working at Mark's, or I guess it was Dick's at the time, working with those guys, to have a pretty solid understanding of what I need in order to run a business like that . . . [Dick's] system, that he had put in place over all those years, was built on efficiency, trying to find the quickest way to generate a really quality product," he recalls. After moving, Todd began to slowly improve his new studio space and tried to get a sense of the market both locally and nationally (primarily, at least at first, through online sales). When I spoke with him about this endeavor in 2013, he discussed his hopes for expanding his facility and said, "I swore that I would never borrow money to do this, so I'm putting it together as I make sales." He was indeed able to do so, slowly and steadily, and after living in Goshen for about three years he was even able to invest in building his own wood kiln on his property.

By moving back to Goshen, Todd hoped to find a good market for functional pottery, and he also appreciated having fellow potters nearby: "That's one of the good things about being in Goshen—Justin is here, Mark and Dick are here, so we can bounce ideas off each other quite a bit." Having several potters in the same area can also be challenging, he notes, particularly since Mark and Todd do relatively similar work. "The biggest thing is trying to figure out where to sell without really intruding upon Mark's business. I think if we compete against each other in some ways that's good, in some ways it's a little bit rough on the both of us," he explains. "Justin is sort of unique in that Justin's work is different than what other potters are doing in Goshen, so he doesn't really compete with the same market," Todd later elaborates, as he muses about ways in which his own work is unique—undulating lips and wavy line details often set his vessels apart from the rest (see fig. 2.15).

Reflecting on these challenges, however, Todd also counters the difficulties with a positive outlook: "The more awareness we bring to the area the better it is for everyone. If I can get people to come from my contacts in Chicago, to come down to the tour or to stop by to purchase work, they might realize that they like Justin's work or Mark Goertzen's work more than mine, in the same way that someone who finds out about me through Mark might decide to buy from me. So, the more awareness there is about the community in general, the better it is, we think, for everyone." Additionally, he says, "Almost all of us are Mennonite, so that whole sense of community and working together in sort of a service-oriented fashion seems to be another thing that also helps us get along."

Though his studio was established later than the others discussed above, Todd fit in easily when he relocated to the Michiana pottery community, and he was able to find ways to be successful as a potter in this region. He hosted workshops at his spacious studio and was able to develop thriving online sales through Etsy.com, particularly during the holiday season. Todd has also been recognized nationally for his wood-fired work; for example, he was selected as one of *Ceramics Monthly* magazine's

Fig. 2.15. A selection of Todd's wavy-rimmed wares on display during the 2014 Michiana Pottery Tour. The sign reads, "Why wavy rims? Because they are comfortable to drink out of. And they're unique, not your average wheel-thrown pot. Plus, we think they look nice . . ." *(Photo by author)*

2015 Emerging Artists and had his wood-fired pottery featured in the publication. Indeed, much of his reason for building his own wood kiln was because he needed to fire more often in order to meet the growing demands for his work.

Justin Rothshank and Todd Pletcher are by no means the only results of the collegiate and apprenticeship opportunities in Michiana, however. One further example is Eric Strader (fig. 2.16), who has found his own niche in the Michiana market, often producing large runs of customized mugs for nearby breweries and coffee shops. Eric also makes many unique functional pieces using a carbon trapping glaze, and the distinctive "sun spots" on his work set his displays apart. Eric looked to his family for his first introduction to the world of ceramics; his grandfather, Stanley Kellogg, was a well-known Michigan sculptor and potter. Although his process is rather different from Kellogg's mold-oriented work, some of the pottery Eric creates (particularly his pitchers—see fig. 2.16) echo his grandfather's forms. Eric's wife, an elementary art teacher, also helped to reintroduce him to clay during the time that they were dating.

Fig. 2.16. Standing in his studio in July 2013, Eric Strader holds one of his pitchers, not yet glaze fired, which was inspired by his grandfather's sculptural forms. (*Photo by author*)

Fig. 2.17. Founding members Bob Smoker (*left*) and Cindy Cooper (*right*) work at the guild during the 2013 Michiana Pottery Tour. (*Photo by author*)

After moving to Goshen, Eric met Dick Lehman and found that there was an opening at Dick's studio for an apprentice, "so I kind of learned everything from the ground up there," he says. "I learned everything, starting out with mixing clay and glazes, but then also I learned how to throw, making fifty or sixty of one form at a time, which I've always said was the best way to learn," he says. After five years as an apprentice at Dick's studio, Eric began to make pots in his own home and to fire his pottery at the Goshen Clay Artists Guild. Once the guild moved into a new building, Eric took over their old space behind the Maple City Market for many years. As of 2014, though, he had shifted to working in a basement studio in his home in Goshen, and he had also begun to build a new studio on family property near Kalamazoo, Michigan, where he expects to relocate in the future; by 2015 he had already moved his large gas kiln and was doing all his glaze firing there, while still living in Goshen.

Like Eric, Michiana potter Bob Smoker (fig. 2.17) also draws a strong connection between the guild and his ability to pursue a ceramics career.

Bob was one of the founding members of the Goshen Clay Artists Guild in 1998, renewing a love of clay that had grown stagnant for nearly twenty years while he pursued other jobs and raised his family. Bob had originally come to love clay as a high school student in Pennsylvania and later studied ceramics at both Hesston College in Kansas and Goshen College in Indiana (as noted above, he introduced Dick Lehman to ceramics while studying there under Marvin). After many years in the guild, Bob finally "quit his day job" in 2010 and decided to pursue ceramics full-time, and for a while he was the only guild member who worked full-time making ceramics in the guild space. Both Eric's and Bob's narratives of their involvement with the Goshen Clay Artists Guild point toward another important aspect of the Michiana pottery community: the existence of a guild facility in Goshen has allowed many potters to continue working in clay after their formative experiences as college students and/or potter's apprentices.

GATHERING AT THE GOSHEN CLAY ARTISTS GUILD

The establishment of the Goshen Clay Artists Guild has been significant to the development of a robust ceramics-oriented community in the Michiana area because it provides a space for those who do not wish to (or do not have the resources to) work in clay full-time, as well as for those who do not wish to or cannot take on the expense and responsibility of setting up and maintaining their own studios. When I spoke with members at various points in the early to mid-2010s, they stated that the guild had been maintaining a membership of around twenty-five to thirty members, at least half of whom are quite actively and regularly involved in making pots. Nestled on the bank of the Millrace Canal and situated just behind the local farmer's market building, the guild is currently located in a generously sized building (fig. 2.18), which includes a large workspace with twelve wheels and many worktables, a glazing area, a glaze materials room, a kiln room, a photography room and small library, and a kitchenette. The Millrace Center was developed by local philanthropists David and Faye Pottinger, and in addition to the Goshen Clay Artists Guild the complex of buildings also includes suites for other local artists' guilds, including the photographers, jewelers, painters, and woodworkers guilds. Regarding this project and others, David Pottinger

Fig. 2.18. The Clay Artists Guild building, which replaced their former location behind the Maple City Market in downtown Goshen. *(Photo by author)*

has said, "We're trying to turn [Goshen] into a community where our local people don't have to go out of town for what they want, whether it's food or entertainment or community gathering" (McGurk 2011).[12]

The Clay Artists Guild is definitely a central location for the Goshen pottery community to gather and to learn; throughout the year clay-related classes and workshops are held frequently in their facility. In fact, these adult classes, which are open to the public, often lead to the addition of new guild members.[13] Marvin Bartel has reflected on the establishment of the guild, saying, "I was very pleased when that got organized, because I was still teaching, and every time somebody graduated and didn't have a place to work, then I'd feel bad because, you know, they wanted to work and they didn't have a place to work." He went on to explain, "There were some, like Dick Lehman and so on, that could . . . they'd just figure out a way to get a studio and get going, but that's a pretty major choice to make. So there were a lot of people that wanted to keep doing something else, but also see whether they could do pottery." Clearly there was a growing need for a community space.

Now, members of the guild have access to the facility any time they wish, with the exception that they are asked not to work during class

Fig. 2.19. Founding member and guild director Fred Driver stands with some of his in-progress pottery at the guild in May 2013. *(Photo by author)*

times. In an interview in 2013, guild director Fred Driver (fig 2.19) described the range of member involvement, saying, "There's only one guild member, Bob Smoker, who is a professional who [makes pottery at the guild] full time. The rest of us go from half time down to just . . . paying for a space, actually. Some want to try and support the arts so they pay for a space but they don't actually work here." The guild is run on a voluntary basis, with a few members like Fred in leadership roles and others involved in various committees.

In addition to hosting classes and workshops that are open to non-members, the guild also interfaces with the broader Goshen community through various sales and events throughout the year. Guild members have the option of selling their work at the guild's booth at the farmer's market space, which is only a few steps away from the front door of the guild; to do so, members must take shifts sitting at the booth and pay a small commission percentage to the guild. Additionally, over the course of a year the guild traditionally holds two sales of member work, one in

Fig. 2.20. Guild members Patricia Burns (*left*) and Eric Kaufmann (*right*) take a turn at the sales counter during the 2013 Michiana Pottery Tour. (*Photo by author*)

fall and one in spring. Their fall sale has now been incorporated into the Michiana Pottery Tour, and they have been included as a location on all Michiana Pottery Tours as of 2018. The guild also organizes a soup benefit every year. Each member makes a few or several bowls for the occasion. Then customers come to the event and purchase the bowls, in which their soup, provided by the potters and/or by local restaurants, will be served; after the meal the bowls are theirs to take home. Each year, the benefit raises around $10,000 for a local homeless charity, and by 2013, the potters were serving between seven and eight hundred bowls of soup at each event. "It's a good benefit, and we really like to stay in touch with the city, with the community, rather than just be an isolated group of potters," says Fred. The guild's desire to make their artistic output relevant and helpful to their broader community is clearly related to trends in the growing Goshen arts scene; to paraphrase David Pottinger, it is about making Goshen a better place for its residents by providing what is needed locally.

Indeed, the guild's members connect with the community in many ways beyond their membership activities. Two members, Eric Kauffman

Fig. 2.21. Cindy Cooper (*left*) and Dick Lehman (*right*) work together to stoke Justin Rothshank's wood kiln. (*Photo courtesy of Justin Rothshank*)

(fig. 2.20) and Cindy Cooper (fig. 2.17 and 2.21), teach ceramics classes at local high schools and have been responsible for inspiring a younger generation of Michiana potters. Cindy has also worked with Zach Tate to offer a summer wood-firing workshop for high school students for at least four years (fig. 2.21). Regarding her relationship with her students, Cindy says it is important for her to identify as an artist first and a teacher second; she appreciates the catharsis she finds through her artwork, and she enjoys being able to share that understanding with her students as they begin to identify as artists as well. Cindy finds "a beautiful connection" among potters, perhaps a closer connection than what is found in some of the other guilds. She attributes much of that communal feeling to the fact that the potters must all work closely together—artists in the guild and students in the school—sharing space and equipment, working out of the same glaze buckets, and so on. In this kind of environment, getting along with one another and having a mutual understanding of the work is crucial.

VOCATIONAL HABITUS AMONG MICHIANA POTTERS

All of the places of learning that I have described in this chapter can be analyzed as spaces where "legitimate peripheral participation" takes place. This heuristic developed by Jean Lave and Etienne Wenger is meant to shift analysis away from the distinction between intentional instruction and learning; instead, they focus on the process of learning and the relations between the participants ([1991] 2011, 36–41). I evoke this here because learning occurs in many forms and in many places in Michiana, and it often occurs outside of intentional teaching moments. The vocational habitus that I believe is developed among many of the Michiana potters comes out of learning experiences where they are legitimate peripheral participants—this does not mean that there are potentially illegitimate participants but rather that they are relevant and related to the experience. The implication, then, is that there are power structures in this learning relationship, and there may be reasons why the person doing the learning is kept from more full participation (for example, in this case, lack of knowledge, skill, or experience). There is also likely no true "center" of the community or possibility of "complete" participation, but Lave and Wenger do make the distinction of "full participation," a term that is parallel to Becker's "integrated professionals," indicating a fullness of ability to participate in the given artistic activity and related art world (Becker [1982] 2008, 228–29). In this ongoing process of learning and identity development, similar habits, perspectives, and preferences emerge, and they are developed and maintained in dialogue with other participants in the tradition.

Throughout my conversations with many of the Michiana potters about their beginnings in clay and their experiences working in shared spaces, a number of themes slowly began to emerge. Readers will likely have noticed the repetition of values such as creativity and experimentation, awareness of space, collaboration between artists, frugality and efficiency, and service to others—threads that I will now pull together and analyze more closely in the following pages. These are not technical skills but instead are a "combination of dispositions demanded by the vocational culture," as prescribed by the concept of professional habitus (Colley et al. 2003). Those who are central to the Michiana network of potters all express similar values in the processes of their work and have a similar understanding of the embodied experience of being a potter, all of which leads to a sense of community among them.[14] Indeed, many express their desire to stay in this particular location due to the similar mind-set of those whom they will see and interact with on a regular basis. As Colley et al. point out, this connection is inherent in Bourdieu's argument, since field and habitus are co-constructing; the field conditions the habitus, and the habitus helps to constitute the field as a valuable and meaningful world worth working in (Colley et al. 2003, 478). The potters' continual (or at least oft-reoccurring) presence in each other's lives helps to reinforce their shared identity. My focus, therefore, is on the localized values that the Michiana potters trace to particular people and sites where they have worked and learned.

Of all the shared values listed above, first let us turn to creativity, which may seem an obvious value for an artist to hold. This term is perhaps better understood as glossing for experimentation, or the acceptance of risk in the pursuit of new ideas. Certainly it would be possible for those who do production work to continue to produce the same or very similar objects over and over again and to make a good living doing so. However, the fact that so many of the potters value exploration and experimentation with their materials gives them a common ground for discussion and an admiration for one another that is clear when they talk about their friends and mentors. Numerous times I have heard Michiana potters expressing their esteem for others in the group by saying something to the effect of "I really appreciate their willingness to try new things," with the underlying implication that trying something new is risky and does not always have positive results. When Marvin Bartel has told his students "try it and see," he has done so knowing that the consequences could potentially be somewhat destructive or wasteful of materials, but that potentiality is balanced by the prospect of the student (and teacher, in some cases) discovering a new technical aspect of the material, or being driven toward a new expressive development in their work. Similarly, Cindy Cooper and Merrill Krabill both express the importance of having their students learn to develop their own ideas and not just replicate what others have created. As professionals, this value of experimentation continues to be expressed by those who routinely take time out of their year—as Dick Lehman and Mark Goertzen recounted and as many other potters do as well—to test new glazes and glaze combinations. While the results of these tests may not be immediately sellable and materials used in tests cannot be reclaimed, it is a worthy opportunity cost because it adds interest in the work for the potter, and it furthermore has the potential of leading to new designs that may be of value to clients and collectors. Additionally, the fact that many of the potters continue—well after their time as students or apprentices—to find the time and the funds to attend workshops is another testament to their desire to continue learning about their craft and to try new approaches.

Developing a sense of space is another clear theme in discussions about learning to become a potter, and it is one that may be unfamiliar to those who do not often create or work with substantial physical objects. Marvin Bartel provides the first example here when he discusses Jeff Unzicker's first large pot; Jeff's disregard for the next steps of the process and places like doorways and kilns where the pot would need to fit are both inspiring (as it is exciting to see a student experiment) and reflective of a common learning experience, since students must learn to plan ahead for the entire process and develop a sense of how pots will fit into existing equipment. The importance of planning ahead for space will also become clear in the chapter 3 discussion of sharing space in a wood-fired kiln. Given that shared studio and kiln spaces are very common—students (and sometimes teachers) work together in college studios, mentors and apprentices work together in professional studios, guild members work together at the guild space, and so on—it is also important that the potters in these environments are comfortable working closely with one another and are able to negotiate using the space simultaneously. As Cindy Cooper, high school teacher and guild member, has described it, potters often feel a sense of community because they so often must "work on top of one another." And, in this regard, it is certainly easy to imagine that one who does not desire to work in the company of others, or who is not comfortable with or adept at the social navigations necessary (taking turns with materials or equipment, developing shared standards for the care and cleanup of the space, potentially bumping into one another in cramped quarters, and so on) may be more likely to leave the shared space in question. Colley et al.

address this aspect of developing vocational habitus when they describe attrition from certain vocational training programs. Vocational habitus "is relational and dynamic, co-constructed partly by the dispositions of the students themselves as they construct their own identities. The vocational habitus must be a 'choosable' identity for the individual," and thus when a student is not able to transform their personal habitus and orient themselves to the vocational habitus, they are likely to decide they are not right for the job and will often decide to pursue other work (2003, 488–89). This certainly points to the usefulness of a possible comparative study; interviewing those who have trained in the Michiana area and subsequently chosen to move and work in other areas of the world would likely provide further insights as to the kinds of values or work habits that are likely to pull one away from this area. Developing a working space where one can work comfortably and efficiently is also crucial.[15] This is reflected in Mark Goertzen's comments that Dick's studio "felt" right and looked as he had imagined his own studio someday being; he lists this feeling for the space along with the development of friendships as being his main reasons for ultimately staying in Michiana.

Along with the ability to work in the same space yet on different ceramic projects, there is also the possibility of working collaboratively in order to complete a single pot or series of pots. This is quite common in apprenticeship arrangements, when the various tasks of creation may be divided among members of the studio; repetitive throwing of smaller objects like cups or bowls may be left to apprentices while more complex decorative work might be left to the master potter, for example. Or, apprentices might mix clay and glaze, split wood, and help to load and unload a kiln, thus clearly contributing to multiple aspects of manufacture, while the hands-on creation of the studio's output of pots might be undertaken by another more experienced member of the team. The work can be shared in many different formations, but in any case, there is a clear need for each potter involved to be comfortable handing the results of their work on to someone else and to have trust in the other to complete their own work with skill so that the end result can be one worthy of pride from all—to the extent that Dick Lehman has stated he feels the result was better than he could have created alone. While this arrangement is primarily seen at the Old Bag Factory studio under

Dick and later Mark (which has contributed to the learning experience of many in the area), Justin Rothshank has also had a number of apprentices in his studio, where they work in return for the opportunity to learn from him and to have space to create their own work.

Justin also provides a strong example of another kind of collaboration in clay: when established professional artists combine their skills to create finished pots or sculptures with elements of both artists' work. Justin has coordinated with a variety of other potters to create in this way, both locally, with potters such as Todd Pletcher, and farther spread around the country. His collaborators have included Eric Botbyl (owner of Companion Gallery in Tennessee, where many of the Michiana potters have been given the opportunity to exhibit their work) and Greg Stahly (Goshen College graduate and former Dick Lehman apprentice, who now teaches in Michigan), among many others.[16] Often, the other potter will create the ceramic form using their own idiosyncratic methods, and then Justin will decorate the surface with glazes and his distinctive decals (fig. 2.22). As discussed above, this kind of working relationship requires a sense of trust and an appreciation for the effects created by the potter with whom one works. The finished piece will be reflective of both individuals, and the hands of each of the individuals who contributed to the piece are often clearly recognizable by pottery connoisseurs familiar with those artists; by choosing to work together, each person is indicating a willingness to be associated with the other in a rather permanent form. This format also requires the artists to work together to negotiate sales of the resulting artwork, agreeing on how (or by whom) the piece will be displayed or advertised, how the income will be divided between them, and so on. However, I have rarely if ever heard a potter express concern about the sales of such work; the primary focus when discussing collaboration is generally on appreciating one another's work and having an opportunity to gain a new perspective on one's forms or decorative approaches via working with each other. Seeing the results that arise from another person's input can be a great source of new ideas that can be later incorporated into one's individual work.

The concepts of frugality and efficiency also show up often when the potters discuss their approaches to their work. Reusing materials in the Goshen College studio is common practice, and they are even planning

Fig. 2.22. Pots made collaboratively by Todd Pletcher and Justin Rothshank, on display in Todd's studio in spring 2013. These have Todd's distinctive wavy rims and Justin's recognizable poppy decals. *(Photo by author)*

to use the bricks of their old wood kiln to build a new kiln soon; many potters do this in order to avoid the expense of purchasing brand-new bricks and to avoid wasting any bricks from old kilns or factories that are still in usable condition. Merrill Krabill specifically tries to instill the value of "learning to work with what you have," knowing this will help his students later when they begin their careers. Marvin Bartell also expressed a concern for his students as they attempt to continue pursuing pottery after leaving college; being able to do so without needing to buy lots of expensive equipment is important, and this is one of the main purposes the guild serves within the community. A sense of frugality is also reflected in Todd Pletcher's decision to never borrow money to establish his studio, instead working hard to make the money he needs to expand his facility. Efficiency is similarly important; any practice that is wasteful of time, money, or materials can be detrimental to the potter's ability to achieve their goals. In this regard, Todd expressed his admiration for Dick Lehman and Mark Goertzen's studio practices, which he learned from while working for them at the Old Bag Factory. And Dick has discussed some specific ways of implementing efficient practice in his studio, particularly his ability to create a semicircular layout for glazing that is easy to navigate. Furthermore, the studio layout that allows the potters to continue working while also maintaining an awareness of their display space—which allows them to quickly serve customers, either in answering questions, giving demonstrations, or making sales— is both efficient and frugal, since they do not need to employ a separate person to stay at the sales counter (fig. 2.23).

Service is another clear value within this community, often linked to the Mennonite faith and Goshen College. In *Mennonite Entrepreneurs*, Calvin Redekop, Stephen C. Ainlay, and Robert Siemens address the seeming contradiction between an entrepreneur's goal of accumulating wealth and the traditional Mennonite commitment to the collective good. They suggest that while it may seem peculiar for those of the Mennonite faith to run businesses and focus on economic prosperity, doing so is rationalized if one's work can be viewed as a form of service to the community and a way of achieving collective goals (1995, 86–92). None of the Michiana potters have expressed any dissonance between their work and their faith; most note that finding ways to be of service to the community is a key part of their ceramic practice. Tom Unzicker's service trip to Tanzania was a crucial aspect of his entry into the world of clay (described on p. 110), and Justin's community project in Philadelphia remains a strong aspect of his personal history with the arts. The Goshen Clay Artists Guild's soup benefit also provides assistance

Fig. 2.23. This image, taken in August 2012, approximates Mark Goertzen's view of his display area while he is working at his wheel. The sales counter is immediately to the left of this image, allowing him to easily step over to assist customers. (*Photo by author*)

to those in need in the Goshen area. Even Dick Lehman's discussion of selling clay at a loss to those he mentored at the Old Bag Factory is an indicator of his willingness to sacrifice potential income in favor of facilitating learning opportunities for others; he also regularly provided for his apprentices to attend ceramics workshops and conferences while they worked for him. Certainly teaching is a main form of service within this group; many directly take on the title of teacher or professor, while nearly every other potter has mentored apprentices and/or taught in the form of community classes or workshops.[17] As Marvin and Cindy have both expressed, identifying as both an artist and a teacher is a benefit; it not only provides an observable example of a working artist for students but it also allows for teacher and student to build a deeper connection. Sharing their discoveries and excitement with one another is a value that goes much deeper than simply teaching technical skills.

I also cannot fail to mention that working in these communal spaces along with students or apprentices is a strong part of identity maintenance for teachers and mentors; while students are undergoing a process of "becoming," those who teach are finding ways to express what they believe to be the best parts of themselves, intentionally foregrounding valued aspects of their identities as artists and potters in the hopes that these aspects will be taken on by those they mentor. And, as I have mentioned, even those who teach often find time to continue their own education through workshops or research into new processes; the education that happens within this network of potters is not linear but instead is often complex and constantly occurring among members of the group who take on a variety of roles. This aspect of co-constructed identities and identity maintenance through teaching and learning is also quite important in the context of wood firing; although students and those who are otherwise very new to wood firing often take part and learn quite a lot at firings, teaching and learning is not always straightforward and chronologically predictable. For example, it is not always true that the oldest or most experienced potter can tell the others how best to manage a wood-fired kiln. Instead, it is more often the case that all the potters who are present at a wood firing are, at that moment, learning about the kiln and the idiosyncrasies of that specific instance of firing, and each potter involved is likely to bring insights from their various wood-firing experiences that will be relevant to overcoming challenges at particular moments in the current firing.

NOTES

1. Bordeau's theorizing of habitus and field is substantially more complex than I will engage with here; I use these terms because Colley et al.'s work on vocational habitus provides a useful structure for thinking about educational practices and identity development processes within occupational groups.

2. Some aspects of the values I identify in this chapter may be shared among many in the pottery profession, while others are more specific to Michiana. A more expansive study would be necessary to make far-reaching proclamations about professional potters throughout the country (or the world), but I have attempted to note which values appear to be more broadly applicable and which are likely more localized.

3. This method is described in more detail in "The Art of Motivation and Critique in Self-Directed Learning," Marvin's contribution to the book titled *The Learner-Directed Classroom* (Bartel 2012).

4. See p. 200–1 for an explanation of the quirky name of this building and its origin story.

5. Prices in Michiana range depending on the size and complexity of the piece, but one could expect to buy a mug for anywhere between $20 and $45, a serving bowl for perhaps $45 to $75, a midsize, simple, wheel-thrown vase (around ten to sixteen inches tall) for $50 to $100. Wood-fired work would fall on the upper end of these ranges, and for particularly good work, prices can be even higher (some of Dick's best pieces may now cost up to $1,000).

6. Slam-molding pottery refers to a process where flat slabs of clay are rolled out and then placed onto a mold. The clay and mold are then dropped or "slammed" onto a hard surface such as the floor or a table. The force of the drop makes the clay slump into the mold, thus conforming to the mold's shape. This provides a relatively quick and low-tech way for production potters to make pieces that are all the same size and shape but not necessarily round; it can provide variation in a production line that is otherwise mostly made up of thrown pots.

7. Dick has written in more detail about this experience in his article titled "The Thursday Night Challenge: Stagnation, Deepening and Stoking the Fire Within," published in *Ceramics Monthly* magazine (Lehman 2008).

8. This was true particularly in the later years; Dick recounts that initially he kept a tight hold on the design work, and everything produced was of his own invention.

9. In addition to these three potters who work in the Michiana area, there are dozens of others who are now farther spread. See Appendix II for a complete list of those who have worked under Mark and Dick as well as those who have worked with Justin Rothshank, who provides apprenticeship experiences in his Goshen studio.

10. Justin has described this experience in much more detail in an article titled "Union Project," published in *Ceramics Monthly* magazine in 2007 (Rothshank and Stephenson).

11. See appendix II for a list of Justin's interns over the years.

12. The Pottingers' influence on the arts scene in Goshen is discussed in further detail in chapter 5.

13. It is worthwhile to note that the membership of the guild is primarily adults older than college age, and the guild typically does not cater to students; this is one of the

reasons that Zach Tate has found there is a need in the community to establish a youth arts space, discussed in chapter 5.

14. Colley et al. also stipulate that "how to look" is part of the definition of vocational habitus, and I could delve into this further. However, the images included in this chapter already do much of the work for me: readers who look closely will notice that the clothing worn is practical, typically consisting of jeans, T-shirts, and aprons, and clothing and skin are often marked with clay or glaze. Furthermore, discussions of appropriate clothing are so prevalent in technical literature and training that it seems unnecessary to recount here.

15. C. Kurt Dewhurst also discusses the alteration of physical work environments, but he does so in regards to industrial work settings where workers often have little or no ownership or control over their place of work (1984).

16. Justin has also explored collaborations on objects other than pots. For example, he worked with Troy Bungart to create ceramic ferrules for Troy's brushes and worked with John Geci to apply decals to blown glass.

17. To provide a succinct list, this includes Cindy Cooper, Eric Kaufmann, and Len Cockman at local high schools and Marvin Bartel, Merrill Krabill, and Bill Kremer at local colleges (along with Chad Hartwig and Zach Tate, who have worked at Notre Dame with Bill). To my knowledge, those who have taught workshops but are not included in the above list of teachers include Dick Lehman, Mark Goertzen, Justin Rothshank, Todd Pletcher, and Troy Bungart. Furthermore, younger potters such as Maddie Gerig have taught children's classes at Goshen Youth Arts. There are many others who teach in the community as well yet are less central to this text.

THREE

THE COLLABORATIVE PROCESS OF WOOD FIRING AND THE MICHIANA AESTHETIC

DOCUMENTING SOCIAL ASPECTS OF WOOD FIRING

When I arrived at Mark Goertzen's kiln on the morning of June 28, 2013—camera in hand, camera bag and notebook stowed away in a large tote over my shoulder—I immediately heard Bill Hunt's enthusiastic greeting: "Document us, Meredith! Document us!" Bill, a well-established potter and former editor of *Ceramics Monthly* magazine, was one of the potters who had travelled a substantial distance (from Columbus, Ohio) to join the Michiana potters in this summer firing of Mark's kiln. His greeting, perhaps emphasized in jest but genuine nonetheless, brought a smile to my face and a renewed energy to my work as I embarked on my usual routine of taking photos and asking questions about the progress of the firing. Some of us chatted casually about documentation that day, about the benefits of a "pseudo-outsider" (myself) whose main purpose was to systematically note all that goes on during a firing. It is certainly the case that potters can be great documentarians themselves (and indeed, the details of the firing are often recorded in firing logs and with photographs—see fig. 3.1), but as a folklorist, my interest was in more than the mechanics of the firing. I was curious about the sense of community that I had observed in Michiana and the fact that it seemed to center around an enthusiasm for wood firing.

But first, precisely what do I mean when I refer to wood firing and wood-fired pottery? Countless pots throughout history have been fired in kilns that have used wood as fuel; this book is not meant to speak to every occurrence of this. Instead, I am referencing contemporary long wood firing, which is distinct in both its technical details and the results

Fig. 3.1. Dick Lehman makes notes about the progress of a wood firing in June 2013; notes often include details such as the temperature and how much wood is being added to the kiln but sometimes expand to include weather conditions and other observations. *(Photo by author)*

that it can produce. As a point of reference, readers should be aware that stoneware pottery is often fired in less than a day using gas or electric kilns. The right wood kiln can also be brought up to the necessary temperature (around 2200 to 2400° F) in about twelve hours.[1] However, such a quick firing in a wood kiln does not allow for very much of the wood ash from the fire to fall on the pots, and for many potters, attaining a natural wood ash glaze is the primary appeal of pursuing wood firing. Yes, burned wood can quite literally become glaze, which is essentially glass—this is a constant source of astonishment for the uninitiated. The chemistry that creates such a transformation is complex, but suffice to say, wood contains certain minerals, and at such high temperatures the ash from the burning wood containing those minerals will fly through the kiln (hence the term "fly ash"), stick to the pots, and combine with molecules on the surface of the clay. Since the wood ash is allowed to build up over time, the melted ash will often run down the sides of the pot, completely coating the pot in this natural and unpredictable glaze. Then, as the kiln cools, the melted ash will solidify into a glassy glaze surface, which is referred to as natural wood ash glaze. A long wood firing is thus necessary to allow sufficient ash buildup; firings may last anywhere from three days to over a week, even up to two weeks.

Additionally crucial for understanding the social significance of this process is the fact that in order to maintain such high temperatures, the intense fire is constantly consuming huge amounts of wood (fig. 3.2). This requires that the potters "stoke," meaning they add small stacks (perhaps an armful, up to a wheelbarrow-full) of firewood to the kiln as often as every ten to fifteen minutes, all day, every day during the firing. Therefore, it is necessary for potters to work together, often taking shifts of four to six hours each, since the kiln must be attended at all times during the firing. Wood firing is thus no easy job, and it often leaves everyone involved physically exhausted, yet creatively reinvigorated. Most importantly, while each potter makes unique styles of pots, for many it is their collaboration at the kiln that allows them to pursue wood firing: building kilns is easier and firing more often and for longer periods of time is less exhausting when the work is shared among multiple people. Furthermore, by sharing their skills and knowledge about the process, each person is able to learn from the experiences of others to produce

Fig. 3.2. The red-hot interior of Mark Goertzen's kiln, midway through a firing in August 2015. A partially melted cone pack can be seen toward the bottom left. *(Photo by author)*

better pottery and refine their individual style. Coming together at the firing contrasts with many potters' everyday experiences of working alone in the studio, and it allows time for socializing while or between stoking, bringing them closer together as friends and providing time for the exchange of ideas. These many aspects combine to define a process that is generally more successful and enjoyable when it is taken on in partnership with others.

It is generally acknowledged in the world of ceramics that collaboration is necessary in the context of long wood firing (fig. 3.3), and it was my awareness of that fact that led me to arrange a two-week research trip to Michiana in summer 2013, with the purpose of documenting two simultaneous wood firings in the area—an impressive feat given the

Fig. 3.3. Bill Kremer helps to stoke his kiln, along with many of his friends and students, during a firing in November 2015. *(Photo by author)*

number of people needed to fire each of the kilns. What intrigued me
most, however, were not the technical aspects of firing, which the potters
themselves do a good job of documenting in logbooks and by taking photographs of the pots before and after the firing. Instead, as a folklorist, I
wanted to focus on the social dynamics that occur in this environment.
In my initial conversations with the Michiana potters (at this point, I
had completed six formal interviews in the area), I found that when I en-
quired as to why they pursued wood firing, they spoke of their enjoyment
of the social and collaborative aspects of it just as much as—if not more
than—their appreciation of the aesthetics that could be achieved by this
method. I found this particularly notable because it is not an aspect of
firing that is addressed in-depth in the existing literature on wood firing.

There is no shortage of documentation of wood-fired pottery; the
tremendous variation in methods and styles from around the world and
throughout time has been addressed in a variety of books, which have
often fallen into two general categories. First, there are many contemporary textbooks and articles discussing wood-firing techniques, primarily

written by potters and intended to educate students of ceramics or fellow studio potters.[2] Additionally, there are scholarly accounts, primarily from folklorists and students of material culture, which describe wood firing traditions as they have been transmitted in specific regions.[3] While the historical work done by these scholars—for example, as John Burrison describes, "the task of reconstructing the lives and work of four hundred humble artisans who, for the most part, escaped the notice of chroniclers" (2008, xxxi–xxxii)—is crucial to broadening the historical record of ceramic traditions, it leaves much to be desired when one wishes to examine the social lives of contemporary ceramic artists. In these varying approaches to the topic, the focus is all too often on the links between types of kilns, technical considerations, and resulting aesthetics: essentially, the exploration of what kind of kiln and firing process enables the potters to achieve the aesthetic qualities they personally prefer and/or that are favored within their art world, in Howard Becker's terms ([1982] 2008). There is acknowledgment, certainly, that long wood firing is challenging and usually requires the potter to have assistance from others in order to fire the kiln for multiple days, but when I began this research project, I found there is really no critical analysis of the social engagement that occurs between potters during a firing event.

For example, Ben Owen is quoted in *The Potter's Eye* as saying that long wood firing is a good opportunity to collaborate with other potters, to learn from each other, and to enjoy the camaraderie of working together (Hewitt and Sweezy 2005, 211, 218). Yet within this substantial book about wood-fired pottery, this is the only section of any significant length that discusses the appeal of the social aspects of wood firing. John Burrison, too, makes note of certain social gatherings that have happened around the creation of pottery; for example, he describes how friends and neighbors would often gather at the potter's residence for a meal and games during a firing (2008, 10–12), and he notes that potters do visit one another, participate in shows and festivals together, and feel "a sense of occupational kinship" with one another (2010, 95–96). However, in both cases, there is little elaboration on these social connections.

One place where I was able to find more personal accounts of social interactions around wood kilns is in *Wood Firing: Journeys and Techniques*, a book that brings together various articles about wood firing that have been published in the trade magazine *Ceramics Monthly*. Multiple articles in the book feature at least a paragraph or two about such aspects as the importance of friends and neighbors helping to fire the kiln, the hospitality involved in providing food or beverages to those stoking, and the discussions that happen in regards to making decisions about the firing process. Even still, in a book of twenty-five articles about wood firing, I was astonished to find that only a fifth of the articles spent any time discussing communal aspects of the work (*Ceramics Monthly* 2001). How is it that such a gap in the literature about wood firing has come to exist? I suspect it is, to a certain degree, tied to the prestige of the individual artist in the contemporary fine art world, a precedent that is difficult to move beyond when the artist at hand wishes to be seen as just such a prestigious individual (a worthy goal, certainly, with attendant financial and social benefits). Or, is this lack of engagement with social aspects of wood firing the result of the work of editors and publishers who find more value in texts about technical information than about social dynamics? Perhaps. While these questions were not the focus of my research, they certainly stand in support of the value of a folkloristic study of wood firing, an approach that integrates both individual and social concerns while still attending to process and aesthetics.

Another tremendous source of documentation of contemporary wood firing comes in the form of Coll Minogue and Robert Sanderson's book, *Wood-fired Ceramics: Contemporary Practices*, which surveys wood-firing potters (mostly in the United Kingdom but also in mainland Europe, Australia, New Zealand, and the United States). Most of the potters featured in the book tend to do shorter (ten- to twelve-hour) firings, and it therefore makes sense that there is less need for collaboration, and most do not mention having assistance with their firings. However, one section of the book features potters with "Oriental Influenced Kilns" and a tendency to utilize longer firings—most falling in the range of ninety to one hundred hours (around four days), with a few examples of weeklong firings—quite similar to what can be found in the Michiana area. In this section of the book, "teams" of people needed to fire the kiln as well as the firing schedules or shifts that they use are almost always discussed alongside the technical aspects of the kiln and firing. However, only one potter's profile includes a further discussion of the kind of social navigation involved in a group firing: in the case of the kiln owned by Torbjorn Kuasbo, the authors mention that he prefers to have his pots in a certain place in the kiln to get particular effects, and thus others (colleagues and students) who are involved must place their pots elsewhere in the kiln (2000, 79). Such an arrangement exists at most of the Michiana kilns, as well.

Minogue and Sanderson's book also includes one final section on "Community Kilns," which offers a very nice breakdown of the possibilities for how such shared kilns might be organized:

> In some instances the kiln in question has come into being as the result of the efforts of a committee or society, specifically formed for that purpose. In other instances, a group of friends—all potters—come together and build the kiln, on property belonging to one of them; or an individual potter has built the kiln alone (perhaps working slowly, over a number of years, as time and finances allow), and then invited a group of friends to help fire it, subsequently forming a regular 'firing team.' In other cases, the kiln is to be found at an institution which provides facilities for adult education. . .
>
> What all of these joint ventures have in common is a high level of commitment from those participating and an equally high level of satisfaction, which makes everyone involved in a firing look forward to the next one. Each firing provides an opportunity for a unique experience—not only is there a sharing of the physical activity, but there is also involvement in working towards a common goal. (138)

What follows in this section of the book (a mere five pages) is a brief description of a few community kilns, with very little detail shared about the groups involved. The book's focus continues to be on the type and size of kiln and general technical firing details, without information on the way the group of potters come together nor the social dynamics within the group as they fire together. The little that these authors do have to say is certainly in line with what I have found in Michiana—commitment and satisfaction, sharing of the work, looking forward to the next firing—yet it seems there ought to be more to say about precisely how these groups come together, how they navigate the shared work, and why they continue to work in this fashion. These were the kinds of inquiries that guided my fieldwork during wood firings in Michiana.

In comparison to the previous chapter, which discussed the development of a sense of community within educational contexts, the rest of this chapter is devoted to the analysis of a special, intense, collaborative event that the potters may share only a few times per year; while wood firing may not occur often, it is nonetheless quite important to the shared identity and social cohesion of the Michiana potters. My first objective is to explore the historical connections this area has with wood firing traditions elsewhere in the world, and I will then elaborate on how and why wood firing initially became popular among potters in this area as well as ways the practice has grown and changed over the years. A later section of this chapter moves into the present, exploring the aesthetic qualities that the Michiana potters currently seek to develop in the objects that they create, how those values move from one person to another, and how and why those aesthetics are also recognizable in other, non-wood-fired pots created by this group. Of note regarding wood firing in Michiana is the fact that many of the potters in the area primarily sell pots that are made using other production methods (i.e., applied glazes and the use of gas or electric kilns), yet as a whole the group expresses a greater enthusiasm for the work and the results of wood firing. In many ways, wood firing provides a liminal space where the potters step away from their usual routines and participate in challenging, collaborative work that, in its intensity and uncertainty, forges bonds between individual artists. Physical challenges of wood firing will also be addressed in relation to this sense of liminality, since the shared embodied experience of the firing is often of primary concern to the potters involved, and thus it plays an important role in the way they organize their work. Finally, this chapter will address the fact that many visual aspects of the Michiana Aesthetic are aesthetic features sought by a broader group of contemporary potters and collectors who wood fire around the world; therefore, I will explore how the term functions for the potters as a way to evoke a feeling of community and positive collaboration, not simply a way to denote an exclusive visual effect that could not be achieved by outsiders.

HISTORICAL AND INTERNATIONAL CONTEXTS FOR WOOD FIRING

It is essential to acknowledge that the wood-firing process in Michiana has grown up with inspiration from other times and places. In particular, it has been heavily influenced by longstanding traditions of wood firing in Japan; the kilns many potters in the US use today are based on Japanese

Fig. 3.4. This chalkboard sign was included in Todd Pletcher's display at the Michiana Pottery Tour in 2013. The quote reads, "'Have nothing in your house you do not know to be useful or believe to be beautiful.'—Wm. Morris." *(Photo by author)*

designs, and many of the aesthetics pursued through wood firing have been inspired by Japanese pots. This and other international connections have been major influences on the trajectory of contemporary American ceramics, and in order to explain the Michiana tradition it is necessary to paint a broader picture of some of the historical movements that preceded it. Two artistic movements since the late nineteenth century have provided substantial influence: William Morris and the Arts and Crafts Movement that began in England, which influenced Yanagi Soetsu, the founder of the Japanese *mingei* movement.[4] Both of these major developments have powerful echoes in the world of American ceramics today. William Morris was a prolific writer and designer; his work still resounds with contemporary artists and craftspeople, including some of those in Michiana (see fig. 3.4). In reaction to the Industrial Revolution, Morris and others promoted the integration of design and production, the use of natural materials, and the beauty of designs based on natural themes.

The American engagement with the Arts and Crafts Movement is well summarized by Charles Zug in *Turners and Burners: The Folk Potters of North Carolina*: "Behind the specific admiration for oriental ceramics lay the general philosophy of the Arts and Crafts Movement, which had originated in England during the third quarter of the nineteenth century and spread to the United States by the 1890s. Speaking out against the de-humanizing tendencies of an ever-enlarging industrial system, adherents like John Ruskin proclaimed the dignity of 'handiwork'.... And in order to escape the debilitating effects of mass production and specialization, English artists looked back beyond the Industrial Revolution," turning to the Middle Ages for inspiration. "America, unfortunately, lacked a medieval past," so some turned to Native American imagery or wares, while others looked to their European heritage or living folk pottery traditions (Zug 1986, 410–11).

Subsequently in Japan, Soetsu Yanagi developed the mingei move-ment along similar lines—a movement that would also have strong influ-ences on American pottery. As his good friend, potter Bernard Leach, has said:

> It would not be entirely amiss to describe Yanagi's position in Japan as relatively comparable to that of Ruskin and Morris in England. In both cases a deep and comprehensive statement was made regarding work and the qualification of work by beauty, against a background of rapid industrialization. In each case the creative thought behind the resulting movements ... may be regarded as counter Industrial revolutions. Morris and his followers felt that there was no genuine heartbeat left in work and so they set out to print and weave and deco-rate with their own hands.... Fundamentally, human beings, whether Eastern or Western, need belief, free play of imagination and intuition in their homes and workshops or they become starved. All the cog-wheels and electronic brains cannot assuage these human needs in the long run.... Basically this is not so much a revolution against science and the machine as a seeking of a means of counterbalance by employing man's first tools, his own hands, for the expression of his inner nature. ([1972]2013, 90–91)

Mingei objects needed basis in utilitarian purpose, to be made of locally available natural materials, and to be made in large numbers. Yanagi and his followers believed in the ideal of the "unknown craftsman," a selfless creator whose skill was born out of the cumulative knowledge of gen-erations of unknown artists, a person with no particular artistic intent, who focused on the good of the community rather than sales benefit-ting only himself. These philosophical ideals also gave way to aesthetic ideals, based a great deal on Korean ceramics and Japanese folk crafts; the emphasis was on simplicity and rustic beauty (Moeran 1981). These ideals were quite subjective, based in intuition, and yet the objects that

Yanagi collected and the philosophy he praised have had a tremendous influence on the trajectory of ceramic productions.

Two very close friends of Yanagi, Bernard Leach and Shoji Hamada, were particularly influential in spreading mingei ideals within American ceramics through their extensive writing, travels, workshops, exhibits, and so on. And, as Mark Hewitt and Nancy Sweezy have lamented, "One of the many results of Leach's proselytizing about the beauty of other ceramics was that contemporary American potters in the 1960s and 1970s who had an interest in functional pots bypassed American vernacular traditional pottery . . . and looked with Leach to the East for inspiration and technical knowledge. Models of the very types of pots that Leech so admired in Japan and elsewhere in Asia were already in America's own backyard, but were consequently largely ignored by contemporary potters" (2005, 167). This does not, of course, mean that American potters were trying to make Japanese (or, more broadly, Asian) pots. As Nancy Sweezy describes in her discussion of southern pottery, "Although a potter may have been inspired by the shape of an Asian storage jar, his turning habits, his clay and glazes from local sources, resulted in a unique interpretation and not a replica" (1994, 26). Even those who did not dig their own clay in their backyards were likely to find North American clay and glaze sources to be both more cost-effective and more familiar. I would add, as well, that consumers play a role in these unique interpretations; different lifestyles necessitate different kinds of implements, and when a potter's main source of income is from functional ware it can be awfully difficult, for example, to convince someone who does not participate in the Japanese tea ceremony that a tea bowl is a useful object.

It is also important to note that an Asian influence on pottery in the US is not only a historical one; it is very much a contemporary link as well. Studying abroad has become a mainstay of the ideal American collegiate experience (not to mention middle or high school programs that are becoming ever more prevalent).[5] Furthermore, many aspiring artists—potters included—are encouraged to pursue international experiences, often through artist-in-residence programs. There are clearly socioeconomic factors at play in whether such an opportunity is feasible for an artist to pursue, and many artists must rely on family support or scholarship or grant monies (or some combination thereof) if they are to pursue such opportunities. Many students and aspiring potters do find ways to go abroad, and when they do, they are likely to be drawn to locations that have longstanding and well-known ceramics traditions. Japan, of course, ranks high in this area, but vast numbers of other opportunities are sought around Europe and Asia. Though Japan has not been the only destination for the potters of Michiana, two programs in Japan have been of particular interest: Togei no Mori (also known as the Shigaraki Ceramic Cultural Park) in Shigaraki, Japan, and the International Workshop of Ceramic Art in Tokoname (more commonly known by its acronym, IWCAT) in Tokoname, Japan. Although IWCAT is no longer in operation, both programs have hosted hundreds of ceramic artists, both emerging and well-established, from dozens of different countries over the years. Shigaraki and Tokoname are significant in that they are both recognized as locations where pottery of many kinds—but particularly wood-fired pottery—has been made for hundreds of years.

THE BEGINNING AND DEVELOPMENT OF
WOOD FIRING IN MICHIANA

Why has this tradition developed in Michiana? The history and geography of the region provide some answers. Wood firing requires vast amounts of wood; it would be strange to find a wood-firing tradition in an area that is not heavily wooded. While to some the American Midwest evokes a sense of farmland, of which there is much, Michiana also has plenty of forested areas. Looking to the source of this landscape and thinking in terms of geographical study, one finds this area has been defined by glacial activity. Cold periods in the Pleistocene epoch produced continental glaciers that covered much of what would become the northern United States; their latest advance, around ten to fifteen thousand years ago, contributed to the creation of the Great Lakes, the flat plains and gentle hills that lay near to and south of those lakes, and the excellent soil that developed throughout much of the Central Lowlands. Later, burning practices undertaken by the Native American population further contributed to the soil quality (Trimble 2010, 16, 22–23). Furthermore, the Great Lakes and other large waterways such as the Ohio River were crucial means of transportation for native peoples and European

Fig. 3.5. This image from a wood firing at Mark Goertzen's place in summer 2013 shows only a portion of the huge amount of wood needed for a long wood firing. *(Photo by author)*

settlers alike. In the area that would eventually become known as Michiana, groups of Algonquin-speaking Native Americans were the first to meet European settlers; conflicts with the white settlers eventually drove out most of the native people who had once called the area their home, and a flood of white immigrants in the early nineteenth century set the stage for the predominantly white inhabitance of the area for the next two centuries (Kilar 1993, 973–77).

For these new residents, much of the appeal of the land came from the aforementioned presence of good soil and large supplies of wood; the wood was necessary for fuel and building, and as the forests were cleared, more farmable land was created (Worster 1993, 1145–49). European settlers, coming from areas with similar resources, found this particularly appealing. The town of Goshen stands as a subtle reminder of this history; it was named after the biblical land of Goshen, in large part due to the fertile land that white settlers found there when they arrived (Baker and Carmony 1975). While the land is still farmed to a large degree, the forested areas found in the Midwest are believed to be only a shadow of the once intimidating forests that covered this land. Still, what has regrown provides a crucial resource for the potters now pursuing wood firing in Michiana, since the wood of multiple trees is needed to sustain the multi-day wood-firing process (fig. 3.5).

Tom Unzicker is often credited as being one of the first to spark an interest in wood firing in the Michiana area (fig. 3.6). Tom built a wood kiln in the area in the early 1990s, and he, along with others like Mark Goertzen and Dick Lehman, all began experimenting and learning about wood firing around then. Mark Goertzen recalls this time, saying, "I wood fire because [Tom Unzicker] at Goshen College in the early nineties, very early nineties, was interested in wood fire. He probably influenced both Dick and I to be somewhat in the woodfire realm, because he built a kiln and we sort of learned all about it together, and then he kept building kilns around the area." Marvin Bartel also recounts Tom Unzicker's early interest in kilns, which came at least in part from a service trip to Tanzania after his freshman year of college. While there, Tom worked with women in a local village who wanted to develop a kiln and glazes to add to their traditional style of unglazed pottery. Marvin recounts that Tom had very little knowledge of kilns and glazes before embarking on the project and soon wrote to his teacher asking for help. Marvin responded by sending a package of books and materials, and by the end of the yearlong trip, Tom had helped to build a kiln and developed sustainable glazes from local materials that the women would be able to continue to use after his departure. "He came back and knew exactly what he wanted to do. He was just totally committed to ceramics at that point," Marvin says, speaking to the impact of the trip on Tom's professional trajectory. Tom recalls that after the trip, he started looking more specifically at Japanese-style kilns and has since built kilns based on *noborigama* and *anagama* styles used in Japan.

When I spoke with Dick Lehman about his initial endeavors in wood firing, he recalled that while he did have a small wood kiln, he did not actually find wood-firing results to be very interesting at first—the results included a lot of browns, muted colors, and so on. However, he says he found inspiration to continue wood firing when his friend Jack Troy (a very well-known potter) showed him a catalogue: "There was one Japanese potter's [wood-fired] work that I just found astounding,

Fig. 3.6. Longtime friends Mark Goertzen (*left*) and Tom Unzicker (*right*) discuss the results of Mark's recent wood firing in September 2015. *(Photo by author)*

because they weren't brown pots. There were pinks and greens and blues and purples, oranges, yellows, golds. They were all natural, there was no applied glaze, long firings, ten-day firings, hotter temperatures than most American wood firers were doing." What he had seen was a catalogue of Kanzaki Shiho's work, and he eventually reached out and contacted Shiho. When they first started corresponding, Dick recalls, Shiho was beginning to learn English, and he was "tough to understand at that point, but I was highly motivated to get to know this man who made these remarkable pots." Over the many years since their initial correspondence, Dick and Shiho have visited each other a number of times, have fired together and exhibited their work together, and they've developed a strong international friendship.[6] These factors explain much of the early interest in wood firing in Michiana; it was a new style of firing to try out together, supported by Tom's interest in building kilns, and, at least on Dick's part, there developed a results-oriented interest in the kinds of effects it could produce.

The size of the wood-fired kilns in Michiana, the volume of pottery fired in the kilns, and the length of the firings are constant sources of remarks from visitors who are unfamiliar with the process; they often find the scope of the endeavor quite impressive. Moreover, the scale is an important factor in why wood firing has become a collaborative rather than an individual practice in Michiana. Both Bill Kremer, longtime professor of ceramics at Notre Dame, and Dick Lehman both relate stories of the challenges of attempting to wood fire by themselves.[7] Bill, for example, tells a story of getting heat stroke while attempting a twenty-four-hour firing alone one summer. "We had a wood kiln ... we'd always share it, there would always be a group, but there wasn't much room in the kiln when you have five or six people putting their work in a small catenary kiln," he says. So, when he received a request for a number of large pots, he decided, "I'll fire this myself, I can do that, I'm not going to share it with others." Later he elaborates, "It was in August, really hot, and I'm firing it along and it got to be, this was a twenty-four-hour firing kiln, and you can drive in your car for twenty-four hours, right? And get somewhere." Unfortunately, he did not account for the difference in exertion between driving and firing. "So I was firing and it was really hot, the kiln's hot, and I'm starting to feel a little bit dizzy. Pretty soon, I can only deal with wood that's up on top of the pile, I can't bend down anymore or I might not get back up. I'm feeling a little nauseous." He goes on to explain that his wife came out to the kiln that evening and thought he looked awful, so she told him to go in the house for a nap; she and their two daughters would keep firing for him. "I remember going into the shower and I just felt this draining out of me, this awful heatstroke feeling. I got up, after I did sleep for a while, and then it's dark out and wasn't so hot anymore. And we managed to get it fired off. But it was, the next day I still felt bad, and I just thought well, I'll feel better the next day. And it took a whole week!" Bill's narrative is quite illustrative as to the benefits of a collaborative wood firing—having someone else take over the stoking will, at the very least, provide the potter with an opportunity to cool off, rest, and recover, hopefully avoiding heat stroke or worse.

Speaking to the appeal of firing collaboratively, Bill also talks about how his experiences firing the small wood kiln as a group led to his later decision to build a much larger kiln: "There was a real collegial, great interactive experience firing that [small] kiln. It was just a one day firing, but it was probably one of the best experiences I'd ever had with ceramics, and it had to do with that kiln—arguing about how to fire it, drinking a lot of beer, staying up all night. So I decided I would build a wood kiln. . . . I decided to build something that was much bigger than I could fire myself." The kiln Bill Kremer now has is about thirty feet long (see fig. 3.7). He often mentions that it is large enough for twenty people to comfortably sit inside and use as a sauna (while it is not being fired, of course), and it works well for firing his tall ceramic sculptures. Later in our conversation, he added, "It was a great idea, it was really a good thing to do, because every year we have this real coming together. I always look forward to it." To my knowledge, as of fall 2017, Bill and his group of Notre Dame students and Michiana potter friends—a constantly varying group—had never missed an early November firing of the kiln over the seventeen years since it was built.

Though Bill's students from Notre Dame do not often make their homes in Michiana after graduating, his presence has still been a tremendous influence on the Michiana community. His current assistant at Notre Dame, Zach Tate, attributes much of this influence to the diverse group of potters and artists Bill has worked with over the years

Fig. 3.7. Bill Kremer poses beside his large wood kiln, along with some of his large wood-fired sculptures. Photo taken in June 2013. *(Photo by author)*

(including notable ceramic artists like Peter Voulkos, who once came to fire the large wood kiln), the stories that Bill enthusiastically shares about his experiences, and, of course, the fact that his huge wood kiln draws in a large crowd of area potters and friends to participate in a firing every fall. At one time, he also fired the kiln in the spring (an idea that Bill and Zach revisited after a particularly successful firing in the fall of 2015 but ultimately decided against pursuing).

In his own attempt to wood fire mostly without assistance, and still with great results, Dick Lehman was able to develop a kiln and firing process for wood firings that were between a week and fifteen days long, yet he could manage these, for the most part, by himself—a feat for which he is well known in the broader world of American ceramics. Over the years, Dick had built two different small cross-draft kilns that could be fired quickly and without much ash accumulation, and he had come to the realization that he was not satisfied with the results.[8] He truly wanted to create pots with "the luscious flow of natural-ash glazes in a wide spectrum of colours" that resulted from days-long wood firing processes. However, he explains there were challenges in accomplishing this:

> Certain real and genuine limitations stood in my way. I really didn't have the money to purchase some property where an anagama-style kiln could have been built (and I was reasonably certain that my neighbours would not be agreeable to seeing a giant anagama growing out of my diminutive kiln shed). And if I had had the property, I would not have been able to afford the materials to build an anagama (or to take the time to scrounge for the materials) . . . let alone, I worried, the skill to build and manage such a large kiln. But worst of all, the time requirements of my commitments (to my wife and children, to my production studio, to my employees, to my customers) seemed to preclude the possibility of regularly spending eight days in a row firing a kiln, instead of working in the studio. (Lehman 1999, 17–18)

Despite these limitations, Dick still found a way to build a kiln that fit his needs. The small kiln he ended up with—a modification of his existing cross-draft kiln—had a huge firebox, which he could stoke himself only about five times a day, putting in a huge amount of wood that would slowly burn until the next stoke.[9] "My thinking at that point was, okay, I've been through the parenting thing, I know how to get up and do the night feedings, I can do this," he recalled with a laugh during one of our interviews. "So in theory I could keep working at the pottery studio and be firing my kiln for as long as I wanted. I would schedule the rest of the firing, the final three days, for a Friday, Saturday, Sunday," since the last few days needed more regular stoking at ten- to fifteen-minute intervals, and therefore required not only greater attention from himself but assistance from others as well. As for the results? "The effect was a snowstorm's worth of dry ash on the pots from that preheating. That would melt . . . just building up massive amounts of ash on these pots. And suddenly I was making the kind of pots that I'd most admired. . . . And here I am doing it in my side yard in Indiana, and working at the same time. That's been my approach to things, to see if there's a way to do more than one thing at the same time," Dick states.[10] Even given how successful the process was, it is notable that these beautiful results could not be achieved without family and friends to help finish the firing over those final thirty-six or more hours.

Additional kilns have been built in Michiana over the years, and today wood firing is something that a majority of the area potters are engaging with in some fashion. Some have their own kilns and routinely fire two to three times a year (or more often, when they are able); others only occasionally make work and participate in a firing hosted by another potter. Two of the main kilns operating in the area in recent years (leading up to and during my fieldwork in 2012 to 2018) are owned by Mark Goertzen and Justin Rothshank. After firing with both Tom Unzicker and Dick Lehman in the '90s, Mark decided to build his own kiln on his property about ten years ago. The kiln, fondly called Dante, is a catenary arch kiln large enough that Mark usually relies on at least two or three other potters, if not more, to help fill the kiln with pots and to fire with him. "That kiln has always been about community," he says, referring to the fact that he built it with the help of others (both potters and non-potter friends) and always fires with the help of others. For Mark, like many potters, the partnership is also with the kiln, and he sees it as an active participant in the creation of his work: "I do like that interplay of doing as best as you can and then offering it over to the fire," he says; in giving up direct control of the pot, he strives for "more of a collaboration with the kiln itself." Collaboration, both with the kiln and with other potters, is a constantly reoccurring theme in the Michiana discussion of the wood-firing process.

Fig. 3.8. A group of potters work the overnight shift at Justin Rothshank's kiln during the summer 2013 firing. *(Photo by author)*

Another locus for wood-firing collaboration in Michiana is Justin Rothshank's kiln (fig. 3.8), which was built in 2010. Justin's approach to wood firing as a social endeavor is quite clear when he writes about his kiln:

> I have a 2-chamber wood kiln, with the rear chamber for soda. I fire it 3–4 times a year. I chose to build a large-ish kiln because of my interest in working with other regional clay artists. The wood kiln is a way for me to connect with other makers. I usually fill the rear chamber with my own work, and share most of the front chamber with 4–6 other artists who are interested in wood firing. Each firing can hold 300–500 pieces so there's plenty of space to go around, and ample time for exchange of ideas and community building." (Rothshank 2014, 27)[11]

He mentions these benefits often when we talk about wood firing, and he has also described to me the fact that his wood-firing network stretches beyond the Michiana region and into other parts of the Midwest: "I have been fortunate to have friends from Pittsburg and Missouri and Michigan who have come to help both build my kiln and fire my kiln," he says (though a local faction is nearly always present at the kiln as well). And undoubtedly, Justin's connections both near and far have helped to expand the wood-firing possibilities in Michiana. During our first interview in the fall of 2012, Justin lamented the small group—only five people compared to a usual fifteen or more—that had been on hand for his most recent firing, attributing the deficiency to a firing of Mark Goertzen's kiln the previous month. As soon as the next summer, however, the two kilns were fired simultaneously. Each of the firings in summer 2013 were lit on the same Thursday and shut down on the same Sunday, and both locations had ten to fifteen potters involved, plus even more friends on hand to help with the stoking. The volume of people and work involved speaks clearly of a regional enthusiasm for the process as well as the power of the Michiana tradition to have drawn participants from throughout the Midwest.

While such enthusiasm may not be infinitely sustainable—indeed, many smaller firings involving just four or five potters have occurred since that monumental summer of 2013—there are other signs of a growing passion for wood firing in Michiana. Len Cockman, who teaches art at Northridge High School in Middlebury (about a twenty-minute drive to the northeast of Goshen) has built and fired a small wood kiln with some of his students. Moey Hart, owner and manager of Northern Indiana Pottery Supply in Goshen, made plans to work with Goshen College on rebuilding the old Goshen wood kiln (originally built and run by the Unzickers and other students in their time) on his property, for the students to use. His good friend Troy Bungart will undoubtedly be involved in the project as well; Troy is very dedicated to exploring wood firing and has put forth a great deal of effort to attend and participate in wood firings at many kilns around the country, traveling as far and as often as he is able. And, as I mentioned in chapter 3, Todd Pletcher built his own wood-fired kiln (fig. 3.9) in the summer of 2015 and promptly fired it at least four times in the six or so months after it was completed. Todd's kiln is the only down-draft train kiln in the area, and it is different from the other kilns in that it holds less work, fires in a shorter time, and offers more predictable firings. While his kiln still has some areas where the pots get a great deal of ash accumulation, it also produces rather different effects than the other kilns, including rich reds and oranges, and a more distinct front (with more significant ash deposits) and back (with very little ash) to the pieces. This variety was part of Todd's reason for

Fig. 3.9. Todd Pletcher's newly built kiln, just before being unloaded in September 2015. *(Photo by author)*

building the kiln; having the opportunity to try something different is appealing when there are already a number of established kilns in the area.

There have also been other changes within this group, and some kilns and people who were once active are no longer. For example, in the early 2000s Tom and Jeff established Unzicker Bros. Pottery in Thorntown, Indiana, a small town quite a bit to the southwest of the Michiana region. There, they had a nine-hundred cubic foot kiln that they would work together to fill and fire about three times per year, only rarely including other potters' work. While their distance from the Michiana community meant they were less involved with the group, they were still near enough to maintain significant friendships and to visit regularly. In fact, Tom and Jeff were both included in the inaugural Michiana Pottery Tour in 2012, where they exhibited their work on Mark Goertzen's property. Soon afterward, though, Tom moved to Newton, Kansas, with his family because his wife received a job offer there. He established a new studio and wood kiln, and a number of the Michiana potters travelled to visit his new place. However, the even more extensive distance means he will have less presence among this group, particularly compared to the early days of Michiana wood firing.

It is also worthwhile to note that Dick Lehman no longer has his own wood kiln—his was taken down over ten years ago, and the bricks were reused by Mark Goertzen in building his wood kiln Dante—yet Dick still remains one of the most active wood-firing potters in the area. He seems to be involved, to some extent, in nearly every wood firing in Michiana, particularly when they are spaced far enough apart that he has time to make a substantial body of work. Being constantly in the role of visiting participant rather than owner of the kiln, however, has somewhat changed Dick's approach to wood firing. He says there are both benefits and detriments to this situation; missing the kiln he once had and lacking control over the firing process can be major downsides, but at the same time, he appreciates the opportunity to observe and learn from such a wide variety of firing approaches. "Others say that a wood-fired kiln is like a sailboat—the very best wood kiln is the one that belongs to someone else who lets you ride around in it once in a while," he writes, alluding to the additional responsibilities and work that come with ownership (Lehman 2014a, 26). His primary advice to other itinerant firers is to ask many questions prior to participating, with the intention of making sure the experience will be a good fit. He recommends asking about the site and maintenance of the kiln, when and how the wood is prepared, the process used for loading and firing, the atmosphere at the firing, the unloading process and results, and more, to ensure your own preferences and aspirations will fit in with others' expectations. Dick also explains that a big part of his own approach to this experience is to take a wide range of his own pottery to fire, knowing he "will have some works in the least desirable areas of the kiln." He therefore brings both unglazed and glazed pots, some pieces augmented with additional ash, colorants, or fluxes, and pieces made with a variety of clay bodies, so he is well prepared "to accommodate a variety of kiln zones and environments" (28). After many years of wood firing with a variety of kilns and firing groups, Dick is obviously quite adept at navigating the different kiln environments that his pots may encounter; his calm and compassionate demeanor, along with his impressive ability to remember personal details about every person he meets, are also noticeable benefits to the social atmosphere around the kiln when Dick is a participant.

"MORE IS MORE": SHARED AESTHETIC IDEALS AMONG MICHIANA POTTERS

Three of the largest area kilns that the Michiana potters circulate among—those of Mark Goertzen, Justin Rothshank, and Bill Kremer—were all built with community in mind, as the potters have attested. All three of these kilns also have the ability to produce somewhat similar results, particularly regarding heavy natural wood ash deposits, glossy glaze surfaces, and a tendency to cooler rather than warmer colors. The fact that so many of the regular participants who fire these kilns appreciate those aesthetics is no coincidence; their shared ideals allow them to fire together easily since they are all hoping to achieve similar results, and participants therefore have similar ideas of how to run the kilns in order to produce those results. As Howard Becker states, "An art world has many uses for an explicit aesthetic system. It ties participants' activities to the tradition of the art, justifying their demands for the resources and advantages ordinarily available to people who produce that kind of art" ([1982] 2008, 132). Furthermore, "a coherent and defensible aesthetic helps to stabilize values and thus regularize practice. . . . An aesthetic, providing a basis on which people can evaluate things in a reliable and dependable way, makes regular patterns of cooperation possible" (133). Just as students or apprentices who do not like the work environments they find in a particular place are likely to move elsewhere to pursue their vocation (as discussed in the previous chapter), those who do not like the social atmosphere around the kilns and/or the results achieved from the firings are likely to move themselves into different ceramic circles where they *are* enabled to do the kind of work they wish to pursue. It is for this reason that I tend to focus my writing on those members of the group who have been involved the longest; while newcomers certainly play an important role in the vitality of the group, they are often still in a stage of experimentation, seeing whether the region has the right fit for their own idiosyncrasies. Many students and apprentices have come and gone over the years, many potters have visited for a wood firing on occasion, but those who have chosen to settle in the area are the most central to the continuation of the tradition, both socially and aesthetically.

Artistically and visually oriented readers may have already begun to develop their own understanding of the frequently pursued aesthetics in Michiana through the images of pots that have been included thus far. Still, at this point it is worthwhile to take a closer look at those aesthetics and to offer some definitive descriptions of the visual qualities being sought. While most potters in Michiana primarily create the familiar forms of functional pots, there is a balance struck between the similar and dissimilar; the soft, earthy colors and juicy runs of ash from wood firing decorate a wide variety of forms, as each potter makes his own unique mark in clay. Some vessels stand stoic and symmetrical while others speak more of fluid and motion; some surfaces are made smooth and clean, others punctuated with pattern and texture. Indeed, a variety of palettes and sizes abound, but if you look closely, you can find the influence of teachers and friends, firing styles and shared kilns (see "Beyond the Local Occupational Group" in chap. 5 for further discussion of how these aesthetics have been influenced by clients' preferences).

Trained under many of the same masters, with years spent working in the same region (if not in the same workshop) viewing and handling one another's work, it is no wonder many of the Michiana potters share similar aesthetic values. Similar clays, forms, surface decorations, and marks of shared kilns flow from one potter to another; not copying but venerating aspects of the work they admire in others, taking it in visually and tactilely and allowing it to infuse their own work in new ways. Certain visual similarities are easily discernable, and those are clearly evident when a wood firing is unloaded and pots are laid out on the ground mimicking the order in which they sat in the kiln (see fig. 3.10, as well as 1.10).[12] Then, the work of many potters appears as one entity, a large gradient of colors and effects changing just as the flow of the ash changes from the front to the back of the kiln, the fire affecting each person's work in similar ways in similar areas of the kiln. In this moment of contemplation as the potters view the results of their work, they often compare notes on clays and glazes that have afforded them the most pleasing results, sharing with one another inspirations for future experiments.

Fig. 3.10. Pots unloaded from Mark Goertzen's kiln during the 2015 Michiana Pottery Tour are spread out on the ground nearby. (*Photo by author*)

That which is successful for one potter is perhaps not widely advertised, but neither is it a secret closely held; methods and recipes are often gladly shared with close friends who will respectfully turn them to their own purposes. Friendship between potters involves respecting one another's style, and, rather than attempting to duplicate exactly the pots or effects achieved by others, each person tries to expand and elaborate upon their own style by utilizing small aspects of the work they admire.

The cohesive aesthetic shared by many of the Michiana potters goes beyond the simple explanation of shared clays, recipes, and/or processes. For example, when I interviewed Tom Unzicker in 2012, he explained how he and his brother Jeff have run their business quite individually, each person making what they desire, yet a shared aesthetic within their studio developed as they worked together for over ten years; many clients cannot tell the difference between their products (fig. 3.11). "When you're working with someone that closely in the studio, over years, you're not even sure where ideas come from anymore. They just bounce back and forth," Tom says. "I'll see Jeff doing something, and I'll add that, and then he'll take it back and do something better with it, and it goes back and forth," he describes.

Tom's explanation for the process of developing a shared aesthetic is also quite fitting for those working in closer proximity to one another in Michiana; even those who do not work in the same studio together often visit one another and have the opportunity to see and use each other's pots, particularly at wood firings.[13] A similar visual style found among these many potters is not intentionally maintained per se, but it can reflect their close working relationships over the course of many years, their respect for one another's work, and their shared values in the creation of pottery. Occasionally, decorative practices developed during apprenticeship make their way into the later works of a production potter who has set out on his own. Eric Strader uses slip trailing that is similar to decorative patterns that have been used in Dick Lehman's production line, which Mark Goertzen has maintained but also developed and made his own. Patterns cut into Todd Pletcher's yarn bowls are reminiscent of patterns still cut into open vessels at Goertzen Pottery. There is also the influence of Justin's decals, which I observed other potters in the area experimenting with in the mid-2010s. In many ways, the layered and

Fig. 3.11. Pots made by Tom and Jeff Unzicker sit in their studio in April 2012, awaiting the next wood firing. *(Photo by author)*

Fig. 3.12. These pitchers by Justin Rothshank show the decorative style he achieves by combining wood-firing effects with additional layers of decals, which are added afterward in lower-temperature firings. *(Photo courtesy of Justin Rothshank)*

complex visual surface that Justin creates with decals echoes that which many strive for in wood-fired pots: similar to layering on ash, there is an underlying philosophy that "more is more," at least when "more" is done well, and with careful consideration of the resulting effects (fig. 3.12).

Many qualities are shared among pots made within the Michiana Aesthetic, a phrase coined by Mark Goertzen as he observed the shared preference for lots of layered ash, striving for glossy pots with running or dripping natural ash glaze, and a desire to achieve additional colors (particularly in the blue/gray/green range) that go beyond the shades

Fig. 3.13. Detail of a wood-fired bowl by Mark Goertzen, with the gray, blue, and green ash runs and crystal formations often sought in Michiana pots. *(Photo by author)*

of brown for which wood firing is often known. "I've always had a blue kiln," Mark says regarding the results he is able to get in most of his wood firings (figs. 3.13 and 3.14). Todd Pletcher often fires with Mark and Dick Lehman and mentions an appreciation for similar traits: "Especially Mark's last few [firings], the beautiful blue ash that you get. It's different from traditional Japanese style work, you get the browns and the reds with sort of the yellow and the green ash runs from the pine, but Mark and Dick were—Dick in particular before he tore his kiln down—getting really great blues and greens, and that's what I'm always going for." Dick also adds his observations that the Michiana Aesthetic tends toward complex surfaces: beyond layering and dripping ash, the potters often attempt to achieve crystal formations in the natural ash glaze and strive for additional coloration such as pinks, lime or apple greens, purples, and violets (for a prime example of Dick's wood-fired work, see figs. 4.1 and 4.2 in chap. 4). It is worthy of note that Dick's descriptions of wood-fired effects are nearly always metaphors for entities found in nature; sunsets and glaciers, flowers, crystals, and rivers adorn his beautifully poetic descriptions of his work.[14] Often, these results come about due to the Michiana potters' willingness to attempt firings that are longer

Fig. 3.14. Side-fired vase by Mark Goertzen. The bright teal spot near the top of the vase and the bright green spot on the center of the body were formed by drips of glaze that ran down the pot when this side of the vase was oriented downward during firing. These vibrant, glassy drips of glaze are often referred to as "dragonfly eyes." (*Photo courtesy of Mark Goertzen*)

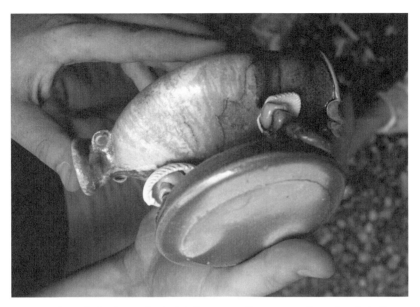

Fig. 3.15. This side-fired piece by Dick Lehman is still on its tripod stand with shells, having just been removed from the kiln after a firing in 2013. *(Photo by author)*

than necessary to reach temperature: with enough time and wood available, they will choose to hold the kiln for many hours at around cone six because at that temperature, fly ash from the burning wood will gather on the red-hot, sticky surfaces of the pots. While many of the Michiana potters speak of inspirations drawn from Japan wood-fired pottery, Dick Lehman explains, "The Michiana Aesthetic at least leans away from the Japanese 'less is more' aesthetic" and tends to embrace a "more is more" philosophy (Lehman 2014c).

Acknowledging that his generation of potters has been greatly influenced by Japanese pottery, Dick once explained in an interview that "I think as a body of potters, ceramic artists in the States are—they're not disconnecting, but they're finding their voice, and they're not just trying to make Japanese brown pots." The idea of side firing pots is another technique used by Dick Lehman and now popular among many of the Michiana potters. *Side firing* refers to the way that the potters set the pots on their sides during the firing—but rather than setting the pots directly onto the kiln shelves, they use clay stands and place shells between the stands and the pots (see fig. 3.15). Many observers are surprised to learn that after being fired in a kiln, the previously impermeable seashells will easily dissolve in water due to the chemical change that takes place at high temperatures. They are, therefore, a great means of creating an easy release between the pot and the kiln shelf or, more often, the firing stand that the potters make to hold up the shells and pots. Dick believes Japanese potters in history began using shells due to their chemical properties and easy availability.

In contemporary times, these shells have shifted to a more decorative function in side firing and beyond; discussing the Michiana Aesthetic, Dick indicates the prevalence of a "willingness to frequently reorient the axis of pots during firing, allowing for side-firing, upside-down-firing and 'somewhere- in-between-those-two-orientations firing'" (2014c). The unique decorative patterns made by seashells adorn many of the pots now made in Michiana; this is another good example of experimentation and openness to risk in the work made by these potters, as discussed in chapter 2. "The results achieved by side firing may be process-driven, but they are always just a little out of control—and often just a little more intoxicating than they would be if all the variables were to be under my control. I consider the process of producing this side-fired ware to be as much an act of receiving as an act of making," Dick has written (Lehman 1996). While shells are a prevalent part of Dick's work with side firing, he and the other area potters acknowledge that getting shells can be a challenge when living at such a distance from the ocean. However, their willingness to seek out these resources speaks to their devotion to pursuing these effects. Furthermore, in an effort to localize the side-firing process, Dick has spent quite a bit of time investigating and experimenting with different methods of supporting the pot for side firing; although he has not yet found a replacement that works as well as the shells for releasing from the thick drips of glaze, he has many ideas that he will continue to pursue.

Experimentation with the aesthetics of wood firing also has an effect on the wider bodies of work that these potters create. Many of them find that they are able to derive new ideas for their production lines (or other styles of work) through the results of the wood firing. An article quoting Dick gives one of the best explanations of this interplay:

Over the years, the nonproduction ware and the production ware have definitely supported each other. For example, the skill and facility that I have developed as a production potter—being able to make the clay do what I wanted it to do—have made it easier to make any new forms that I might imagine for the specialized firing approaches. If I had an idea, I could essentially make it; I had the skills to make it.

Out of the risk-taking in the nonproduction pieces, sometimes forms or ways of making would make their way back into the production line. Big spirals with a rib, for example, started with side firing and made its way back into some of our products in the production line.[15] Always when I am working, but especially when I am making nonproduction things, I have an eye out for how what I am doing would influence or improve the production ware. I tend to think that most of the movement was from the nonproduction ware to the production ware. However, most things I made in the nonproduction ware were functional. I did not make very much what I would call pure sculpture, or things that weren't at least derived from function. (Hartenberger 2013)

Dick is not the only one to benefit from concurrently creating multiple styles of work, however. As noted in previous chapters, Mark Goertzen has made some changes and additions to the production line at the Old Bag Factory since Dick's time there, and among the effects he pursues are more dripping, runny types of glazes. Mark describes how there is a direct link between his pursuits in the production line and his work with wood firing, saying, "I get ideas for the wood firing and all of a sudden it will show up in the production work. I try to keep a good number of one-of-a-kind work going, so that I evolve." For example, forms and surfaces that work well in wood firing may also look good with drippy applied ash glazes used in the production line. Todd Pletcher has also discussed how refreshing wood firing can be, as it often leads him to incorporate new ideas in his production line of pots, which is generally fired in an electric kiln; he tends to create more unique objects for wood firing rather than the long runs of identical vessels that he makes for his production line, and he often tries variations of the forms and surfaces in order to best take advantage of the flow of wood ash within the kiln. Sometimes, variations that he has used for his wood-fired vessels then begin to inform the design of his production line. He knows this happens among other potters as well and describes, for example, "Justin often says that the wood fire works for him as a way to sort of experiment, and drive some creativity into his production line. I utilize it in the same way in terms of how it affects my production line. The wavy line, for instance, was something that I was playing with specifically for wood firing, that I liked enough to start incorporating into all of my work" (see fig. 2.15 in chap. 2). Always open to change, the Michiana potters are not afraid to "try it and see," as Marvin Bartel would say, and the wood firing is a crucial influence in this.

COLLABORATION IN THE WOOD-FIRING PROCESS

Wood firing is a very physical process, and therefore participant observation was an important aspect of my ethnographic fieldwork, particularly because I needed to develop an understanding of the potters' embodied experiences of their art. Many scholars in folkloristics have noted the benefits of participating in an activity alongside their collaborators, and they explain the many insights they have gained through a shared sensual experience. For example, Deirdre Sklar's article in the *Journal of American Folklore* special issue titled "Bodylore" describes two different instances when her own physical participation in religious events, alongside her informants, allowed her to gain deeper insights into cultural practices (1994). My fieldwork experiences have also indicated a similar benefit to a participatory approach. My first direct experience with the wood-firing process used in the Michiana area occurred during a fieldwork trip in the summer of 2013, and although I was inclined at first to stay behind my camera and at a safe distance, I was constantly encouraged by the potters to take part in stoking the fire. In the wood-firing process, the temperature in the kiln reaches 2,300° Fahrenheit or higher, and when the door of the kiln is opened, extraordinarily hot flames rush out toward the potters who step up to toss in the wood that fuels the fire. Though they dress in protective gear (including long-sleeved shirts, thick leather gloves, and glasses), the potters who stoke are subjected to intense heat and often find they can only stand at the door stoking the fire for very brief periods of time before feeling as though they are risking bodily harm. While I had a logical, academic understanding of this encounter and similar experiences of extreme heat in my own work with the raku firing process, it was not until I was invited to step up to the kiln and feed the fire myself that I truly understood the intensity of this practice—hearing the rush of the flames and the crackle of the wood, feeling the intense heat on my face, managing my own struggle as I felt a physical urge to step away from the heat—while on the other hand still very much aware that I needed to remain and complete my duty to feed the fire.

Having this firsthand familiarity allowed me to turn to my own embodied experience as I developed various lines of inquiry with the potters and continues to help me understand their answers as I ask them to explain their own somatic ways of knowing what is happening in a wood firing. A close parallel can also be found in Dorothy Noyes's experience of the fiery Patum in Berga, Catalonia, an annual festival that takes place during Corpus Christi and involves dances and elaborate costumes. Despite her initial hesitations, Noyes found that full participation in the Patum was ultimately crucial to her incorporation into the group she was connecting with in her fieldwork in Berga: "My attitude—of body and thus for them also of mind—revealed my distance from the event, so they forced me into intimacy with it . . . I came to understand the techniques of incorporation as reciprocal: the individual is brought into the Patum, and the Patum is taken into the individual. One's change of attitude is then literal and visible to others" (2003, 136). Similarly, as my participation affords me membership into the wood-firing community, it lends credence—from the potters' perspective and from that of my readers, I hope—to my ability to comprehend and interpret their activities.

In order to understand the deep social significance of wood firing within this group of potters, one must understand the intense and challenging process of wood firing, particularly the knowledge and preparation, technical skill, and physical labor that are necessary for a successful wood firing. As I describe this process in the following paragraphs, it is useful to think of the wood firing as a kind of liminal space where the potters step away from their usual routines and participate in collaborative work that forges bonds between these individual artists (and a more direct analysis of the liminality of this event will be provided in the next section of text). Wood firing is something that may happen, for these potters, only a few times per year. And—this is a key point—currently none of the Michiana potters are making a living solely selling wood-fired pottery. Those Michiana potters who work in clay full-time usually have an additional production line where they make glazed and electric- or gas-fired wares, and this is where the majority of their sales come from.[16] However, when you speak with them about their art, their greatest enthusiasm is for the wood-fired work, and they put a great deal of time and effort into making sure wood firing continues to be a part of their production.

The preparation of making pots for the wood fire may take place over the course of weeks or months prior to firing, and this part is largely an individual endeavor. The potters then shift into a collaborative mode when they bring their work to one person's kiln and begin to navigate the kiln loading process together (fig. 3.16). Often five or six potters (or more) will fire their work together, and while the owner of the kiln or the more experienced potters may get preference as to where their pots are placed, overall they must arrange works so that the entire kiln is evenly loaded and conducive to the movement of the flame. And, at the same time, each individual pot should be carefully placed so that the ash will fall onto it in the manner the potter desires. From the point when the kiln is loaded to the moment it is unloaded and all is cleaned up, the overall process may take up to three weeks: loading can take hours or may occur over the course of a few days; firing can take anywhere from a few days to a week; cooling the kiln again takes a matter of days; and unloading requires a similar amount of work and time to that taken with loading. Considering that all of the potters involved need to schedule time away from their usual activities producing pots (or other professional work, as the case may be), as a matter of convenience the wood-firing activities of loading, firing, and unloading are often spread out over three to four successive weekends. This kind of weekend schedule is a great accommodation for those who must attend to their regular jobs through the week, but it can also be a challenge for those who travel from afar to be a part of the firing; driving a substantial distance three weekends in a row is often not temporally or financially feasible. Therefore, more distant participants may choose to ship bisque ware to be loaded into the kiln without their presence, or they may choose not to attend the unloading, instead picking up finished work at a later visit or having those pots shipped back to them. In any case, the weekend-oriented arrangement is much more conducive to regular local participation.

Fig. 3.16. Many potters help to load Justin Rothshank's kiln before a firing in June 2013. (*Photo by author*)

As for the specifics of the firing, often the kiln is warmed overnight or for a day or so, keeping the temperature around 200 to 300° to ensure the pots are dry and warm. Then, a more substantial wood fire is lit and built slowly over a few hours; often this occurs in the morning on the first day of firing and is done by the first shift of potters (though it is common for many others who are involved in the firing to attend the lighting). Finally, the fire will grow much stronger, and the potters will begin gaining temperature much more quickly. By then the kiln takes almost constant supervision and must be stoked approximately every ten to fifteen minutes until it reaches an overall temperature of around 2,300° or more.[17] Although it is possible to reach the necessary temperature for a complete firing in only a day or so, most of the Michiana potters are relying on natural wood ash glaze to develop the complex surfaces on their pots, and only occasionally do they apply any glaze prior to the firing.[18] Therefore, the potters will often choose to hold the kiln at a lower temperature (perhaps around 2,000° or lower) for many hours or even days to allow the wood ash to build up on the surface of the pots; it will then melt and drip down the pots once higher temperatures are reached. Not only is this process time consuming, but the fire is consuming impressive amounts of wood as well. A three-day firing might use around six cords of wood, and the wood must be split—yet another task often undertaken by the potters. To understand the scale of the fuel used and work needed to split this much wood, one can consider this comparison offered by Justin Rothshank: the same amount of wood burned in a wood stove could easily heat a moderately sized home throughout the winter months.

To manage the long hours of a firing, which often occurs over three or four days in the Michiana kilns, the potters who have placed pots in the kiln will work in groups and stoke the kiln in approximately six-hour-long shifts. These are often divided into early morning, midday, evening, and overnight shifts, though schedules can vary depending on availability; many also stay long past their required hours or will sometimes choose to drop by outside of their designated shift. Friends and family gather as well, keeping the potters company, helping to split wood, and sometimes taking their turns stoking the fire. Typically, each scheduled shift overlaps the shifts that fall before and after for an hour or more, providing a sense of continuity; the overlap allows the new crew to hear about the previous shifts' goals to hold or raise the temperature, get a feel for the kiln and the rhythm of the stoke, and so on. For example, Bill Kremer says he prefers to have three on a team who take six-hour shifts, and halfway through each shift new people come on: "by the time I leave, you'll have picked up the feel of the kiln, understand what the cycle is—they'll be watching the dials and get a sense of what it is. The kiln is always changing, it never stays the same. Just when you think you've got it figured out, you don't," he says, speaking to the necessity of paying close attention to the pyrometers (i.e., "watching the dials") and other visual indicators of the internal status of the kiln while on shift. The schedule of six-hour shifts with overlap is very common at Mark Goertzen's and Justin Rothshank's kilns as well.

Mimicking the apprenticeship structure, the wood firing offers another opportunity for mentoring within the pottery community (fig. 3.17). Those who own the kilns tend to take the lead, as their familiarity

Fig. 3.17. Mark (*left*) and his assistant Royce Hildebrand (*right*) stoke together during a firing in summer 2013. Mark often has assistants from his shop take shifts at his firings, and he is careful to train them on how to safely and correctly stoke the kiln. (*Photo by author*)

with the kiln runs the deepest. Occasionally a different kiln boss is chosen; sometimes Dick Lehman has run a firing of Mark Goertzen's kiln, for example. In either case, well before the firing can begin, it is the kiln boss or owner who goes through the process of inviting participants, setting a schedule, and organizing shifts for stoking. Just as the energy of apprentices is utilized to increase production in the studio, during a firing the "young bucks" are often relegated to the challenging overnight shifts. Though they may complain about the late hours and lack of sleep, they often revel in the opportunity to make their own choices while stoking the fire, feeling a bit rebellious outside of the direct supervision of the more experienced potters. Of course, it is not always the case that enough younger potters are available to take the overnight shifts; sometimes, this is the least desirable shift among the group. I have also observed situations where the kiln owner will be the one to take on the additional challenge and responsibility of staying up overnight to care for the kiln.

During most shifts, if a decision about the firing cannot be reached communally, the group will often defer to the wisdom of the kiln boss or the most experienced potter present; even in this relatively democratic process where decisions are continually discussed and often reached as a group, there remains a subtle structure of leadership. Through these many aspects of the process, wood firing functions to bring together a group of potters and friends who have a vested interest in the success of the firing. However, not all moments are devoted to stoking the fire, splitting wood, teaching, or discussing the firing; there are also many quieter moments between stokes that can be filled with conversation and camaraderie. Often accustomed to working individually in their own studios, taking part in wood firing gives the potters an invigorating opportunity to converse with others in their profession during the many hours of loading, shifts of stoking, and labor of unloading the kiln. While pottery is, of course, a main topic of conversation, the potters also tend to share many of the same hobbies, and they will often delve into a variety of topics of common interest around the kiln. All of these aspects of social interaction play into the development of a strong sense of community among the potters, a quality of wood firing that becomes even more explicit when analyzed through the lens of liminality.

WOOD FIRING AS LIMINAL SPACE

The concept of liminality was first introduced by Arnold van Gennep in relation to his study of rites of passage. He claimed that rites of passage mark the movement of an individual or group through particular phases in their lifecycle and suggested that all such rituals have a three-fold structure, including the pre-liminal (rites of separation), liminal (rites of transition), and post-liminal (rites of incorporation) (van Gennep [1909] 1960). The idea of liminality was taken up by Victor Turner decades later. Turner proposed that these in-between periods offered a time of withdrawal from one's usual sense of identity and modes of social operation and therefore served as a time and place of great ambiguity, out of which new perspectives could arise. Furthermore, with the breaking down of established structures, a sense of spontaneous communitas, or feeling of togetherness and community, could form between participants who were together undergoing this transformation (Turner [1969] 1997). Over the years, the idea of liminality has been applied to moments and groups of varying scales, to encompass many different kinds of periods of change. In applying *liminal space* to wood firing, I am specifically using the term to indicate an event with a defined temporal and spatial frame, involving certain processes and patterns of behavior that are usually present, along with a sense of the unknown and of challenge undertaken as a group. As described above, wood firing is clearly a time of intense change—for the pots, most clearly, but also for the potters, since they are laboring in anticipation of a new body of work while simultaneously developing new or deeper friendships and new insights into the wood-firing process.

There are, of course, certain contrasts with how the concept of liminal space has been utilized in the past. For example, wood firing could only rarely be considered a rite of passage. While the first firing that a potter participates in is often remarked upon and given special attention, particularly in regard to educating them about the process and training them to stoke appropriately, it is not often a key element of the event. From my observations of the Michiana group, however, I can say that having participated in wood firing is a definite prerequisite for one's centrality to the Michiana pottery community; those who do not participate tend to be on the outskirts of the network, not as well connected as others who do engage in wood fire. Having experienced the intimate physical challenge of stoking the fire, one becomes a part of the group. Dorothy Noyes expresses a similar sentiment in *Fire in the Plaça* when she explains, "I had but to participate as they did. I could have their experience by living in their bodies, and I could do this by eating what they ate, dancing what they danced, and, in general, by spending time with them: acquiring a history in common with them" (2003, 31). As a researcher of wood firing—and in a position of inexperience similar to some of the potters' apprentices—I felt the need to participate in the stoking and thus appreciated the benefits of acceptance into the group.

While "wood firing as rite of passage" is not quite the appropriate analytical approach here, wood firing can be seen as a kind of ritual, if not necessarily in a religious or spiritual sense.[19] For example, some

Fig. 3.18. Mark (*left*) hands out small ceramic cups of bourbon to those who are about to help fire his kiln in August 2015. (*Still from video recording made by author*)

kiln owners in the Michiana area have distinct rites through which they begin or end a firing. Mark Goertzen always has a special bottle of bourbon that is opened and shared among the participants at the point when the fire is lit (fig. 3.18). He pours a small drink for each person and then a small offering into the kiln, saying, "May this warm your stomachs, and my stomach, and Dante's stomach," referring to the fire that will soon blossom in the belly of his kiln, Dante. The bourbon bottle typically stays at the kiln site throughout the firing, and if any is left at the end, it might be shared among those who help to close up the kiln when the firing is over. As kiln boss in summer 2013, Dick Lehman made a similar offering of espresso, brewed at the kiln site in a travel espresso maker. Sake offerings, left atop the kiln in ceramic sake cups (in a manner similar to what would be done in Japan), have also been made at Mark's kiln. Similarly, Bill Kremer ended his 2015 firing with a special offering to the kiln. He has a very large spoon made by Peter Voulkos that he filled with salt and left sitting above the front arch of the kiln throughout the firing (fig. 3.19). At the very end of his firings, Bill and the other participating potters usually salt the kiln to add to the effects of the wood ash. This time,

Fig. 3.19. A very large ceramic spoon full of salt and a sign saying "Just hot enough!" over the arch of Bill Kremer's kiln in 2015. *(Photo by author)*

I observed that after copious amounts of salt were placed in the kiln at each of the stoke holes, the salt from the spoon was ceremoniously tossed in during the last stoke.

There are other notable similarities to van Gennep's original use of liminality; his tripartite structure, for instance, fits loosely with the threefold loading, firing, and unloading stages of the firing. During loading, the potters both leave their daily routines and begin to give up control of their pots as they are placed in the kiln; during firing, they work together in a relatively democratic process of stoking and making decisions about the firing, and they are distinctly aware of the transition their pots are going through; during unloading, the pots are unveiled in their new, final form, and the potters begin to accept the results of the firing, deciding how they will incorporate these pots into the body of work that they display, and simultaneously incorporating their new knowledge of the process into their aspirations for future wood firings (fig. 3.20).

The sense of transition and ambiguity that both van Gennep and Turner discuss in the liminal phase is quite easily applied to the clay objects included in the firing, since firing is a volatile process and pots

Fig. 3.20. (*Left to right*) Bob Smoker, Fred Driver, and Justin Rothshank look over the results of a summer 2013 firing of Justin's kiln. (*Photo by author*)

may not survive or turn out to the potter's liking (there is somewhat of a Schrödinger's cat feeling to this situation). Furthermore, the potters feel a close kinship with the work they have put into the kiln and therefore also encounter their own sense of transition and uncertainty during the firing. The work that they get out of the kiln will in many ways determine what they do next. Will they have pots they love to display and sell in upcoming shows? Conversely, will they have to cope with a lack of wood-fired inventory? Will the experiments they try in this kiln turn out well? Will they find new inspirations and thus find themselves making modified forms in preparation for the next firing? All of these questions and more remain unanswered as they strive to fire the kiln to the best of their ability, consistently stoking the fire, trying to make the best possible decisions about how often to stoke, when to rake the coals, whether more air or less is needed, and so on. Throughout all of the intense physical and mental work demanded by the kiln, each potter hopes they are making the best possible decisions within the idiosyncratic circumstances of that particular firing. Changes in the weather (humidity, atmospheric pressure, and so on) can affect the trajectory of the firing. Conditions of the available wood (drier versus recently cut wet wood, hard woods like oak versus soft like pine) can change how the fire burns. Too much air means oxidation (areas in the kiln where the pots may turn white and the ash glaze surface will not achieve the rich colors afforded by reduction), but still, air is needed for combustion and cannot be cut off too much. On and on, a cascade of decisions to consider, to discuss with others around the kiln, while the possible results of the firing—the result of the pottery's transition, and thus the transition of each of the potters—weigh in each person's mind.

A key part of the firing experience, Bill Kremer believes, is the state of mind that occurs while firing: "One of the jokes with that kiln is, how many times are we going to have to fire this thing in order to finally get it to where it is . . ." He pauses. "Well, the ideal [exists] when we're firing it. Everyone has high hopes, expectations, and that's why we gather together, and that's why we're—it's almost like a religion or something, and that's the chapel. Of course, once we unload it there'll be a few good things, but [at that point] it's just another firing, so to speak." With the firing completed, the potters shift their focus to the next firing, to another opportunity to pursue the ideal, and begin discussing plans for the next firing—when to have it, what new ideas they will try. In Bill's description, every stage of wood firing is always oriented to the future; he states often during the firing, "We are living in the ideal," or perhaps "living *for* the ideal." Prior to and during the firing, the main consideration is the future results that will be attained, and after the firing, once those results have been seen, the potters' thoughts are immediately consumed with planning the next wood firing, with an eye to achieving even better results the next time. Mark Goertzen also expresses a similar sentiment about how each firing fits in with other firings: "The enjoyment of wood firing is also the puzzle of it. Since nothing is guaranteed look-wise, that's the fun of it. How this firing will go in the puzzle, and who gathers, and talking about how we should be firing it, that's all fun for me," he says (fig. 3.21).

It is crucial to note that the dynamic of uncertainty and attentiveness to the future does not only concern the individual potter's relationship

Fig. 3.21. Between stoking, Mark Goertzen (*left*) and Troy Bungart (*right*) discuss the firing of Mark's kiln. Photo taken during a firing in August 2015. (*Photo by author*)

with their own pots. Turner's concept of communitas is also quite relevant, given the heightened sense of empathy, friendship, and camaraderie that tends to be present around the fire. As this is a collaborative endeavor, with the pots of friends, colleagues, students, or apprentices also included in the kiln, each potter also feels empathy for the others involved, particularly since their fates are linked. Too many mistakes during firing could mean every potter participating leaves with poor results and negative feelings, just as a really successful firing can generate great pots, good sales, and additional enthusiasm for working together in the future. And smaller interactions during the overall firing can be just as meaningful. For example, if someone has a great insight that solves a problem, their reputation or social status can rise a bit within the group. On the other hand, if someone does not show up for their shift or acts irresponsibly while in charge of the kiln, they jeopardize their relationship with friends or mentors who are relying on them. If wood is thrown into the firebox with too much force, it can hit the stacks of shelves and pottery, knocking over and breaking the work of many potters. Due to the significance of these and other individual actions to the fate of the entire

Fig. 3.22. Bill Kremer (*left*) and Dick Lehman (*right*) study the pyrometer together under the rare circumstance that the kiln is firing hotter in the back than in the front. Photo taken during a firing of Bill's kiln in November 2015.(*Photo by author*)

group, a sense of togetherness is heightened as each potter understands his potential to affect all others who are involved.

Given their consistent attention to these details of the firing, whatever shared sense the group has about the likely outcome of the firing, whether positive or negative, always affects the mood of the present (fig. 3.22 and 3.23). When the firing appears to be going well, group decisions can seem easier, and conversations can turn to topics external to the firing—discussions of new designs for forms, or of family, friends, or current events; often there are jokes and laughter and lighthearted moments shared around food or beverages. Yet when the firing stalls—when temperatures do not rise as predicted, or if they drop, or if concerns arise about conditions within the kiln—the atmosphere among the potters becomes more serious, with quiet moments of contemplation around the pyrometer or the kiln log, earnest voices discussing the possible solutions, and shared stories of solutions found in past firings. In either case, whether positive or negative, friendships are deepened through these conversations and experiences, as individuals share personal details about themselves, finding commonalities both in ceramics and in other aspects of their lives.

Physical aspects of firing are also key to the sense of community and empathy developed at a firing. Given the extreme heat of the fire, consequences such as burns, heat stroke, and dehydration must always be kept in mind, and since all participants take part in the stoking, they have a shared embodied understanding of the extreme heat and sense of urgency that is felt as you step up to fuel the fire. As I explained previously, when the potters open the door of the kiln to add wood to the fire, extraordinarily hot flames rush out of the kiln toward the potters who are stoking. Though they dress in protective gear to mitigate the heat and danger (see, for example, the welder's mask and gloves worn by Mark Goertzen in fig. 3.18 and the thick gloves, long sleeves, and apron worn by Dick Lehman in fig. 3.24), they are still subjected to intense heat and usually find that they can stoke for only brief periods of time before feeling as though they are risking bodily harm. The urgent, instinctual reaction to step away from the fire and avoid injury is counteracted by one's knowledge that the fire must be stoked, that one's duty to the group and the kiln must be completed. Thus you stay at the fire and complete

Fig. 3.23. Mark often makes wood-fired pizza for his guests, as he did at this wood firing in August 2015. Here, he is in a particularly good mood because the firing has been
going well. (*Photo by author*)

Fig. 3.24. Dick Lehman stands in front of Mark Goertzen's kiln during a firing in July 2013. He is wearing a protective apron and gloves given to him by his good friend, Japanese potter Shiho Kanzaki. *(Photo by author)*

your task, and you know that when others take their turn at stoking, they, too, have likely felt this same struggle and have chosen duty over instinct. Burned clothing is common, and underlying a conversation about one another's burned sleeves is a sense of proximity to the fire, implied but not spoken: "I reached into the kiln and so narrowly avoided burning my skin!"

The idea that intense physical experiences lead to feelings of empathy and community among participants is well supported in anthropological and psychological studies of ritual. A prime example comes from research done by anthropologist Dimitris Xygalatas and his colleagues. Building on Émile Durkheim's notion of collective effervescence, this study of the *paso del fuego* (fire-walk) in San Pedro Manrique, Spain, involved tracking the heart rates of both fire-walkers and spectators.[20] During the fire-walk, participants walk over hot coals, often carrying a loved one in their arms. The study found "an astonishing level of synchrony in heart-rate activity, extending from fire-walkers to spectators of the event . . . the closer the social ties between two people, the more their heart rhythms were synchronised." Xygalatas also compares the paso del fuego with the Hindu religious festival Thaipusam in the Republic of Mauritius, which involves body mutilation and piercing. There, the researchers found a direct link between the amount of pain experienced by the participant and/or perceived by the observers and the amount of money they would thereafter donate to charity; the more pain, the higher the donation. Overall, Xygalatas concludes that "empathic reactions to the suffering of others and the joint experience of suffering forges strong communal bonds. As the Spanish fire-walkers told me, when you perform this ritual, 'everyone is your brother. The next day, you see another fire-walker in the street, and you know you've been through this together, you've bonded, you have a different relationship to this person.' The cumulative effects of this transformative process can cement the social fabric of these communities. Collective arousal plays an important role in shaping social behaviour and identity." Furthermore, while he acknowledges that "social cohesion is not the conscious goal," Xygalatas shows that it is a major benefit garnered from many kinds of physically challenging rituals (2014).[21] While his research focuses on religious rituals that purposefully entail a great deal more pain or bodily harm than a typical wood firing, the mechanisms at play are remarkably similar. Shared physical challenges lead to empathy among participants, and the sense of community felt around the kiln is a major benefit to the group. Although the analysis regarding liminality and embodiment is mine, the idea that wood firing is a source of community cohesion among potters in Michiana is broadly acknowledged by those who participate.

Readers who are familiar with contemporary wood-fired pottery in America will likely notice that the aesthetic, physical, and social qualities of wood firing described in this chapter are not completely unique to the Michiana area. Long wood firing is always a challenge, and the effects sought and achieved—including side firing, heavy drips of melted ash, even the wider variety of natural ash glaze colors—have been successfully pursued by those outside of the region. Indeed, a regionalist approach can go only so far in the assessment of visual qualities appreciated in Michiana, both because these are not completely unique to the place and because there is still quite a lot of variety in the works produced by area artists. Each potter has their own preferred forms, textures, and so on, and even though these are often influenced by others in the area, each artist maintains a distinctly individual style.

So, why continue to refer to the *Michiana Aesthetic*? It is perhaps best to think of the Michiana Aesthetic as a reflection not just of visual qualities but also of community: the participants have shared values, as previous chapters have established, and because they seek at least *similar* visual results, they have the ability to fire a kiln together in a way that, when successful, will produce results that all participants will be pleased with. It is perhaps even more profound to point out that the aesthetics being pursued in Michiana have much more to do with social aspects than they do with geography. As those who have studied folk arts are often well aware, the aesthetics found in places such as North Carolina or Japan are often closely tied to the natural resources, such as clay or shells, which are available in the area in addition to the wood for wood firing. Certainly, the Michiana potters could choose to move to places where they could dig local clay or pick up shells from a nearby ocean, yet they remain in *this* place because the social connections they have here are more important, and the material resources they need can be brought in from elsewhere. The use of the regional designation, Michiana, in the definition of their aesthetic reflects the fact that this is where their main artistic influences and friendships lie. They choose to be in this area because they can work with people whom they respect and care about, and their aesthetic preferences and artistic processes have been, in most cases, deeply influenced by those people.

NOTES

1. The times and temperatures given here are estimates only and are provided to assist a nonexpert audience in understanding this process. The concept of "heat work"—meaning that the chemical effects achieved in the kiln result from a combination of temperature and how long that temperature is held—is crucial for a more specialized understanding of the process. It is because of this combination of both time and temperature that the potters often use cones (small implements that are made of the same materials as clay and glaze and are designed to be placed in the kiln and melt at certain intervals) to judge the progress of the kiln, rather than just looking at the temperature displayed on the pyrometer.

2. For example, see *Ceramics Monthly* (2001), Minogue and Sanderson (2000), Rogers (2003), and Troy (1995).

3. Relevant examples include those that document pottery traditions in the southern United States and Japan. See sources mentioned previously (Burrison 2008 and 2010; Sweezy 1994; Zug 1986; Mecham 2009), with the addition of Louise Allison Cort's *Shigaraki: Potters' Valley*, which provides an in-depth look at a longstanding regional tradition in Japan (2001).

4. Translated as "folk crafts" or "folk arts."

5. While the 2014 Open Doors Report on International Educational Exchange published yearly by the Institute of International Education (IIE) indicates that fewer than 10 percent of all US college students study abroad at some point in their undergraduate education, top public institutions boast upward of a 40 percent participation rate in study abroad, and some private institutions have over 80 percent participation (Institute of International Education 2014). Furthermore, in a 2012 poll commissioned by NAFSA: Association of International Educators, 63 percent of respondents indicated they believed international education is "very essential" or "moderately essential" to the educational experience (NAFSA: Association of International Educators 2012).

6. Dick has written extensively in trade magazines about his friendship with Kanzaki as well as other Japanese mentors and friends whom he has interacted with during his long career. An account of his publications (and the text of many of the articles) is available on his website: http://www.dicklehman.com/html/writing/index.html.

7. Notre Dame is home to the other prominent ceramics program in the Michiana area (in addition to the aforementioned program at Goshen College), and the program has been headed by Professor Bill Kremer since it was established upon his hire in 1973. While this is an important source of ceramics education in Michiana, the Notre Dame students are not often as interconnected with the professional potters in Michiana as the Goshen students are—hence the lack of discussion of this particular program in the preceding chapter. Where Goshen College provides a flow of people out into the local

ceramics community, Notre Dame tends to pull local potters inward, to firings at the Notre Dame wood kiln.

8. Cross-draft kilns come in many different sizes, shapes, and designs, but all rely on heat moving "from the inlet flues on one side of the kiln chamber to the exit flues along the opposite side." In other words, air goes from openings near the firebox, through the kiln, then out through the chimney on the other end of the kiln, passing through the pottery in the process (Olsen 2011, 83).

9. For more details of the large firebox Dick added on to his cross-draft kiln, see his article "An Approach to Long Woodfire" (Lehman 1999).

10. Dick discusses this balance in his work (between his production line and wood firing) in much more detail in his article "Side Firing: Where the Life Is" (Lehman 1996).

11. When Justin references "the rear chamber for soda," he is referring to the way that he adds soda to this separate part of the kiln to produce different surface effects on the pottery. The "soda" used by potters is often either sodium carbonate (soda ash) or sodium bi-carbonate (baking soda). When one of these substances flies through the hot kiln and falls onto the pots, it combines with the silica in the clay to form a sodium-silicate glaze; this is very similar to the way that wood ash interacts with the pottery to create glaze. Some potters who wood fire also choose to add soda or salt to the kiln to create additional glaze effects on the finished pots.

12. This practice is not standard among all wood-firing potters but has been done at every unloading of Mark Goertzen's kiln that I have attended and has also been done at Todd Pletcher's kiln. It is a useful method to see where different effects occur in the kiln from front to back, but some potters may instead rely on photos taken in the kiln before unloading each shelf or stack of pots.

13. Their collections of one another's pottery also play a large role in the maintenance of this aesthetic, an aspect of the community that will be discussed in detail in the following chapter.

14. For a particularly profound insight into the aesthetics Dick has been able to achieve in his work, see his article "Toward a Vocabulary for Wood Firing Effects" (2004).

15. A rib is a wide, flat tool that potters often use to smooth out surfaces or to create patterns while throwing or hand building. Here, Dick refers to the way the rib is held against the surface of the pot as the wheel turns: by applying pressure and moving the rib inward or outward, the potter can make a raised spiral pattern on the surface of the clay. In firing, the glaze interacts with the raised pattern and creates noticeable color variations on the finished pot.

16. The dichotomy I suggest here of production line and wood-fired work is a broad generalization and is not found among all potters who pursue wood firing.

17. For those who are more familiar with ceramics, it may be of interest to know that most Michiana potters tend to attempt to achieve cone twelve in the front of their kilns and at least cone ten in the back. When they hold temperature for ash accumulation, they may attempt to do so at cone six to eight, though of course all of these details can vary substantially depending on the idiosyncrasies of each firing.

18. The most common application of glaze is a "liner glaze" on the interior, which provides a smoother, functional surface on the inside space where little ash is likely to fall. This is particularly common on forms like cups or mugs. Some potters also add

glaze on the exterior of pots, particularly those pots that will sit in the back of the kiln and therefore receive less of the fly ash.

19. Although Bill Kremer often speaks of a definitive link between wood firing and religion, and additional potters do profess a sense of spirituality in regard to the kiln and the process, many take a much more secular and pragmatic approach. It would be inappropriate to impose a sense of religiosity upon all participants.

20. *Collective effervescence* refers to the idea that when a tribe or society comes together to perform a collective action, they will feel a sense of unity (and concurrent loss of individuality); for further details, see Émile Durkheim's *The Elementary Forms of the Religious Life* ([1912] 1995).

21. The article cited here is intended for a more general audience. Further scientific details of the fire-walking study can be found in "The Fire-Walker's High: Affect and Physiological Responses in an Extreme Collective Ritual" (Fischer et al. 2014).

FOUR

COLLECTION PRACTICES: MAINTAINING THE AESTHETIC

My interest in potters' collections goes back to an interview that I conducted in 2012, when I asked Dick Lehman to describe to me the people or types of pottery that had been most influential in the development of his personal style. After mentioning the influence of his first (and only) ceramics professor, Marvin Bartel, and publications such as the trade magazine *Ceramics Monthly*, he listed as one of his main influences the collection of pottery that he had acquired from other artists: "I reasoned that surrounding myself with the good work of others was another facet of my education, since I didn't really have one," Dick explained, referring to the fact that he was a religious studies major rather than an art student in college. "And that has resulted over the years in a pretty significant collection of work. I've largely stopped collecting at this point." He pauses, then continues: "I'm just not buying much anymore. I'm starting to see the downside to a collection is, how do you dispose of it? That became a little more focused during, since my [lymphoma] diagnosis in 2004. There were points along the way when I wasn't quite sure I was going to live, and so, all of those end of life questions, you know. Is this going to be a problem for someone? Is it going to be an asset?" he says, elaborating on his thought process at that time. Fortunately, as mentioned previously, Dick has been in remission for some time now. And, soon after mentioning these concerns in the interview, he reiterated the importance of his collection: "I figured that if I surrounded myself with enough beautiful work, I might make more beautiful pots."

Dick had indeed amassed a substantial personal collection, including some of his own best pieces, works by artists he admires, and works by his many former apprentices; the ways he acquired, utilized, and eventually sold parts of the collection are all important aspects of this chapter. The inquiry that follows is primarily concerned with the role of collecting and collections in the lives of contemporary potters. For the purposes of this text, I will define *collecting* as the practice of physically bringing together various artistic resources into one's personal space, typically the home or studio. Specifically, I will look at how pottery owned by these artists constitutes a primary resource for the development of new artwork and, simultaneously, the development of the professional and social status of the potter. While intangible or less-tangible collections (via images, sketches, or online sources, which in their two-dimensionality contain less information than three-dimensional pots) often serve similar functions as creative resources or as a means to reify social connections, I intend this chapter to primarily focus on the importance of collecting, displaying, and utilizing tangible pots (with one small deviation into the possibilities of online display). I will then briefly follow the line of reasoning that Dick set forth and look at what can happen to these pots after they move out of the hands of the initial collector; I will address how small, private collections can move into the public sphere, particularly when they are brought into museum collections.

Why do we need to understand artists' collections of artwork? The answer is multifaceted. Of interest to art historians, museum curators, and others involved in the collection, preservation, and display of artwork is the fact that so many contemporary artists are collectors, and they may often have substantial collections that could eventually be donated or sold to art museums and similar institutions, and thus will enter the public record.[1] As many in the field have lamented, when looking at historical works of art one is often faced with a tremendous loss of information: lack of provenance, no knowledge of how a piece was made or by whom, where it was made, which archaeological dig or obscure location it was found in, and so on. The contemporary potters whom I work with, however, tend to view their personal collections as just that: intensely personal and therefore reflective of many interpersonal relationships.

Without a doubt, this is true for those who work in other mediums as well. They know when and where they have purchased pieces or received them as gifts, they know who made the piece and (usually) which techniques were used, and with this knowledge they would be able to provide a strong written record that could be preserved along with the artwork in their collection. The problem, I believe, is that so much of this information can seem so very straightforward and easily traceable in the present. However, if it is not recorded along with the collection of objects, it can become more and more obscure as the years go by. Artist-collectors (as I will demonstrate here with the case study of potter-collectors) therefore represent an ideal opportunity for ethnographers to work in the present toward having a more complete historical record in the future. This chapter is not intended to provide an exacting, pot-by-pot provenance for any particular potter's collection, but it will provide examples of the kinds of information that can be gleaned through discussion with artists about their collections.

To further the argument, a study of artists' collections also provides a strong counterpoint to the famous collections brought together by wealthy patrons of the arts, which make up so much of the art historical canon today. While these elite collections do have their place in our understanding of fine art through the ages, such collections may tell us only about the aesthetic preferences and social relationships of one or two wealthy people; they often tell us relatively little about the everyday lives of the middle- or lower-class people who make up the majority of the world's population.[2] Therefore, it is valuable to find ways to embrace those who may not previously have been included; inquiring into the collections of artists is a key way that we can further the written record regarding specific artworks.

Finally, and perhaps the most important reason I argue that we should pay attention to artists' collections, is that by examining the collections that these potters have gathered into their lives (alongside a study of the art that they are engaged in producing), we can elicit a much deeper understanding of their values, their social networks, and their creative processes. While these kinds of meanings are more difficult to elicit when working with historical records, contemporary artists are present and able to speak directly to the value of these collections in their everyday lives. Thus, by asking questions about how a collection represents aesthetic ideals, friendships, artistic kinship, and so on, we have a wonderful opportunity to understand the context in which a potter creates the work that they believe to be their best. Similarly to previous chapters, the following discussion of contemporary potters' collections draws on my own fieldwork in Michiana, but here I have also broadened the study to incorporate other written records of the lives and work of contemporary American potters, in order to analyze two main roles of these artists' collections of pottery: I will consider both how the collected works constitute a primary visual and tactile resource for the development of new works, and I will analyze how the act of collecting and displaying collected works can function as a resource for the development of the social and professional status of the potter. I will begin with the potters' collection of their own work and then move outward, following the social life of the object.

COLLECTING ONE'S OWN WORK

The example that falls closest to home, so to speak, is that of a potter keeping their own work. Art historian Krzysztof Pomian defines a collection as "a set of natural or artificial objects, kept temporarily or permanently out of the economic circuit, afforded special protection in enclosed places adapted specifically for that purpose and put on display" (1994, 162).[3] While this definition does not fit all cases, it is indeed applicable when potters intentionally choose to set aside examples of their own work, preventing those pieces from entering economic circulation. It seems, from my observations, that pieces on both ends of the spectrum of quality are often kept in the potter's possession; successful personal works may be kept as representations of an ideal and as a resource for future creations and, at the same time, pieces seen as flawed and/or those works that lack economic value in the current art market are also kept out of circulation, thereby helping to maintain a positive public reputation.

On one end of the spectrum, personal work judged to be of high quality is sometimes kept due to a sense of pride, as a representation of an ideal, and as a resource for future designs. As was previously mentioned, one of Dick Lehman's techniques for inspiring new work involves surrounding himself with good work; he primarily speaks of this in terms of collecting works from other potters, but over the years he has also kept a large number of his own pieces that he viewed to be particularly successful. He decided to part with a portion of this personal collection in 2014, when celebrating his "40th anniversary of pottery-making" and simultaneously raising funds to support the construction of his new studio. In a mass email sent to promote the sale, he commented on his collection: "I have saved the very best until the very end [of the sale]. . . . Here are pieces that have inspired me over the years of my making. Some have been in my personal collection for almost a decade . . . others, for a bit shorter period of time: all are among my favorites." In a later message, he hinted at their value, noting, "These are large and major works . . . they cost a bit more . . . but you save more as well. Perhaps these will qualify as 'important gifts'. . . for parents, siblings, children . . . dear friends and colleagues . . . or perhaps even to treat yourself." The works featured in this special sale were some of the more expensive offerings from Dick, often costing around $1,000. Dick has often chosen to keep these pieces aside as representations of the ideal he is striving for as a potter, and the description of this piece (shown in figs. 4.1 and 4.2) that he included on his website is particularly illuminating as to his personal attachment to the work:

> All-natural-ash wood-fired surfaces always seem to outstrip even my most hopeful anticipations . . . running ahead, pointing the way, revealing new faces, and somehow reintroducing me to my very best self.
>
> This large jar was side fired for 15 days in my wood-fired kiln. I used Chinese Elm from our property that had been blown over in a big storm. On this pot are the salt and metallic salts that these Elm trees had soaked up from our very soil . . . making a natural ash glaze never to be duplicated. This is about as 'domestic' a pot that I can make.
>
> The piece was sidefired on sea shells. One of the wads holding the sea shells is firmly fixed to the surface of the piece. For a while, that chunk of clay bothered me . . . the piece wasn't 'perfect' . . . but after living with it for a bit, I have come to see it as genuinely PERFECT, just like it is.
>
> The range of colors and crystals, and naturally-produced glaze so beautiful . . . a gift from the firing . . . colors and textures I've never reproduced since taking down the kiln almost 15 years ago.
>
> This has been a 'keeper' for me . . . now it's time for it to find a new home.
> (Lehman 2014b)[4]

Fig. 4.1. Tsubo (view number one), wood-fired for fifteen days, all-natural-ash glazing, no applied glaze, by Dick Lehman. Approximately twelve inches tall. Note that the Japanese word *tsubo* can be translated as jar, pot, or vase but often is meant to refer to a piece of similar proportions and size to this one. *(Photo courtesy of Dick Lehman)*

Fig. 4.2. Tsubo (view number two), wood-fired for fifteen days, all-natural-ash glazing, no applied glaze, by Dick Lehman. *(Photo courtesy of Dick Lehman)*

Although he has now sold a large portion of this personal collection, Dick still continues to keep some of his own idealized work as both a reference point and a point of pride.

Dick is not the only one to participate in this kind of activity. For example, at the unloading of his wood-fired kiln in summer 2013, I saw Mark Goertzen pull out a large vase that he and his wife, Suzanne, were both extremely pleased with, and they immediately began to discuss their desire to keep the piece for themselves rather than selling it. As I described in the previous chapter, the results of the wood ash falling and melting onto the pots are quite unpredictable, and exact effects (such as thick drips and runs of this natural glaze or crystallization of the glaze) are challenging to achieve. Therefore, pieces that come out of the kiln with exceptionally good results are particularly coveted. "Of course," Mark noted at the time, speaking generally about some of the pieces he keeps for inspiration, "the question is whether to keep them at the studio or at home." In other words, which location is a more useful or enjoyable place to keep a high-quality piece that offers inspiration for future work? Mark often spends more than forty hours per week in his studio in Goshen, Indiana, where he and customers could view the impressive piece, but he likewise spends much of his time at his home in Constantine, Michigan, where he, Suzanne, and their visitors could enjoy viewing and using his work. Indeed, both locations are well adorned with Mark's own pots and pieces from other potters. What further emphasizes the impact of keeping some of his own best work within his own space are remarks Mark made approximately a year after many of his pieces were purchased by Mr. and Mrs. Haan for inclusion in their museum.[5] "I feel a big loss," he said during a 2015 firing of his wood kiln, expressing his hopes that the newly completed pots would be up to his standards. "I'm hoping some good things come out [of this firing] so I can live with some again. I really do miss them." Fortunately, many great pots were produced in that firing, which not only provided Mark with new work to sell but also enabled him to renew his personal collection.

Many potters whom I have interviewed prefer to keep artwork in both their studios and their homes, often utilizing functional wares for functional purposes. More often than not, visitors in a potters' kitchen are served beverages in the potters' own handmade cups and mugs; I speak here from experience, since this has often been the case during the course of my fieldwork. Dick Lehman, Marvin Bartel, and Todd Pletcher were some of the first to invite me into their homes and serve me beverages in cups and mugs they had made themselves. And, potters themselves often eat off of their own wares on a daily basis. North Carolina potter Mark Hewitt, for example, discusses having lived and worked with Michael Cardew, who had many pots in his home: "We got to know what Michael's favorite pots were and why," he says, emphasizing the importance of living with and talking about the work (Mecham 2009, 61). Mark now makes a habit of living with and using his own wares, as evidenced by an image illustrating his essay in *The Individual and Tradition*, which is captioned, "The table set with Mark's stoneware in the home of Mark and Carol Hewitt, Pittsboro, North Carolina," (Hewitt 2011, 465). The usual explanation offered for this—a method that many of the Michiana potters have mentioned—is that using functional ware is the best way to evaluate it; a potter might make a few samples of a new form and then use them himself or with guests in order to elicit feedback on the new form's functionality and comfort (or lack thereof). Making just a few pieces for purposes of evaluation is different, of course, from making a large set of one's own dinnerware, a significant undertaking which can reflect a sense of pride and a desire to utilize (and demonstrate to visitors) the fruits of one's efforts.

It is important to note, however, that potters do not keep their own works only when those pieces fit within an artistic ideal that is generally accepted within their broader art world; some pieces may be appreciated and kept by the potter even when they lack economic value within the current art market. While this does not necessarily mean the potter views the piece to be of poor quality, it often does reflect their knowledge of their customers' preferences. For example, at the unloading of Justin Rothshank's wood-fired kiln in the summer of 2013, I was able to observe the great enthusiasm expressed by many of the potters involved as they pulled pots out of the kiln that were covered in thick, rough deposits of mostly unmelted ash. "Crusty!" they would exclaim, referring to the rough, unmelted ash surface (figs. 4.3 and 4.4). While these are not the kinds of pots one will often see displayed for sale at the Michiana Pottery Tour, they are still sometimes coveted and kept by the potters, who

Fig. 4.3. "Crusty" pieces unloaded from Justin Rothshank's wood-fired kiln in July 2013. *(Photo by author)*

Fig. 4.4. Looking inside the two pieces to the left of this image, one can see they are both covered in a thick layer of unmelted ash. Photo taken after a firing of Mark Goertzen's kiln in September 2014. *(Photo by author)*

recognize that these works might not have a high economic value. It is possible that attempting to sell such a "crusty" piece might damage their reputation among a customer base that they have built based on their ability to produce works often described, in contrast, as "juicy" (referring to the thick, smooth, glossy, colorful drips of glaze that can be achieved in a long wood fire). However, the rough and crusty pieces do have value among the potters who are interested in the chemistry of the technique and who wish to explore the full repertoire of effects that can be produced by a wood-fired kiln, even when those effects might include rough surfaces that are not, to many consumers, as pleasant to handle.[6] Often they will seek out these thickly coated, "crusty" pieces by placing work in the firebox of the kiln, where more of the ash from the burning wood will gather, sometimes burying pieces that have been set off to the sides.

While a cursory glance at the idea of collection indicates the simple idea that objects are chosen for their appeal to a person and likely reflect personal aesthetic ideals and high economic value, a collection can, upon deeper analysis, reflect much more complex choices and deeper cultural values. As described in the above discussion, potters often choose to keep pots that they find visually and technically appealing, sometimes doing so even if those pieces do not fit a broader aesthetic ideal shared by their customers. Howard Becker addresses trends such as this when he says, "Judgments of value not held jointly by members of an art world do not provide a basis for collective activity premised on those judgments, and thus do not affect activities very much" ([1982] 2008, 134). Therefore, it is understandable that while "crusty" results may be of interest to some individuals in the group, those included in the broader art world do not seek out such results, and therefore Michiana wood firings are still primarily aimed at producing "juicy" results. The primary outcome when results like this are produced is a change in the individual potter's personal collection; such pieces are kept in the home or studio, admired by the potter but perhaps not as likely to be utilized for serving food or beverages to others.

When looking beyond personal works that are kept, however, a consideration of pots made by other artists further complicates the act of collecting. This category includes items given as gifts and mementos of special occasions, pieces kept as samples from admired artists, works that serve as representations of creative kinship (i.e., teachers and students), and pieces used as a means of forging a deeper connection with other artists, often through display or even via the financial support that can be supplied through the purchase of the pot. All of these potentialities will be discussed in the remaining sections of this chapter.

GIFT GIVING AMONG POTTERS

The first example to consider regarding collected objects that were made by other artists is perhaps the most intimate: that of objects exchanged among artists who have collaborated in various capacities and have close personal relationships. Trading pottery of similar size and/or value is a common practice among potters and is often a means of growing one's collection. Potters also give one another gifts of pottery quite often. Giving gifts during and in relation to wood-firing events is, in some ways, the epitome of this method of collection building. Among the potters whom I have worked with in Michiana, giving gifts around the kiln is a prevalent means of expressing appreciation for the assistance provided and the new connections made during the firing. Often these gifts are in the form of pots or small amusing figures left at the kiln site, but the exchange of goods around the fire also extends to food, T-shirts, photographs, and other tokens of friendship.[7] The exchange of pottery is particularly relevant to this chapter since these gifts can contribute substantially to the collection of pots owned by a potter. These gifts may serve as artistic inspirations and representations of an ideal aesthetic (similar to the pieces of their own work that potters might keep); however, having been chosen by another person to be given as a gift, their presence in a potter's collection is more likely to reflect the perceptions of the giver rather than the recipient.[8] Additionally, while these gifts may sometimes serve as creative resources, often they have a parallel purpose in representing a variety of social connections, and the exchange of such gifts can serve numerous social functions.

I have often observed these kinds of exchanges in the course of my fieldwork, particularly at wood-firing events, and the kinds of work exchanged there can be loosely divided into three categories: (1) completed works that are good representations of the potter's personal style or of the results of that particular firing, (2) works from the firing that have fused together in interesting ways, and (3) pieces made at or specifically for the wood-fired kiln that now serve as kiln decorations. Generally, these kinds of exchange do not involve a monetary aspect since, most often, these items are given as gifts. For the most part, these gifts are given as mementos of friendship, as physical markers of the ephemeral experience of having overcome the challenges and joys of firing a wood kiln together.

I was not fully a participant in the firing of Mark Goertzen's kiln in the summer of 2013, since I was not on the shift schedule and had no work of my own included in the kiln, but the potters accepted me as one of the group; my purpose was to document their work, to gain a deeper understanding of the process of wood firing and the social interactions entailed in that situation. While in some ways an outsider, I was present at the kiln nearly as often as any of the potters who took shifts in the firing. I also helped to stoke the kiln and stayed later than necessary on more than one night to talk with those who were on shift. Therefore, I was included in many social exchanges around the kiln, including the toast when the fire was lit and the informal giving of gifts at the end of the firing. As the kiln was being unloaded, on the morning of July 6, Bill Hunt came out of his small trailer (where he had been staying during the firing, having driven in from Ohio to participate) holding a number of small cups he had made prior to the firing. He set them out on a table and then proceeded to give a cup to each potter involved in the firing. Many of the potters then offered him small tokens of their own from the recent firing: a cup, a mug, a bowl, a small figure. In the midst of all this, Bill turned to me and indicated I ought to have one as well; I was honored, and my own collection of cherished pots thereby expanded. Other exchanges among the potters present occurred as well, as they compared the results each had received from the kiln.

A few months later, Dick Lehman approached me at the wood-firing symposium I organized at Indiana University and handed me a small mug that he had made. He said it had come out of the wood firing I had attended that summer and explained, "You ought to have a piece that

Fig. 4.5. Two pairs of fused wood-fired vessels that came out of a summer 2013 firing. *(Photo by author)*

you helped to fire." This piece has become a constant reminder of both the beautiful results of that summer's firing and the connections I was able to build around the kiln at that time. An additional piece from Mark Goertzen has also become a beloved part of the collection in this manner, given after my husband and I helped to fire his kiln in summer 2015, and many other wares both received and purchased adorn our home.

Another representation of the potters' collaboration at a particular wood firing sometimes comes in the form of pieces that have fused together in the firing. As described in the previous chapter, wood firing can be a somewhat volatile process, and sometimes pieces will tilt over or fall off of their wads or stands during the firing, occasionally leaning into other pieces and then fusing while the natural wood ash glaze is hot and sticky. Once the kiln cools and the glaze has hardened, there is often no way to disconnect stuck pieces without causing irreparable damage to their surface or structure (see fig. 4.5), and they therefore cannot be used or sold. To further complicate matters, more often than not the two or three pieces that have stuck together will have each been made by different potters. Rather than discarding these accidental collaborations, the

Fig. 4.6. Figures near Mark Goertzen's kiln in September 2014. *(Photo by author)*

potters will often have a discussion among themselves to decide which of those who were involved in the accident will be allowed to keep the result or, alternatively, whether they are willing to attempt to break the pieces apart (if the point of adherence is small enough and could potentially be sanded smooth afterward). While these pieces may not be the most pleasing aesthetically and can be an upsetting loss of work for the potters involved, they can also offer a point of comedic relief and a reminder that the wood-firing process involves giving up a great deal of control, leaving works up to the caprice of the kiln. Displayed at the kiln or in the potter's home, the piece becomes a memento reflective of that working relationship and the collaborative firing of the kiln that brought together both the potters as friends and the combined pottery forms.

Visiting the kilns of many wood-firing potters around the state of Indiana, I have observed that these kilns are usually surrounded by vessels that suffered various accidents in the firing (cracks, breaks, or the abovementioned conjoining of separate forms). Furthermore, the kilns are often decorated with small clay figures on the top of the archway over the kiln door, such as the ceramic spoon over Bill Kremer's kiln (fig. 3.19) discussed in the previous chapter. In many cases, these figures were constructed by potters on shift during the firing, using spare bits of clay or wadding (a highly refractory clay substance formed into balls and placed under pots to help keep them from sticking to the kiln shelves) found around the kiln (fig. 4.6). These decorative pieces might be made in relation to a conversation or joke made around the kiln, and they are not necessarily examples of the potter's best sculptural work. Quite often they are left unfired, the bone-dry clay becoming highly fragile and easily broken. Their ephemeral quality is appropriate for the setting, however, since the group coming together around the kiln is likewise ephemeral; it is rare for the exact same group of potters to fire together more than once, even though certain friends may attend much more frequently than others. Left as mementos that will sit at the kiln site in perpetuity (likely until they are accidentally broken), these clay figures serve as reminders of the presence and assistance of collaborators at the firing—people without whom the wood firing would not be possible, nor nearly as enjoyable.

COLLECTED POTS AS PHYSICAL RESOURCES AND
REPRESENTATIONS OF ARTISTIC LINEAGE

Beyond the practice of giving and exchanging pottery as gifts, another place where we can examine the close interpersonal relationships between potters is in the collection of works that are representative of one's artistic family tree. Many pottery traditions have been passed down through families, and many of these have been the subject of study for folklorists and art historians; well-known examples in the United States include families in Georgia and North Carolina as well as extensive Native American traditions. Caroleen Sanders in North Carolina, for example, learned the art of pottery from her mother and others in her family and still has a collection of her mother's work that she can reference in her own creative endeavors (Mecham 2009, 130).[9] Similarly, Wanda Aragon learned from her mother, Frances Torivio, and others in her family (Duffy 2011, 201). However, for Wanda, finding pots from others further back in her ancestry was a challenge; in her search for Acoma pots made by her ancestors, she began primarily with a collection of sketches and photographs acquired through museum research. However, these resources were not enough, and she was inspired "to keep searching for the old pots themselves, to see and touch them in order to appreciate their subtle qualities and true colors, consider them from all sides, and understand the structural systems of their designs"—feats that were not possible with static, two-dimensional images (203). This statement highlights the importance of having the physical pot in one's collection; aspects such as balance, texture, and weight are not experienced visually as well as they are tactilely.

While many potters do keep images and sketches as resources for creative inspiration, collecting actual pots is just as important—if not more so—because it gives the potter a deeper understanding of the form. David Stuempfle echoes this experience when he says, "I kept buying books to learn from, and going to museums and, at one point, I just had to buy some old pots to hold." Tactile interaction with pots is, however, still only a small part of the experience for David: "'the main connection I have to the tradition is the human one—and I got that through Vernon and Melvin and others in Seagrove,' he says emphatically" (Hewitt and

Sweezy 2005, 255). Although contemporary pottery traditions (such as those in North Carolina and Michiana) are not as often passed through families, teachers and students often speak of one another in terms of kinship and generational relationships. Feeling a close affinity to those who have been their teachers or mentors, students or apprentices, potters often desire to collect and display works from these important figures in their lives. There appears to be a great deal of variation between whether these pieces are acquired as gifts or through trade or purchase, but no matter how they are acquired, there is a strong commonality in the practice of collecting pieces that are representative of one's artistic kinship. For example, when I have spoken with Dick Lehman, Marvin Bartel, and Bill Kremer—all potters who have dedicated much of their time to educating others—they have all spent significant time pointing out works around their homes that have been made by students or apprentices and explaining those students' accomplishments. Having these pieces on display gives the teachers an opportunity to express pride in their students and, less directly, to express pride in their own teaching skills; the success of the student (often related when verbally describing the creator of the artwork at hand) is reflective of the effectiveness of the teacher.

Collecting and displaying ceramic pieces reflective of one's past— in this case, as a parent, child, teacher, or student—both tells a visual narrative of education and kinship and simultaneously gives the potter an opportunity to verbally relate those stories of the past that are most important to their identity as an artist. If someone inquires about a piece on display in their home or studio, or adorning their kiln, the potter has an opportunity to verbally express their feelings for the maker, explain the story of how they received the piece, and tell of other important aspects of that relationship. Thus, not only does the object itself reflect an intimate relationship, but that object also provides the potter with the opportunity to share personal details with someone who has been invited into the private or semiprivate space where the potter works and/ or lives. All of these objects are situated somewhere between the categories of memory objects Barbara Kirshenblatt-Gimblett has suggested. She defines souvenirs and mementos as objects that are "from the outset intended to serve as a reminder of an ephemeral experience or absent person" (1989, 331). I would argue most items in a potter's collection do this. However, collections of mugs, for example, could also fit under her rubric for "material companions," as they are incorporated into daily life, used often, and valued for their continual presence in one's life (330). Furthermore, in her discussion of miniatures and models, Kirshenblatt-Gimblett notes that "such objects are a medium of exchange and focus of interaction—a talking point" (335), an observation that holds true for nearly all pots in a potter's collection. When I have visited the Michiana potters, I have seen pottery on display throughout their homes; pots sit outside in gardens, in yards, on porches, and indoors throughout the house, displayed in various fashions. Often large pots or sculptures sit on floors or tables, and smaller pieces are placed on counters and shelves, while functional wares might be found in cabinets or on countertops. Work that was made to be hung often adorns the walls as well. While living rooms, sitting rooms, or dining rooms are popular locations for the largest or most significant conversation pieces, it is not uncommon for pottery to line the shelves in bedrooms or bathrooms as well. Marvin Bartel, for example, once took my husband and me on an extensive tour of his home, where every room holds objects that signify relationships with students, teachers, and other artists whom he has known; even the floors and walls in some rooms are covered in tiles that Marvin himself made.

This trend of expressing relationships through collection and display exists well beyond the Michiana potters, and it is relatively well-documented by folklorists working with potters around the United States. For example, looking to the past, Kim Ellington speaks with fondness of a potter in his own artistic lineage, Sam Propst, who lived just down the road when he was young and who worked with Kim's mentor, Burlon Craig. Kim, now a renowned potter in his own right, owns a large, broken five-gallon jug made by Propst, which Kim calls "my ghost pot, because it haunts me. It'll keep coming back whenever I'm making something. I'll think about how damned thin [walled] that Propst is.... And there is not a single pot that I will make of five gallons that I don't see that this thing doesn't echo.... My god, the man set a standard that is unequaled." Kim's biographer, Charles Zug, explains that this is typical in the North Carolina tradition: "For Kim and his contemporaries, all of whom collect these old utilitarian vessels when they can afford them, these ghosts from the past continue to instruct and inspire—and also serve as the basis for future work," (Zug 1986, 38–39). Again, this approach to collecting echoes Pomian's discussion of the varying purposes of collections, as he says that objects can act "as go-betweens between those who gaze upon them and the invisible from whence they came" (Pomian 1994, 171). While this can be a useful perspective in discussing deities or people from faraway lands, as Pomian does, objects function in similar ways to represent those who were once close and have now moved away or even passed on. Potter's collections are often clear representations of those social relationships that are—like the often limited engagement of older generation with younger or teacher with student— no longer present in their everyday lives.

PURCHASING WORK FROM OTHER POTTERS

In Daniel Miller's ethnography of shopping, he provides an example of a mother who takes her children to a toy store as a way of rewarding them while on a shopping trip. Despite entering the store with the intention to only allow the children to play, not to purchase a toy, she does indeed decide to buy a small item at the end of the visit due to a feeling of obligation toward the shop, which she has used for entertainment purposes (Miller 2001, 20). This example clearly illustrates the idea that purchased items may not always be a part of our personal collections due to a deep affection for the form, function, or aesthetic value of the object, but instead may have come into our lives due to a particular social function. As discussed in previous sections of this chapter, it is common for a potter to own pieces that were received as gifts or selected as representatives of close interpersonal relationships, and not all of these pieces necessarily fit that potter's personal aesthetic ideals. This holds true even in the case of works the potter purchases. Objects come into an individual's possession for complex reasons, and in analyzing a collection, one must keep in mind that any item in the collection is likely tied to complex social interactions and cultural values held by the collector.

As I demonstrated above, work is often acquired by a variety of means when a close interpersonal relationship exists between potters; gifts are given, and teachers and students often seek to collect work as representations of their relationship. A slightly less intimate example of collecting among potters involves the purchase of another's work, particularly under the circumstances when a close interpersonal relationship does not exist. There are many reasons for a potter to purchase another's work. Generally a purchase offers financial support to other artists, which can be very meaningful in supporting junior or less-established artists. Often making a purchase gives the potter an opportunity to own pieces that display strong workmanship or admired aesthetics. Sometimes, the purchase of a piece can represent the potter's admiration for the work of a well-known artist; the large financial commitment necessary to purchase expensive pots can represent proof of the potter's seriousness in their respect for the other artist, as well as the felt necessity of having an object at hand as a physical declaration to others of that significant feeling. However, the idea that a potter will only purchase and own a piece that represents their exact aesthetic ideals is much too simplistic; many other factors are at play. In the pursuit of their personal collection, each potter will usually reflect upon concerns relating to financial priorities, space available for storage and display of collected work, and even the social ramifications (whether positive or negative) of being associated with other artists' work.

The annual National Council on Education for the Ceramic Arts (NCECA) Cup Sale is a useful situation within which to analyze these complex purchasing choices. The Cup Sale takes place each year during the NCECA annual conference; it is a one-day sale consisting of donated works brought in by potters with a range of experience in ceramics, and the sale of the donated cups raises funds to support scholarships, residencies, and other opportunities provided by the NCECA organization for its members. The result of this format—where both beginner and experienced, relatively unknown and very famous potters donate—is that it has become a place where potters enthusiastically acquire works made by others, often arriving in the early hours of the morning in order to be one of the first in line when the doors open, and therefore able to purchase works made by popular artists before they are sold. Already the idea of a purchased piece offering direct financial support to another artist is clearly oversimplified, since the proceeds of this sale go to an organization rather than to an individual artist. Additionally, since the

Fig. 4.7. Michiana potters Troy Bungart (*left*) and Moey Hart (*right*) pose for a photo while firing Mark Goertzen's kiln in September 2014. (*Photo by author*)

potters are purchasing within this specific context, the form of the pot has already been determined; whether or not a cup is of interest to the potter, if one chooses to purchase from this sale it is the only form one will be able to acquire.[10]

At the 2014 NCECA conference in Milwaukee, Wisconsin, I had an opportunity to talk with Troy Bungart and Moey Hart, two Michiana potters who had dubbed themselves the "Troy and Moe Show" (fig. 4.7). Although neither is a full-time professional potter, both are quite enthusiastic about ceramics and particularly wood firing, and their enthusiasm and willingness to participate in nearly any wood firing that is happening in their area adds great energy and helps to maintain the Michiana tradition of wood firing. At this particular conference, Troy and Moey explained that they were planning to arrive at the Cup Sale in the early hours of the morning, well before the doors would open, in order to get prime spots in line and therefore have an opportunity to purchase cups donated by the potters whom they admire most. This was, for them, a rare occasion where small pieces by well-known potters around the country would be available for purchase, and it was therefore an opportunity to own a cup or mug that they might otherwise not be able to easily acquire. Soon after the Cup Sale, on March 23, 2014, Moey posted several images on Facebook, each one featuring a new mug that he had purchased, along with the comment, "Some of my finds from NCECA this year. I'm so proud to own these! Can't wait till next year!" In another post on the same day, he also boasted that he had arrived so early that he was the fourth person in line for the sale that morning.

These cup forms, and more specifically mugs, have taken on further significance among potters who participate in online dialogues about pottery on Facebook, Instagram, and similar online networking platforms. In the mid-2010s, potters began to participate in a custom of photographing a mug, either by itself or in a "selfie" of themselves holding the mug, and posting the image on a Monday with a message that denotes the post as part of the "Mug Shot Monday" trend. The hashtag used for participation in this trend is generally written as #mugshotmonday.[11] The images can take many forms, but more often than not, in my observations, the mug shown in the image has been made by another potter.[12] Furthermore, Facebook gives users the ability to "tag" other users in images; these tags are attached to a specific area of the image (often someone's face, though in this case the tag would be attached to the mug), and then the user can add text in the form of the other user's name, which links to the person's profile page. This means that whenever a mug is posted, it can be linked to the Facebook page of both its maker and its owner. This online display of one's collection is a prime illustration of the function of a contemporary collection in developing and maintaining social relationships. In this case, ceramic works are reconstituted as new objects when they are represented in images, and the circulation of those images leads to social interactions in the online format; once posted on Facebook or similar sites, images can be "liked," commented on, and reshared, and each instance of interaction is generally visible to both users' online group of friends or followers.

While this kind of activity might be common among those who are "real-world" friends who connect outside of the online community, it also provides potters with an ideal situation in which they can reach out to others with whom they might not yet have a close interpersonal relationship and demonstrate their interest in the other potter via the

Fig. 4.8. Image of Moey Hart holding his recently purchased mug made by Ted Neal. Posted on Instagram and Facebook, May 1, 2014. *(Photo courtesy of Moey Hart)*

display of pots owned. This was indeed the case with Troy and Moey, as I observed after their purchases during the 2014 NCECA Cup Sale. Specifically, one of the seven mugs Moey had purchased was made by Ted Neal, who is currently a professor at Ball State University in Muncie, Indiana, and who is well known among potters for his kiln-building skills and his industrialized style of wood-fired ceramic forms. Soon after the 2014 NCECA conference concluded, Moey and Ted became Facebook friends. About a month later, Moey posted a new image of Ted's mug, appropriately tagged with the name "Ted Neal," and he furthermore mentioned in the text that he often uses the mug (fig. 4.8). Ted

Fig. 4.9. Todd Pletcher (*left*) and Ted Neal (*right*) work together building Todd's wood-fired train kiln in August 2015. (*Photo by author*)

commented on the image, saying, "Thanks for the props. Enjoy!" Over the summer months, I noticed that Ted, Moey, and Troy all began interacting more and more in the Facebook format, liking and commenting on one another's posts.

Finally, these interactions culminated with Troy and Moey visiting the Ball State University ceramics facility in late August 2014 to participate in a firing of the train kiln (a type of wood-fired kiln) that Ted had built. It is quite likely that this firing collaboration would not have happened without the development of their friendship on social media and the many interactions over the previous months, which seems to have served as proof of Troy and Moey's dedication to wood firing: photos of the two of them firing at least three different wood kilns, owned by friends in the Michiana area and beyond, were posted during the summer; these were a visible and easily accessible reminder to other potters of their serious interest in the technique as well as their likely reliability when participating in wood firings. The Ball State firing event was well-documented on Facebook, including a post by Troy captioned "Loading the Ball State train kiln with Ted Neal, Tim Compton and Moe" and followed the next day with a post by Ted saying, "A nice candle, and it's not even my birthday.[13] Thanks for all the help #troyandmoeshow." Thus, at the conclusion of a successful firing, their friendship was ostensibly solidified. Furthermore, a year later, Michiana potter Todd Pletcher hired Ted Neal to come to his property to lead the building of his new train kiln; during the course of my research, this was the most recent addition to the wood-fired kilns in the Michiana area (fig. 4.9). Indeed, during the building of this kiln in August 2015, Ted confirmed to me that his initial introduction to the Michiana group was primarily through his online contact with Troy and Moey. Although Ted's home base is Muncie, Indiana—around a two-hour drive from Goshen, and certainly not part of Michiana—he is close enough that Troy, Moey, and later Todd, were all able to visit Muncie and help to fire the Ball State kiln, therefore building relationships that would have otherwise been much more challenging to develop in person if they lived at a greater distance.

COLLECTING FOR PUBLIC DISPLAY

Discussions of collecting thus far in this chapter have generally entailed personal collections that are displayed in a manner that could be called private or semiprivate; works kept at home or at a potter's studio function on the level of interpersonal relationships and are not often brought to the attention of a broader audience. Even items shared in an online format often have a limited circulation among those designated as "friends" or "followers" depending upon the kind of website one is visiting, the connections that exist between users, and the privacy settings utilized by those users. However, a potter's collection is not necessarily limited to this realm. Potters' studios, for example, take a wide variety of forms: some individuals' studios are quite private and their products are sold elsewhere, while some potters invite customers into their studios and have a showroom for sales; still others are very social, collaborative spaces where many potters work and sometimes sell together. In some cases, therefore, a potter's collection kept at the studio is apt to be more public than other types of personal collections. The idea of analyzing the collection found in an artist's studio is not a new one in the study of art;

for example, Sarah Burns notes that one way critics in the late nineteenth and early twentieth centuries were responding to the work of fine artists was to consider not just their artwork but also their personalities and particularly their studios; perception of the artist and their workspace was thus inextricably tied to perceptions of their artwork. Many critics that Burns cites were concerned with ways the artist's personality was reflected in their working spaces, which in turn led artists to feel they needed to try to cultivate "artistic" and intriguing spaces in which to sell their artwork (1996, 55–59).

A nonconsumer situation also worthy of consideration is the college or university setting, where artworks collected and displayed by the professors are used as teaching tools and seen by many students over the years. While a potter's collection might often be considered rather private and meant for personal use, a teacher's collection brought into the classroom is certainly intended for a broader audience. Examples of this abound; in Indiana alone, I have encountered such collections at Goshen College, Ball State University, Earlham College, and Indiana University, and I know of the existence of many others. At Ball State, for example, Ted Neal and Vance Bell have made a point of collecting works from former students, previous visiting artists, and well-known figures in the world of ceramics; these pieces sit on the shelves of the studio as visual references for students (see fig. 4.10, for example). This is not a unique approach in teaching ceramics, as is also evidenced by the study collection that Karl Martz helped to create for students at Indiana University. Martz, who had studied briefly with Bernard Leach, Shoji Hamada, and Soetsu Yanagi at Black Mountain College in North Carolina, was no stranger to the intense Japanese influence on American pottery at the time (McKimmie 2009, 68). It follows that the Indiana University Art Museum collection now includes works by Japanese potters that were acquired by Martz while he travelled in Japan in the early 1960s—pieces that were obtained specifically to enhance the collection available to art students at the university. The potters whose work Karl helped to bring into the museum include Tsuji Seimei and Toyo Kaneshige, who are known internationally; Martz's presence likely had other impacts on the collection as well. In this case, the pots acquired by the potter have moved further into the public realm; while they were not being exhibited

Fig. 4.10. Part of Ted Neal's mug collection on display at Ball State University, posted on Instagram and Facebook with the hashtag #mugshotmonday. Original caption reads, "Includes works by Daniel Anderson, David Eichelberger, Matt Repsher, Deborah Schwartzkopf, Chris Gustin, Troy Bungart, Mel Griffin, Ben Bates, David Peters, Dick Lehman, Markus Urbanik, Linda Christianson, John Neely, Kyla Toomey, Michael Kline, Jennifer Allen, Matt Long, Adam Knoche, Collette Spears, Adam Phillip Knoche, Lorna Meaden, Diner Mug, David Bolton, Doug Peltzman, Chris Pickett, Brandon Whitacre and Daniel Ricardo Teran." *(Photo courtesy of Ted Neal)*

in the early to mid-2010s, some have been in the past, and as part of the collection they are available for students, scholars, and others to view upon request.

Although Karl Martz passed away in 1997, his legacy as a teacher lives on, in part due to his actions as a collector and his contributions to the museum. This brings us back to a consideration of Dick Lehman's concerns about the fate of a potter's collection, mentioned at the beginning of this chapter: what does (or should) happen to a potter's private collection once he is no longer around to benefit from it? As a set of items brought together to meet idiosyncratic creative and social needs, it seems the potter's collection is potentially rendered obsolete upon their death. Indeed, the creative inspirations for which they were meant and the narratives evoked by those objects would, if not recorded, pass on along with the potter. However, that does not mean that these objects necessarily cease to be useful when they are no longer in the hands of their initial owner. Dick Lehman, for example, decided to be proactive about selling some of his collection, a significant portion of which was purchased by Bob and Ellie Haan for inclusion in their collection of Indiana ceramics.

When I first met them, the Haans had been longtime collectors of Indiana art; they amassed a substantial collection of paintings by T. C. Steele and others from the Hoosier Group as well as a number of other nineteenth- and twentieth-century Indiana painters. More recently, in the early 2010s, they began to collect examples of contemporary pottery made by Indiana residents, which complements their older collection of historical Indiana pottery made by the Overbeck Sisters, former Rookwood Pottery designer Laura Fry, and the abovementioned Karl Martz, who, in addition to teaching at Indiana University, also worked as a potter in Brown County, Indiana for many years.[14] All of these artworks are currently housed in the Haan Mansion Museum in Lafayette, Indiana (fig. 4.11).[15] This museum was also the location of the Indiana Ceramics Celebration held on October 24 through 26 and November 1 and 2 in 2014. I was able to speak with Bob and Ellie about their collecting goals and the process by which they had acquired this substantial collection.

In discussing their quest for Indiana pottery, Ellie Haan stated that she and her husband started the collection by meeting and purchasing from just one or two potters; they then followed the suggestions of those potters in their pursuit of others, onward and outward until they had met and purchased from a network of over two dozen significant Indiana ceramic artists. Their focus was on teachers and those who had settled down to work in Indiana for significant periods of time; rather than brief

Fig. 4.11. The exterior of the Hann Mansion Museum in Lafayette, Indiana, in October 2014. *(Photo by author)*

visitors to the state, they wanted to collect those who had become part of the fabric of Indiana life and who had therefore had a strong impact on the visual presence and future direction of ceramics in Indiana. This might mean the exclusion of students who were only in Indiana to study or even very productive potters who did not teach. To the Haans, the significance lies in the tracing of tradition—a genealogy of Indiana potters, one might say.[16] Just like the potter-collectors discussed in the above sections of this chapter, the Haans have brought their own aesthetic preferences, cultural values, and historical perceptions into the development of their collection and museum. As Marvin Bartel commented at the 2014 Michiana Pottery Tour (soon after the Haans purchased dozens of pieces from his home), their tastes often run to the traditional instead of the modern. A glass-topped table that Marvin had made, for instance, was too "contemporary" or "modern" for their taste, and the Haans passed it up in favor of a piece that would fit in better with the style of their early twentieth-century mansion and the period furniture and artwork it already contained. In her consideration of the development of museums in late Renaissance culture, Paula Findlen says, "As a repository of past activities, created in the mirror of the present, the museum was above all a dialectical structure that served as a meeting point in which the

Fig. 4.12. Part of the Haans' exhibit of Dick Lehman's pottery, displayed on a piece of
period furniture in their home/museum during the Indiana Ceramics Celebration in
October 2014. *(Photo by author)*

historical claims of the present were invoked in the memory of the past"
(2004, 161). Furthermore, the museum was "a conceptual system through
which collectors interpreted and explored the world they inhabited"
(162). These observations are no less true of many museums today, and
they are clearly reflected in the collecting practices of the Haans.

The Haan collection also includes a few pieces made by highly re-
vered potters such as Shoji Hamada. The apparent strangeness of the
inclusion of Japanese ceramics in a museum dedicated to Indiana artists
is first reconciled by the acknowledgment that contemporary American potters have been, in many cases, deeply influenced by the influx of
Japanese ceramics into the United States in the nineteenth and twentieth centuries. Furthermore, these Japanese pieces were part of Dick
Lehman's "study collection"—pieces he had gathered as inspirations for
his own work and as symbolic gestures of respect via ownership for these
potters' work—which the Haans had acquired along with much of Dick's
own pottery. It is, moreover, important to recognize the context in which

these pieces were displayed; unlike many other ceramic pieces that were displayed on open shelves and various items of furniture around the house (fig. 4.12), these small Japanese pieces were included in a rather poorly lit cabinet with other small works by Indiana potters such as Dick Lehman and his former apprentice Todd Pletcher. The Japanese pieces were not clearly labeled as non-Indiana works, and unless one were to look closely and read the small pieces of paper sometimes placed inside or nearby, one might not know at first glance that these pots were made by venerated Japanese potters and once owned by an Indiana potter who has spent a great deal of time in Japan. However, when I inquired, Ellie was quite happy to guide me to this display and explain the history of the pots. As her husband, Bob, explained during the event, since so much of the collection had been acquired in the months just prior to the exhibition, creating labels for all of the pieces was a daunting task for one person (himself) to undertake alone. Most likely, future exhibits will include more thorough labeling.

OBJECTS AND SOCIAL INTERACTIONS

"One of the impressive things about these nineteenth-century pots is how they've come to mean different things to different generations," says David Stuempfle, in reference to the many old North Carolina pots displayed alongside his own in "The Potters Eye" exhibit in 2005. "From utilitarian objects to family heirlooms to cultural treasures—these pots have stood the test of time" (Hewitt and Sweezy 2005, 255). Yet it is not just time that leads to this stratification of significance. Within just one potter's contemporary collection, viewers will find pieces that have just such a variety of meanings; Dick Lehman's collection is smaller now than it once was, but it still encompasses many categories of objects, including pieces of his own that he utilizes every day, pieces from students and mentors who are nearly as close as kin, and pieces from his connections in Japan. Every object in his collection—and in the collections of many other potters—has a multiplicity of meanings and functions in his life. Indeed, in one way or another, we all create meaning in our lives, and, more often than is generally acknowledged, we do so through interacting with objects. This is material culture, "the vast universe of objects used by humankind to cope with the physical world, to facilitate social intercourse, and to benefit our state of mind ... that sector of our physical environment that we modify through culturally determined behavior" (Deetz 1996, 35). It would be a gross oversimplification to say that potters collect pots for only one reason or another. Instead, to echo the words of Dick Lehman, they surround themselves with beautiful and meaningful pots in the hope that it might make them better potters. Developing as a potter involves much more than attempting to mimic ideal pots of those who have gone before; those who are successful collect ideas that they like and remix elements to create a style of their own. And aesthetics are only part of the picture, since social relationships are also key to the professional development of a potter; strong relationships with teachers and mentors, friendships with those who help to fire one's kiln, pride in one's students, and careful navigation of new social and professional relationships with other potters are crucial as well.

Looking at the way that these social interactions are reflected in and reimagined by the possession of objects can shed light not only on the life of the individual potter but on the broader social structure she or he lives in as well. People often root ephemeral, cerebral moments in the physical world through an association with more permanent objects, attaching stories and deep personal feelings to lasting, physical items that can be seen, felt, and sensed in so many ways that a memory cannot. In the most intimate sense, in the interactions between individuals and objects they behold, emotions are reflected and memories are brought into physical form; we express our sense of self through objects, and in doing so, our physical relationship with the world intertwines with the invisible network of human, social relationships that sustain us.

NOTES

1. This is precisely what Dick Lehman chose to do with much of his personal collection, in large part due to the end-of-life concerns mentioned earlier. His collection will be discussed further in a later section of this chapter.

2. Warren Roberts, folklorist and scholar of material culture, indicated that in the past there has often been a tremendous problem "with the work of most of those who write about the way in which people used to live: Because many writers ignored the vast majority of the population, the nontypical five percent of the population is represented as typical," leaving another 95 percent of the population either misrepresented or underrepresented in written works. Here, he is discussing the tendency of historians and museums to "assume that all people in the past lived in mansions or in large towns" (1996,

viii–ix). I certainly count myself within the line of scholars whose stated goal is to give credit to the ingenuity of a broad spectrum of people and to expand the historical record to embrace more of those who may not previously have been included.

3. This definition, while useful in this analysis of potters' collections, is problematic when applied to the broader world of collecting. For example, objects in collections can have huge economic impacts for collectors, museums, museum-goers, insurance companies, and more, even when they do not physically circulate. Furthermore, collections can and do circulate, passing from one owner to another through various means, or being sent out on loan from one institution to another. The ways and means of display vary so greatly, dependent upon the collector's circumstances that it is, perhaps, too broad to say that the latter part of the definition even applies directly to all the examples that are included in this text. Nevertheless, Pomian provides a useful place to begin in considering the nature of a collection.

4. All ellipses in these quotes have been preserved from the original statements written by Dick Lehman. No edits or abbreviations have been made from his original email and website text.

5. See the section titled "Collecting for Public Display" later in this chapter for further details on this museum.

6. It is sometimes possible for a potter to re-fire pieces that do not come out of the kiln as desired, with the hope of melting the ash and adding more ash, ending up with a pot that is up to their usual standards. However, this can be risky, and re-fired pots will often break in a second firing, which also puts nearby pots at risk for damage.

7. Of course, the purpose and emotion behind a gift can be much more complex, a point evoked by Marcel Mauss's seminal study *The Gift*, not to mention those scholars who have followed in his footsteps (Mauss [1954] 2000).

8. A useful comparison can be found in Robert Georges's article "You Often Eat What Others Think You Are: Food as an Index of Others' Conceptions of Who One Is," which explores the social dynamics of serving food to guests and how the host's perception of the guest's preferences often prevails over the preferences the guest would have expressed, were they given the opportunity (Georges 1984).

9. There are a number of other brief references to collecting in *The Living Tradition: North Carolina Potters Speak* (Mecham 2009), but this was not a topic on which the interviewers focused much attention. This includes Jennie Bireline's mention of looking at other pots in her home while making (31), Charles Davis Brown's brief anecdote about a large vase that he made with one of his mentors many years ago (49), Vernon Owens's discussion of an old churn that is "just perfect" (97), and an interview with Hal and Eleanor Pugh, who have collected sherds left by a potter who worked on their property in the early 1800s (109).

10. It is important to note, however, that the artists' interpretations of *cup* vary greatly; anything from tiny teacups to mugs to large, handle-less tumblers may be found in the sale. Even some so-called cups with tremendous sculptural aspects that render them nearly useless to drink from are included on a regular basis.

11. For those not familiar with the term, a hashtag, which is created by using # followed by a word or set of words—for example, #mugshotmonday—is a marker of topical interest which, when clicked, links a user to other posts recently marked with the same hashtag within that particular social networking website, such as Facebook, Instagram, or Twitter.

12. Another common trend is to promote one's own work, often by posting recently completed mugs that one has made or, alternatively, by posting an image that shows mugs in the process of being made.

13. The *candle* is a colloquialism referring to the flame coming out of the kiln's chimney, which at certain points can signal that the firing is going well.

14. While Rookwood does not have a direct Indiana connection, its location in Cincinnati, Ohio, situates it firmly in the American Midwest. Furthermore, Fry lived a substantial portion of her later life in Lafayette, Indiana, where she taught at Purdue University (Purdue University Libraries, Archives and Special Collections 2012).

15. The Haan Mansion Museum is a complex establishment. To give a brief overview, this substantial structure began its life as the Connecticut State Building in the 1904 World's Fair in St. Louis, Missouri. After the fair, it was moved to Lafayette, Indiana by owners who made minor alterations to the original design and turned it into a private home. As of the mid-2010s, the mansion was owned and lived in by Bob and Ellie Haan. They had slowly turned it into a museum and were planning for an endowment to ensure its longevity after they are no longer able to sufficiently care for it themselves.

16. A similar effort has been made by Vernon and Pam Owens, who established a small museum on the property of their pottery studio, called Jugtown, in North Carolina. As Vernon says, "To have a representation of what Jugtown means for people to come and see—it's very, very important. I mean, you get so much more of a picture [of the history]" (Mecham 2009, 96).

FIVE

MORE THAN POTTERY IN MICHIANA; MORE THAN MICHIANA IN POTTERY

DEFINING ASPECTS OF THE MICHIANA REGION

When Dick Lehman and his wife, Jo, decided to move from their long-time home in Elkhart, Indiana, to a new place—particularly one where Dick could have a designated studio space for all of his pottery work—they asked themselves a critical question regarding the potential location: "Where is our community?" The answer was Goshen, and it was on the outskirts of this town where they eventually bought property and built a new home and studio, which, Dick proudly tells me, Jo designed (fig. 5.1). For them both, being close to a strong network of friends was important; for Jo, being close to the elementary school where she taught was a priority, and for Dick, being close to other potters was also a main consideration. As Dick's narrative of their move attests, Goshen, Indiana, is a particular locus of the Michiana pottery tradition. It is home to the Old Bag Factory, where Mark Goertzen now runs the pottery studio that Dick used to own. It is the place where both Mark and Justin Rothshank continue to train apprentices. It is the location of Goshen College, where Marvin Bartel and Merrill Krabill have taught dozens of ceramics students, many of whom have now settled in the area. And it is host to a number of craft guilds, including the Goshen Clay Artists Guild, where many potters make their work and/or teach classes. In other words, Goshen is in many ways the central node of the broader Michiana pottery network, and the development of a vibrant arts community in recent decades has been a substantial influence in the concurrent establishment of a strong regional pottery community.

Fig. 5.1. Dick Lehman's home (*left*) and new studio (*right*), open to the public for the first time during the 2015 Michiana Pottery Tour. (*Photo by author*)

Two important contexts for understanding the Michiana pottery movement—history and place—are in many ways inseparable; history has a location, and places have history, and we cannot understand one without the other. The task at hand, then, is to understand the history and distinctive features of the region where these potters are living and working, since it can influence each person's lifestyle and products in a variety of ways. The chapter that follows is intended to give readers a more thorough understanding of Michiana as it fits within the broader American Midwest, both historically and contemporarily. It first provides a brief historical overview of the area, including immigration patterns, religious influences, and other factors that have affected the demographics present in the area today, which in turn affect the Michiana potters' experiences of the area. Of significant contemporary interest is an analysis of the area's Mennonite heritage and related tourism as well as the focus on support for small local businesses and the arts in the town of Goshen, Indiana, where a majority of the potters included in this text live and/or work. Furthermore, this chapter looks at some of the additional social connections that the Michiana potters rely upon, including family, friends, clients, galleries and their owners, suppliers of tools and materials, potters who live elsewhere, and publications. These resources may lie outside of Michiana and/or the ceramics community, yet they are close enough to be useful and to make Michiana a viable place to pursue pottery as a profession.

While I've often taken the term for granted in this text, definitions of *Michiana* can vary extensively and are frequently based on the context of its use. Within governing bodies, one often sees the inclusion of particular counties rather than towns (see map 1.1 in chap. 1 for both towns and counties relevant to Michiana). For example, the St. Joseph County Chamber of Commerce refers to its county seat, South Bend, as "the economic hub not only for the county but also for a nine-county, bi-state (Indiana and Michigan) region with nearly one million people. Locals refer to this region as Michiana" (St. Joseph County Chamber of Commerce).[1] On the other hand, the Michiana Area Council of Governments is "the designated 'Metropolitan Planning Organization' (MPO) for the South Bend Urban Area and the Elkhart/Goshen Urban Area"; this organization lists four Indiana counties, and does not include any counties in Michigan (Michiana Area Council of Governments). Additionally, by watching newscasts and weather reports on television in this area one gets a slightly different sense of the region, based on the broadcast area: announcers onscreen often say their report is about and/ or for Michiana, and the maps used often include a selection of counties that reach farther to the east and south.[2]

To complicate matters further, those searching a map are likely to discover that Michiana is also the name of a village in the far southwestern corner of Michigan that sits adjacent to the similarly named Michiana Shores, a town just over the state border in Indiana. Both of these small towns, with populations in the low hundreds, are located on the coast of Lake Michigan. Neither plays a part in the Michiana pottery movement as I have defined it here; those involved are found farther inland, often toward the center or on the eastern side of this ambiguous region. Attempts at official designations aside, those travelling by car— an appropriate mode of transportation in Michigan and Indiana, both of which are known for their automobile manufacturing industries—are likely to develop their own sense of the extent of the region, as signs for businesses with names including *Michiana* dot the highways and county

Fig. 5.2. A view of the St. Joseph River from potter Mark Goertzen's property in Constantine, Michigan, during the fall of 2015. The St. Joseph flows through much of the
Michiana region. *(Photo by author)*

roads throughout the northern third of Indiana and a smaller portion of
southern Michigan. It is a typical Midwestern landscape, with flat plains
and a few small hills or occasional rivers and small lakes where one is
likely to find Dick Lehman, Mark Goertzen, and their friends fishing
when they are not making pots (fig. 5.2). For the most part, outside of
the numerous small towns, one encounters large plots of farmland that
are interspersed with occasional densely wooded areas. As discussed in
chapter 3, these are crucial forests that provide the potters with wood
for wood firing.

Both agriculture and animal husbandry have played a tremendous
role in the economies of both Michigan and Indiana in the last century and more; for example, Michigan is known to be part of the Dairy
Belt—one of the top dairy-producing states in the United States—while
Indiana is considered part of the Corn Belt. Certainly, one is likely to find
both cows and cornfields along the highways of both states, particularly
where the two states blend in Michiana. Corn is Indiana's top crop by
yield and value, closely seconded by soybeans (United States Department of Agriculture). Residents of Indiana and nearby states may recall

the Indiana Beach jingle "there's more than corn in Indiana"—the commercial was ubiquitous on 1990s television, and for many, it highlighted (rather than minimized) the sense that there is indeed quite a lot of corn in Indiana.

While farming remains important to inhabitants of the Michiana area, particularly to the Amish and Mennonite families who grow their own crops and often sell to other local residents and businesses, farming is not the only large industry in Michiana; it also has a long-standing association with automobile manufacturing. Detroit and its long history with the Ford company is not far away, but more directly in Michiana, there have been substantial imprints made by the Studebakers in South Bend and the RV (recreational vehicle) industry in Elkhart County. One local tourism website claims that "Elkhart County manufactures one of every two recreational vehicles on the road today" (Elkhart County Convention & Visitors Bureau 2015b). Additionally, the RV/MH [manufactured housing] Hall of Fame is located in Elkhart; a satirical article by *The Onion* featuring this museum was a source of great amusement for potters at a Michiana wood firing in 2014 (*The Onion* 2001). Beyond farming and automobile production, further analysis shows that the recession (ca. 2008) and national shift to a service economy has affected Michiana as much as many other places in the country. It may be best known to many today as a destination for Amish, Mennonite, and Germanic heritage tourism.

RELIGION AND REGIONAL HERITAGE TOURISM

As I mentioned briefly in chapter 3, the area that would eventually become known as Michiana was previously inhabited by groups of Algonquin-speaking Native Americans. However, conflicts with white settlers eventually drove out most of the native people who once called the area home, and immigration by primarily European peoples in the early nineteenth century set the stage for what is now predominantly white inhabitance of the area. The current religious demographics in the Midwest can be in large part attributed to these settlement patterns; for example, a strong Catholic presence can be traced back to the many early French settlers and missionaries (Kilar 1993, 977). The University of Notre Dame in South Bend, Indiana, a large Catholic research university

and location of one of two substantial college ceramics programs in the
Michiana area, where Bill Kremer has taught for decades, now stands as
a prominent reminder of this heritage. After the French, settlers moving west from their homes in New England brought more Protestant
beliefs to the area. Immigrants coming from both Ireland and Germany
were also substantial contributors to the growth of European influences;
while the Irish were primarily Catholics, the German immigrants were
much more diverse and included Catholics, Evangelicals, Lutherans,
Methodists, and many other religious sects. While this diversity makes
generalization difficult and problematic, social scientists indicate that
"aspects of the German character—rural conservativism, a strong work
ethic, and dogged persistence—became an integral part of Great Lakes
society" (979). Indeed, as the details in chapter 2 attest, persistence and
a strong work ethic are values to which many Michiana potters now attribute their artistic and professional success.

The abovementioned influx of German immigrants was comprised
of many Anabaptists; being heavily persecuted in their homeland for
their views on necessary reformations to the Christian church, they
found great appeal in the religious freedom and availability of fertile
land in the new world. Those who made their way to Indiana were mostly
Amish (named for Jakob Ammann) or Mennonites (named for Menno
Simons) of Swiss and German descent. While the history of these Anabaptist groups is complex in terms of belief and practice, it will suffice
here to say that the Amish initially split from the Mennonites in the
late seventeenth century, and then the Old Order Amish split again in
Indiana in the late nineteenth century, both times due to differences of
opinion as to how best practice their faith. While there is still a substantial group of Old Order Amish in Michiana today, there are also slightly
less conservative groups, such as the Conservative Amish Mennonites
(known since the latter half of the twentieth century as the Conservative
Mennonite Conference). After many splits in the church, it is also notable that most of the Amish who did not split into the Old Order Amish
eventually joined with Mennonites to form a new general conference, the
Mennonite Church, in the twentieth century; this is the same organization with which Goshen College is now associated (fig. 5.3). The merge,
which began in Indiana and Michigan, eventually spread throughout the

Fig. 5.3. This sign on the campus of Goshen College says "making peace with the arts," linking a core Mennonite value with the arts program at the college. *(Photo by author)*

United States and became the largest cohesive Mennonite body in North America (Rudolph 1995).

Religious practice is challenging to quantify, first because it can be highly individualized, but also in large part because figures on membership and attendance are imprecise.[3] Still, it is worthwhile to provide a brief look at some of the demographic data that demonstrates the prevalence of the abovementioned religions in the Michiana area. For example, the Association of Statisticians of American Religious Bodies's 1990 survey of religious adherents shows that counties in northern Indiana have some of the highest population percentages of Amish and Mennonite Church members in the United States.[4] The adherents counted in the survey accounted for approximately half of the total population of Indiana (based upon the national census in the same year). The largest single group to report was the Catholic Church with 26.5 percent of those total adherents, while members of the Mennonite Church accounted for only 0.7 percent of the total adherents in the state of Indiana. The data for Elkhart County, however, reflects substantially different trends: while the Catholic Church is still the largest group, it has only 16.2 percent of the total adherents in the county, while the United Methodist Church (14.7 percent) and the Mennonite Church (14.4 percent) come in at a very close second and third place. This indicates a remarkably dense population of Mennonites compared to the rest of the state (Association of Statisticians of American Religious Bodies 1995). Additional data provided by the ASARB indicates that this trend has continued as late as 2010.

While these statistics indicate that one can define Michiana at least partially in religious terms, this is included here only as an example of the religious demographics of the area and not as a definitive enumeration of religion in Michiana. After all, numbers can do little to indicate individual people's experiences of faith. One should also consider that a tally of those who are members of specific church groups neglects to acknowledge those who attend less regularly or who maintain an individual faith outside of a formal church setting, not to mention those who consider themselves to be secularly affiliated with the "Mennonite heritage," which they often attribute to their upbringing, familial ties, or shared secular values rather than shared religious convictions. In my experience, it is clear that—related to the abovementioned Germanic influence—the larger concentration of many Amish and Mennonites in the area has contributed much to the shared values of peace, acceptance, neighborliness, and service that exist among most members of the Michiana pottery community. A majority of the potters featured in this book do acknowledge close ties to the Mennonite heritage or faith, but whether or not they were counted in a religious census is of little consequence; what matters to this ethnographic account is that, for many of them, affiliating with some aspect of the Mennonite identity is a large part of both their individual approaches to their work and their shared experience as a community. Although not all of the potters are part of the Mennonite faith, there are often strong undercurrents of these values in the narratives they share about their work in clay, many of which were explored in previous chapters. Certainly every potter is influenced by their surroundings, and those who do choose to stay and work in this area are quite likely to share similar values, even if they come to those values via different means.

During my own time in the region, I have found it easily observable that the Amish and Mennonite communities in Michiana have a substantially larger public visibility than most other faith groups. This can, in part, be reconciled by the acknowledgment that some of the more conservative Amish have distinct styles of dress and transportation that visually set them apart when they are out in public (see fig. 5.4, for example). However, most contemporary Mennonite Church members—including the potters in this book who are of that faith—do not ascribe to these traditions. The presence of Goshen College, which is affiliated with the Mennonite Church, also helps to account for the religion's visibility. Trends in the promotion of Michiana tourism also play a large part in the visibility of the Amish and Mennonite faith in this area; signs for Amish furniture stores populate the region's highways with frequency, and attractions such as Das Dutchman Essenhous ("the German eating house") in the town of Middlebury, Amish Acres in Nappanee, and Menno-Hof (a nonprofit visitor center that interprets and presents aspects of Anabaptist history) in Shipshewana all tout their religious associations as well as the availability of homestyle food in nearby or associated restaurants and hand-sewn quilts and other similarly handcrafted items in the gift shops.

Fig. 5.4. The horse, buggy, and numerous bicycles parked outside of the heavily attended weekly farmer's market in downtown Goshen, Indiana are common sights
around the Michiana area. Photo taken during a Saturday morning market in May
2013. *(Photo by author)*

It is clear that these attractions are presenting a kind of staged au-
thenticity, a performance of Amish life as it is imagined to have been
lived in both the past and the present, a gentle introduction and risk-
free encounter for those who are not themselves a part of the Old Order
Amish lifestyle. To this end, themed hotels in the area, such as those
attached to Amish Acres and Das Dutchman Essenhous, advertise handcrafted wooden furnishing and beds adorned with quilts alongside the
convenience of free Wi-Fi and swimming pools. And, despite the emphasis on advertising homemade foods and handcrafted items, a great
deal of mass-manufactured trinkets can also be found on the shelves
of the Essenhous gift shops, often in the form of jewelry, clothing, and
home décor marketed toward women of middle age and older. In relation to Dean MacCannell's model for the designation of tourist attractions, these sites are clearly named, marked with signage, and included
in widely distributed marketing materials, deeming them worthy of attention by outsiders to the community (MacCannell 1976). For example,
the AmishCountry.org website boasts the experience of "a simple life

lived well," and throughout the site, descriptors such as "heritage" and "historic" are found in abundance (Elkhart County Convention & Visitors Bureau 2015a). Those who view the advertising materials and signage so broadly available in Michiana will likely come away with the sense that this is a region where one can purchase a variety of items carefully crafted by artisans who hold themselves to high standards—a regional reputation that is now also supported by the expansion of locally owned small businesses and locally grown and crafted consumables for sale in Goshen, although such goods are promoted in a different way.

FROM PAST TO PRESENT IN GOSHEN, INDIANA

Although it is smaller in size than the neighboring city of Elkhart (located to the northwest), Goshen is the county seat of Elkhart County and is large enough to be well known to residents around the region. A look at the town's history provides a helpful context for understanding the progressive direction in which it has been moving in recent decades. One means for visitors and residents to get a sense of the town's history is through visiting the Goshen Historical Society, located on Main Street and open to the public every Saturday (fig. 5.5). The more permanent displays that I viewed over the course of three years (2013 to 2015) tended to have an institutional focus, highlighting memorabilia from local schools and city services such as police, firemen, and utilities. Additionally, artifacts from numerous businesses are displayed throughout the space and provide the impression that industry and locally owned business is a primary point of historical pride. Further adding to this sense was my experience during a visit in 2013, when a member of the Historical Society took a few moments to point out the exhibits that were most meaningful to him and noted his sadness that so many of the businesses shown are now closed. Upon reading a Goshen history book sold by the Historical Society, I discovered that it includes substantive chapters on industry and local retailers, and additional chapters are consistently peppered with mentions of local businesses (Conrad 1981).[5] These encounters made it clear that for at least some portion of the residents of Goshen, working industriously in a small, locally owned establishment is a worthy endeavor. It is likely that this mind-set has played a part in the success of newly established small businesses in Goshen.

Fig. 5.5. A section of Main Street in downtown Goshen. The Goshen Historical Museum is the second building from the left, situated between Gutierrez Mexican Bakery and Snyder's Men's Shop. Photo taken in May 2013. *(Photo by author)*

Many potters and other artisans whom I have spoken with trace the beginning of the bourgeoning arts community in Goshen to the redevelopment of the Old Bag Factory by Larion and Nancy Swartzendruber in 1984. Built nearly a hundred years earlier in 1895, this large and recognizable building to the northwest of downtown Goshen was at first home to the Cosmo Buttermilk Soap Factory. In 1910, the Cleveland-Akron Bag Company was offered the building for their new endeavor in Goshen, which was eventually operated by their subsidiary, the Chicago-Detroit Bag Factory; after a later merger, it came to be known as the Chase Bag Factory. In the early 2010s, this history was quite accessible to visitors since parts of the building were dedicated to exhibits illustrating the kinds of work done at the factory until its closure in 1982.[6] Machinery, sample products, photos, and testaments from former workers are included in these exhibits. On the exterior of the building, a painted sign proclaims the importance of "BAGOLOGY" in large letters. This term was coined to indicate the company's dedication to the making of bags; the Old Bag Factory's website claims it was used during the heyday of the Chase Bag Factory and means "to elevate the production of bags to

Fig. 5.6. This Old Bag Factory sign in 2012 highlights some of the businesses within, including Lehman-Goertzen Pottery (as it was called in the years between Dick and Mark's ownership), Mishler Sculpture Studio, a quilt shop, a bookstore, an antique shop, a vintage shop, and "working artists' studios." *(Photo by author)*

the level of science" (The Old Bag Factory 2011). Now, the sign serves as a large visual reminder of the building's history within the community, despite having been put to new purposes; after a period of closure in the 1980s, the Swartzendrubers restored the building and opened their own handcrafted furniture store in the space, along with other small businesses (fig. 5.6).

As previously discussed, Dick Lehman opened his pottery studio alongside his friend Larion's furniture store when the Old Bag Factory was renovated. Dick attributes much of the success of this kind of revitalization project to strong, trusting relationships among members of the Goshen community. He recounts, for example, a story about the gas kiln that he built when moving in to the Old Bag Factory: it was a new, fuel-efficient heat-exchange design developed by Goshen College professor Marvin Bartel, and as such, there were no standards or safety regulations on file for inspectors to consult.[7] Dick had trust in the quality of the design and in the many safety features Marvin had incorporated, and the inspector who approved the installation also showed that trust;

Marvin, after all, was the only available expert, and having used the kiln himself, he was able to offer his reassurances about the kiln's safety. When we spoke about this experience, Dick also acknowledged there are probably a number of individuals—particularly city officials—whose willingness to support the arts and trust the intentions and the quality work of the developers or artists involved has played a considerable role in the arts development in Goshen, even though their names might not be as prominently acknowledged in the public record.

Many Goshen residents and artists do publicly attribute much of the growth of the arts in their town to the development of the Goshen guilds, which were established in large part due to the vision and support of David Pottinger and his wife, Faye Peterson Pottinger. While David (now in his eighties) started his career working in plastics in Detroit, he has spent much of the last twenty-five years working toward the improvement of the town of Goshen (O'Hara 2015). He and Faye began by restoring the South Side Soda Shop in the 1980s, and in subsequent decades they have played a substantial role in the preservation and revitalization of many other buildings in Goshen's downtown area (Petry 2012). The couple also provided substantial support for the development of numerous Goshen art guilds. In addition to the Clay Artists Guild, discussed in chapter 2, the Pottingers were also responsible for developing spaces for other artisan guilds in the town. Around the time that the Clay Artists Guild began to grow out of its initial space in the back of the Maple City Market in downtown Goshen, the Pottingers purchased an old lumberyard near the Millrace Canal and developed it into the Millrace Center, which includes space for the Farmer's Market, a local café and bakery, a specially designed new building for the Clay Artists Guild, and buildings for the Jewelers Guild, Photographers Guild, Painters Guild, and Woodworkers Guild. Potter and high school art teacher Cindy Cooper met Faye Pottinger through school connections, and they quickly became good friends; Cindy attributes much of Faye's interest in the arts and the establishment of the Goshen Clay Artists Guild to her background as an art historian. Thinking of the many additional projects that have bolstered the now-flourishing art scene in Goshen, Cindy says an arts-oriented community was greatly desired; it grew intentionally "because so many of us made an effort to make that happen."

Using Melanie Smith's typology of tourism, the kind of experiences being promoted in Goshen could be considered a kind of arts tourism, particularly "the need for the arts to become more accessible to wider audiences, and to promote lesser-known arts activities," while the Amish heritage tourism described previously in this chapter could be considered a blend of both heritage and cultural tourism, since there are strong references to Amish life as lived in both the past and the present (Smith 2009, 13). The other key difference from the heritage tourism discussed above, however, is the Goshen focus toward appealing to local residents: rather than marketing resources to outsiders, the intention is to improve the quality of life for residents by providing opportunities that they find relevant and useful. In this regard, the Pottinger family's influence also stretches beyond real estate: their son-in-law and David's business partner, Jeremy Stutsman, was a longtime city council member and, in 2015, was elected Democratic mayor of Goshen. Stutsman appeared to be a popular choice among Goshen potters. During his 2015 mayoral campaign, he was hailed as a progressive who would continue to support the arts and other important social and economic projects of benefit to Goshen residents.

One of these projects is headed up by Zach Tate, ceramicist and instructor at Notre Dame, who is also the executive director of the newly developed Goshen Youth Arts center (fig. 5.7). He and his wife, Leah Schroeder, are two of the five board members who worked to open the center in downtown Goshen. Just as Dick Lehman described, much of the project has hinged on trust and support from city officials. "The city has been so gracious," Zach said in an interview just prior to the center's opening. However, gaining support was not without its challenges. Eventually, after the group's first attempt to purchase a building for the project fell through, the city agreed to sell them an old and long-vacant home at a substantial discount, with the understanding that they would complete renovations very quickly—a goal with which the organization was happy to comply. "We had a lot of long conversations about what this would look like, this relationship, and eventually began to trust each other on it." Zach emphasizes that the project and others like it represent "an investment in people, not an investment in capital," and he acknowledges that it takes a particular mind-set to give support to such a project. Part

Fig. 5.7. Goshen Youth Arts during the May 2018 "First Friday" event, featuring the Goshen High School Spring Art Show. *(Photo by author)*

of the concern, Zach understands, is that artists can have a reputation for being unreliable; this is an apprehension he has encountered with a number of institutions, including grant funding organizations. "But there's also the fact that the artist is a person that's a thinker, they are a doer," he says in response. "They also have to be very ambitious, they also have to be very clear and concise with what we're doing, and they also have to be prompt. So we want to try to build those attributes up with the city and let people know that if you entrust us with this, we will make good on what we say we're going to do." The project indeed moved forward very quickly, having first taken shape around 2014, when Zach made the permanent move to Goshen after many years of regular visits to the area.

Much of Zach's enthusiasm for Goshen Youth Arts is related to his previous work with youth in the area. When we talked in late 2015, he explained he has taught a summer wood-firing course with Goshen High School teacher Cindy Cooper for four years, and he also taught a summer workshop for children in nearby Mishewaka with potter Justin Rothshank. He described how the Mishewaka elementary school they worked with does not have a designated classroom for art, and therefore "to see [the students] working in 3-D for possibly the first time ever was a really awesome experience. . . . Given the opportunity, these kids can really do some amazing stuff." Although Mishewaka is around a thirty-minute drive from Goshen, Zach had parents ask if they could bring their children to Goshen Youth Arts for classes before the center even opened, and he said he had no intention of turning them away. "It's pretty amazing how thirsty they are for stuff like this," he says of the students.

Ultimately, Zach, Leah, and the other organizers of Goshen Youth Arts hope to make their classes free in order to make them as accessible as possible; in the meantime, they are using a sliding scale based on income in order to help accommodate children coming from lower income families. Offering free classes is a particularly admirable goal given that the most recent data released by the US Census Bureau estimates that approximately one-third of children in Goshen live in households with an income below poverty level (United States Census Bureau 2013). This is not just an issue of socioeconomic class but also one of race; as noted above, the town of Goshen and surrounding areas have been predominantly white for a long time, and it has not always been a welcoming place for people of color.[8] While racial discrimination and/or inequality is not something most Michiana potters experience personally, most are very much aware that such challenges exist for their neighbors and would like to make improvements in that regard. Much of the work that Zach is doing at Goshen Youth Arts to provide affordable arts opportunities to youth in the area is a direct response to the poverty experienced by the region's nonwhite children. He has also mentioned hopes to bring in artists of color as teachers or artists-in-residence so that such students will have the opportunity to learn from artists who look like them. But Zach's goals stretch well beyond the children of Goshen and surrounding towns: "One of the things about this art scene that I'm hoping we can do is not just create the culture of art with kids, not just help kids, but also bring the community together with it. I've got a lot of public art projects in mind," he says, looking to the future.

Goshen has become a much more diverse place over the years, and many residents do appreciate that change.[9] "There are so many cultures at Goshen. I love that," says Cindy Cooper, speaking of her work with high school students. Goshen College also contributes to this change in the local population, with brochures indicating they have 32 percent students of color and 10 percent international students. And while the college strives to be inclusive on campus, they also endeavor to immerse students in other cultures through study abroad programs, in which 80 percent of their students participate. International engagement is a noticeable part of the lives of some of the Goshen College graduates who are now potters living and working in the Michiana region; many have travelled abroad for service trips or for art-related purposes. These statistics are not meant to imply that the problems of structural inequality are any less urgent and challenging in Goshen than they are throughout the United States in the early twenty-first century; however, the sense among the more outspoken residents who take part in the arts and educational networks in the area is that they are working hard to make progress on issues of social justice.

While the growing emphasis on the arts in Goshen tends to be focused inward, on benefits for residents, over the course of my years of research I have also observed increasing media interest in Goshen as an arts destination, both within the state of Indiana and on a national scale.

Fig. 5.8. Crowds line Main Street during the July 2013 First Friday celebration in Goshen while proud owners parade their vehicles up and down the street. (*Photo by author*)

For example, *American Craft Magazine* (published by the American Craft Council) printed an article in July 2015 highlighting potters, jewelers, sculptors, and a variety of other artisans in the area as well as the venues through which they exhibit and sell their work:

> Makers are everywhere in Goshen. They're living and working in the Hawks rental building aimed at artists and entrepreneurs, a former furniture factory where each unit includes extra work space. They're hanging out at one of the three [*sic*] craft guilds in town. They're showing their work—at the indoor, year-round farmer's market or one of the numerous craft fairs around the area or the once-a-month party known as First Friday [fig. 5.8]. Or they're firing a kiln together on the edge of a forest outside of town. A number of artists . . . marveled that other artists who used to tease them about living in the middle of nowhere are now hailing the high level of work coming out of Goshen. (O'Hara 2015)

And the article is quite inclusive, noting others who are working outside of the usual artistic mediums; highlighted are the recently established Goshen Brewing Co., known for its locally sourced food and craft beers brewed on location, as well as Janus Motorcycles, a small company that offers two different handmade models created out of locally sourced

Fig. 5.9. Goshen Brewing Co. sits to the west of downtown Goshen. It opened in spring 2015 and quickly became popular destination for many area residents and craftsmen. Photo taken in August 2015. *(Photo by author)*

parts (O'Hara 2015). Many of the area potters note these same trends in our conversations, claiming that Goshen has become a maker-friendly place, one where they find good friends in like-minded individuals—and not just other potters—who understand the time and dedication it takes to run a small business and/or work in the arts industry.

Furthermore, venues such as Goshen Brewing Co., Constant Spring restaurant and bar, The Electric Brew coffeehouse, and other Goshen shops often provide unique retail opportunities for some of the area potters and other artisans as well (fig. 5.9). Custom ceramic mugs and other handmade pottery vessels featuring the venue's logo are often either available for sale or provided for regular clients who may have their own numbered mugs designated for use within the venue, as has been the case at Constant Spring. These beverage venues are not the only places where the work of local potters is featured in Goshen. At the River Bend Film Festival in downtown Goshen, sculptures donated by Dick Lehman have been presented to award winners as their trophies. Even the tap handles at Goshen Brewing Co. were made by area potters, and many of their employees are craftspeople from around the town who find it useful to hold a steady job alongside their work making and selling art. For example, willow-basket maker Viki Graber works at Goshen Brewing Co., but outside of that work, she is well known for her basket weaving (Watson 2016).

Two additional craftsmen with small businesses have played an important role in the pottery scene in Goshen: Troy Bungart makes and sells handmade brushes and wooden pottery tools, and Moey Hart established Northern Indiana Pottery Supply as a resource for regional potters. Troy's business primarily operates out of his home in Two Rivers, Michigan, where he has a substantial workshop for both pottery and woodworking, and he routinely supplies potters with custom brushes and wooden tools for their creative endeavors. He also sells his wares online and has taught brush-making workshops. Moey's business is located on the west side of Goshen, on his family's large farm property. Part of his business entails routinely picking up or receiving shipments of materials from suppliers farther away in the Midwest and then delivering those materials to Michiana potters. He also began to make slip that is available for sale, and he also sometimes slip casts and bisques items that can be purchased by other artists. Of course, as mentioned in previous chapters, both Troy and Moey are avid potters themselves, in addition to their supply-oriented endeavors. Troy, for example, loves experimenting with shino glazes, and he and Moey often fire a small experimental soda kiln on Moey's property. Both men have close relationships with the other potters in the Michiana community, and it is clear that those who work in the area appreciate having friends like Troy and Moey, who provide local resources for crucial supplies and who are also very enthusiastic and available to participate in wood firings and events such as the Michiana Pottery Tour.

As discussed in chapter 1, the growth of the Michiana Pottery Tour is an indicator of support for the arts in Goshen, and it also highlights the role of the potters in helping to develop this region as an arts-oriented destination. Michiana potter Brandon "Fuzzy" Schwartz, who exhibited his own pottery at Moey Hart's location during the 2014, 2015, and 2016 tours and assisted at Mark Goertzen's kiln in earlier years, offered some insight as to the number of visitors and locations they have come from. While he was quite busy selling his wares and conversing with customers, he also kept some notes about the number of people who came and, when it was mentioned in conversation, where they had come from. At his own booth in 2014, he had over thirty visitors on Saturday and over forty-five visitors on Sunday, including many locals as well as people from Chicago, Illinois; Syracuse, Leesburg, Ft. Wayne, and South Bend in Indiana; and Brooklyn, Buchanan, Kalamazoo, and Niles in Michigan. Fuzzy's count was even higher in 2015 and included over sixty-five visitors on Saturday and over eighty-five visitors on Sunday. That year, he noted additional local visitors as well as people from Chicago, Illinois; Elkhart, Ft. Wayne, and Indianapolis in Indiana; and Ann Arbor, Cadillac, and St. Claire Shores in Michigan. The 2015 tour also brought in some people from locations even farther away, including a woman from Kentucky who was visiting her sister in Michigan as well as "a lady from Alaska visiting family and two potters that live in Florida and spend a few months in Chicago each year." Fuzzy has noted that in these counts he typically does not include "family members or helpers of other vendors" unless they make a purchase at his booth; he is concerned with how many customers and potential customers he encounters in the course of the tour, and thus those who are there only in the capacity of vendor or assistant are of less concern in his data gathering. In addition to seeing a larger number of visitors in 2015 (as compared to 2014), Fuzzy also reported a larger number of items sold.

While the experiences that other potters have shared with me have been more anecdotal, my understanding is that many of them have seen a similar growth in both number of visitors and sales made. But the tour is not just about sales; it is also about bringing in new visitors, encouraging them to enjoy the experience and feel welcome in the future, and educating them about Michiana potters and their pottery, particularly wood-fired work (fig. 5.10). As I discussed in chapter 1, the kiln opening events that Mark coordinates every year of the tour provide an important opportunity for visitors to learn about wood firing. Knowledge about wood firing is relatively uncommon, and even potters who have not wood fired may have relatively little knowledge about the process. Scheduling times throughout the tour when small portions of the kiln will be unloaded allows visitors to plan their tour schedules so that they can see part of the unloading. As the potters work together to pull pots out of the recently fired kiln, they offer explanations to the crowd that

Fig. 5.10. The natural colors of the wood-fired pottery (pieces here by Todd Pletcher) fit in well with the natural displays chosen by the potters and the seasonal leaves that are nearly always present during the tour. Photo taken in September 2012. (*Photo by author*)

gathers, often presenting their own work and explaining what is unique or successful about the piece. These explanations help audience members to better understand and appreciate the aesthetics of wood firing. Furthermore, after the pots are unloaded they are often spread out on the ground nearby, and in between unloading times the potters often gather with their customers and friends to inspect and discuss the results.

Having this time with visitors to emphasize the hard work that goes into wood firing, the impressive chemical processes that turn wood ash into glaze, and the unpredictability of results and the potter's lack of direct control over the final decorative patterns found on the pieces is a great way to cultivate a clientele that will feel connected to the process and hopefully purchase wood-fired pots in the future. Through their enthusiasm at the kiln opening, and throughout their interactions with visitors at other times and locations on the Michiana Pottery Tour, the potters instill their own sense of Michiana aesthetics into a broader community of potential clients. Their efforts help to instill an appreciation for wood-fired pottery, respect for the natural materials used, enjoyment of the look and feel of handmade pots, and appreciation of the skills of the people who make these—all values that fit in well with the trajectory of the heritage tourism and arts development in the town of Goshen.

BEYOND THE LOCAL OCCUPATIONAL GROUP

With the exception of the above section of text about the arts and small businesses in Goshen, the research and analyses I have included in the preceding chapters have almost exclusively attended to the kind of relationship found between those who share a vocation. This book is specifically intended to focus on this group of professional potters in Michiana and those to whom I referred initially as "pottery adjacent full-time," particularly professors and teachers of art as well as suppliers like Troy and Moey who, in addition to the tools and materials they make available to the group, are also heavily invested in making pottery. Sometimes, a similar relationship is also present with those who are particularly invested in pottery as a hobby, to the point that it might be more accurately described as a secondary career; this applies to guild members, for example, who devote incredible time and energy to the craft. What everyone included here has in common is the fact that pottery is central to their identity, takes a substantial percentage of their time and energy, and is a main financial consideration in their lives. However, we must not neglect the many other kinds of supportive relationships that are also present in the potters' lives: family and non-potter friends, consumers (both individual and institutional), suppliers, and a variety of connections with the broader world of ceramics. Both Glassie's model for the study of material culture (1999a) and Becker's suggestions for the study of art worlds ([1982] 2008) demand this, and while many of these connections have been alluded to in the preceding pages, it is worthwhile to elucidate this aspect of the pottery profession in more detail.

Beginning close to home, family and friends are often a crucial aspect of the potter's success. In addition to their partnership in many aspects of everyday life and the crucial emotional support that a spouse or partner usually provides, many spouses and partners are also quite directly involved in the potter's work. A number of instances of this have already been included in this text, but other examples from my fieldwork abound: I remember Jo Lehman bringing food to the first unloading of Mark Goertzen's kiln that I attended; Todd's partner working alongside him to build their new wood kiln; Mark and Suzanne taking late-night shifts stoking the wood kiln together; Brooke Rothshank participating in numerous exhibitions with Justin, selling her paintings. At the 2015 fall firing of Bill Kremer's kiln, one of the participating potter's girlfriends confided in me that there is an ongoing conversation among the potters' spouses and partners regarding the fact that their role is often to reassure the potter as to the quality of their work; having not made the pots, the partners find they are usually less critical of the results and do not see the same little imperfections that the potter might pick out. This woman confided that she will often insist that her boyfriend keep a piece and live with it for a while, because after a couple of weeks, he often comes to love the results as much as she does.

Parents and children play important supportive roles as well, in many cases. Numerous family members are always present at the Michiana Pottery Tours, often helping with sales or refreshments. I have also met Justin's father at a firing of Justin's kiln, and Todd's and Anna's parents at the building of Todd's kiln, and all of their support and enthusiasm for their children's work was abundantly clear. Additionally, those potters who have children often involve their children in their work, to some degree. Dick Lehman's adult son, Scott, and Merrill Krabill's son, Seth, have both sold work at the Michiana Pottery Tour. One of Troy Bungart's teenage daughters often assists him with the brush workshops he runs and has attended kiln firings and pottery tours with him often, sometimes tending to sales at his booth. Both Justin and Moey's elementary-school age and younger children are often present around the studio and at kiln firings. And Justin's eldest son, Layton—no more than six or seven years old at the time—set up a booth of his own selling just-sprouted maple trees that he had dug himself and planted in some of his fathers' seconds (fig. 5.11).[10] Furthermore, as children participate in a potter's everyday life, they also engage with the collections of pottery that I described in chapter 4. Justin has written an article that beautifully describes the influence this collection has on his family life: "Sometimes my three-year-old son, Layton, helps me put away the clean dishes. Often he'll pick up a cup and ask, 'Daddy, did you make this one?' Usually, the answer is, 'no,' and then the question is, 'who made it?' And he'll pose this question to every dish before it goes back on the shelf. And what I think is great about this, are the answers. . . . Virtually all the pieces have a name that goes with them, as nearly everything in our cupboard is handmade by someone we've met, or know" (Rothshank 2012, 28). Justin goes on to recount his own first experience of a potter's studio, when his parents commissioned a set of dinnerware, and the lasting influence it had on him, including some later connections he made with the work of the same potter. He ends the article with remarks that speak to the role family can play in developing an appreciation for art: "While I don't expect Layton to become a potter, I do hope to pass along the same sense of respect for handmade objects that my parents helped to root in me. It feels good to share moments of connection to others in our lives while unloading the dishwasher with my son. I think one of the strengths of the studio pottery movement, and the benefits of buying handmade objects, is this experience. There's a face and a name, and a culture and experience, behind each piece, not just dirt and glaze" (29). While documenting family involvement was not my priority during my fieldwork, it is unmistakably a crucial part of life for the Michiana potters and one I could not do justice to with just a few remarks here. Yet the examples

Fig. 5.11. Justin Rothshank's son Layton (*right*) with a customer at the 2014 Michiana Pottery Tour. (*Photo by author*)

above speak clearly about the significance of family connections in the lives of these potters.

Friendships are often just as crucial as family, and while the con-nections between potters in this occupational group might often be best described as friendships, this does not preclude the existence of many other important friendships; those friends who live nearby are often quite present in the potters' lives. Friends and neighbors often come to help with wood firing and are happy to help chop wood, stoke the fire, provide enlivening conversation around the kiln, and share enthusiasm for the results of the firing—something that I have observed at nearly every firing and kiln unloading that I have attended (fig. 5.12). Many share in hobbies like fishing and sailing or are skilled craftsmen or crafts-women who can help to build a new house or kiln shed; Justin's home, for example, was built by the hands of many friends in the community. Often friendships have formed over shared goals in the community, with all wanting to make Goshen and Michiana a better place for residents; Cindy Cooper and Faye Pottinger's friendship, mentioned previously, comes to mind in this regard. And, quite often, the potters' good friends may be active in the arts or education or may own or work in a small local business, and therefore they share similar concerns and triumphs in their lives.

Another important social connection, which is sometimes (but not always) less intimate than friendship, is that of the potter and their cli-ents. In chapter 4, I addressed the collection of pottery primarily from the potter's point of view, but it is critical to acknowledge that in order to make this a profession and a sustainable source of income, a potter must build a clientele and maintain good relationships with those who routinely purchase and collect their work. While all of the professional potters engage in online sales to a certain degree, and many of them sell their work through wholesale or consignment arrangements at other galleries, face-to-face interactions at their studios and/or special sales events like the Michiana Pottery Tour are still quite crucial. Often, these situations give the potters opportunities to learn quite a bit about how their work is received by others; by observing how a potential customer interacts with a pot, they are able to glean information about whether

Fig. 5.12. Mark Goertzen's neighbors using a hydraulic wood splitter to help split wood for the June 2013 firing. *(Photo by author)*

that pot feels comfortable to hold, has a pleasing texture, has good balance, and so on. Dick Lehman has published an article that describes this kind of interaction quite clearly:

> Several weeks ago a woman came into my studio. She spent the longest time just looking among the mugs: handling, fondling, carrying several around the studio while hugging them. She checked the handles for how they fit her hand. The rims she put to her mouth to see how they felt. Several times she declined my offers of assistance, saying she was "doing just fine." After nearly half an hour she called me to wrap up her choice. She had a satisfied smile across her face, a pleased-with-herself stance . . ." You see, I had one of your mugs for several years. I always started my day with coffee in your mug. But recently I broke it. And, you know, life has not been the same since. I don't mean to be melodramatic, but life for me was better when I started the day drinking out of that mug." . . . For several hours I mused at just how theatrical this customer had been—making a big deal over so little. But then it struck me. I had almost missed the wonderful gift of this curious exchange. Melodramatic or not, was not her response just exactly what I hope for in the making of my pots? Isn't it my fondest wish that the work of my hands will actually change someone's life, that the investment I make in clay will make someone's life just a little better? Of course it is! (Lehman 1993)

Creating work that will elicit such a strong response in a client is the ideal for many potters. And seeing customers react to pots can be a substantial part of a potter's ongoing development.

Tom Unzicker also spoke with me about how clients' preferences had played a role in the development of his style, describing how he and his brother had almost unconsciously shifted their work toward what customers prefer. As Becker says, artists almost always "take the imagined responses of others, learned through their experience in an art world, into account when they complete a work" (Becker [1982] 2008, 202). Tom explained that his own work in graduate school was "gnarly . . . probably more like the traditional Japanese, with the crusty and rough surfaces. But over the years, whether it's conscious or unconscious, [Jeff and I have] just found our customers respond better to shinier, smoother, glossier kind of surfaces and brighter colors." And while it "isn't necessarily what our original vision was," Tom still feels that "it's all worked out somehow. We still enjoy what we're doing. It's interesting, we've probably discovered some things in terms of surfaces and that kind of thing that we wouldn't have otherwise figured out." In that way, clients

Fig. 5.13. (*Left to right*) Steve Hansen, Eric Botbyl, Todd Pletcher, and Troy Bungart. All four fired Todd's kiln together and then exhibited work at Todd's location on the 2015 Michiana Pottery Tour. (*Photo by author*)

can be a driving force in a potter's creativity, whether it is a direction the potter personally foresaw or not.

Further regarding the context of consumption, most potters also maintain relationships with the gallery owners who sell their work. While the Michiana potters all take part in a wide variety of exhibition opportunities—often including juried and invitational exhibits, wholesale or consignment arrangements, temporary individual and group exhibitions, and so forth—there are two galleries in particular that many of the potters exhibit with and interact with on a regular basis. These are the Schaller Gallery in St. Joseph, Michigan, and the Companion Gallery in Humboldt, Tennessee. Both galleries focus heavily on functional pottery, which is a good fit for most of the Michiana potters. Eric Botbyl, the owner of Companion Gallery, is also a potter and has an interest in wood firing; he is friends with many of the Michiana potters and has come to the area to fire with both Justin and Todd. He has also collaborated on some pieces with Justin, and he exhibited some of his own work at Todd's studio during the 2015 Michiana Pottery Tour (fig. 5.13). Although Eric lives a substantial distance from Michiana, he could certainly be included as a more distant node in the network of Michiana pottery professionals. It is clear that the relationship he has with the Michiana potters is mutually beneficial, since he provides them with an opportunity to present their work to a broader audience, and they have provided him with opportunities to collaborate in making pottery.

Of course, we must not neglect those who provide the materials that are needed for the potters to do their work; the potters would have nothing to sell if they could not procure the necessary supplies. I have already mentioned Troy Bungart, who makes and sells pottery tools and brushes, and Moey Hart, who opened Northern Indiana Pottery Supply to serve the pottery community in Michiana. Looking farther outside of the Michiana region, however, there are also suppliers that have been mentioned numerous times as I have spoken with these potters over the years. First, many use clays from Standard Ceramic Supply Company out of Pennsylvania; Moey is now able to provide a central distribution location for those popular clays. Second—and perhaps more important—is the AMACO company (American Art Clay Company, Inc., which also makes Brent pottery wheels), located in Indianapolis, Indiana. The company provides a wide range of clays, glazes, and other pottery supplies to the region's ceramic artists, and a number of the Michiana potters have had beneficial relationships with the company. For example, Todd Pletcher layers some of the AMACO Potter's Choice glazes on his production line and was featured in a video on their website explaining how he gets some of these effects.[11] Justin Rothshank also tested some of AMACO's Low Fire Matt glazes, and his cups were featured on their website.[12] AMACO has also sometimes provided glazes for workshops held by the Michiana potters, particularly for youth classes. Often, relationships like these are mutually beneficial because the potter and the company will promote one another's work; for example, in situations such as those mentioned above, Todd, Justin, and AMACO have posted on social media sites about the projects, which puts each in front of a wider online audience. This kind of mutually beneficial relationship is not exclusive to Michiana; in fact, many ceramics suppliers ask artists to test and use their glazes and then feature the artists in some way in their promotional materials.

I have also hinted throughout this text at the many connections that the Michiana potters have to the broader contemporary ceramics world. Each of the potters has numerous relationships with other potters around the country and even around the world. These relationships take many forms: close personal friendships and ongoing correspondence, workshops taught or attended, traveling to fire kilns together, connecting with former teachers or students, chance meetings at annual NCECA conferences, and so on. Justin Rothshank, for example, has been a tremendous resource and can always point me to new artists with a connection to Goshen and Michiana, even if they are now living out of state. He has also hosted a number of young artists at his location on the Michiana Pottery Tour. For example, in 2015 Stephanie Galli was included, and though she is originally from Detroit and has not lived in Michiana, she is one of many artists to make a connection through this broader network of potters.

When I talked with Stephanie during the 2015 tour, she recounted to me the serendipitous way in which she had connected with the potters in Michiana. In 2011, she had been travelling in China, and on her return flight she met a woman who was returning to Indiana from Korea. As they talked, she discovered that this woman, Hannah, was dating a man whose father was a potter; Hannah's boyfriend (now husband) was Scott Lehman, and his father is Dick Lehman. Stephanie recounted that when she recognized Dick's name, Hannah was not surprised, since many ceramics artists are familiar with Dick's work. However, Stephanie had attended Central Michigan University, where she studied ceramics with Greg Stahly, who had previously worked for Dick Lehman at the Old Bag Factory. Greg and Dick have remained close over the years, and Stephanie said she was quite surprised to make such an unlikely connection on the flight home. She, Hannah, and Scott have become good friends, and Stephanie began to know some of the broader network of Michiana potters through their friendship and eventually exhibited her work there

Fig. 5.14. Stephanie Galli with her display of mugs at the 2015 Michiana Pottery Tour. *(Photo by author)*

during the 2015 Michiana Pottery Tour (fig. 5.14). She finished her MFA at Indiana University in 2016 and soon afterward returned to Central Michigan as a lecturer in ceramics. While Mount Pleasant, Michigan, and Bloomington, Indiana, are both too far away to be considered part of Michiana, both were near enough that Stephanie could maintain a close connection with Michiana.

Other connections are made more directly, through visits to the Michiana area for professional reasons. Dick Lehman, for example, recounts his friendship with famous ceramist Paul Soldner, who had lived in the Michiana area for a short time and whose father was a Mennonite minister. Once, when Paul had been commissioned to install a hot tub at a resort in Lakeside, Michigan, he found that those who were supposed to be helping with the project were drinking a lot and not doing much work. So, Paul suggested asking Dick Lehman to help, saying, "He probably has the Mennonite work ethic." Thus the two of them, along with Randy Schmidt, a professor from Arizona State University, completed most of the project together. Experiences such as this—perhaps short-term but still very meaningful connections—could fill a book, as all of the Michiana potters are very well connected within the contemporary world of American ceramics. It will suffice here to say that these additional professional relationships—with people who are less present in everyday life yet often still quite influential in the potter's work—are worthy of acknowledgment and deserve further attention than will fit in this particular text.

Publications can also play a crucial role in a potter's life, often in a less personal way. Many of the Michiana potters reference articles or books they have read over the years as strong influences in their development; often they have seen new aesthetic elements they wish to incorporate into their own work, have found new techniques to try, or have learned of potential solutions to problems through the extensive reading that they have all done. And with the massive expansion of online resources, many are also turning to websites and social media for these kinds of resources as well. Furthermore, many of the Michiana potters are published authors in their own right; many of their articles and other texts are cited in this book. Their publications, often in trade magazines that focus on the art of ceramics, ensure that their methods and philosophies are available to a wider audience in the ceramics world, further facilitating their connections within this broader professional group. Still, it is those who are available nearby to provide support and collaborate on many aspects of the pottery process who have had the greatest influence on the development of a sense of community among the potters in Michiana.

NOTES

1. In the St. Joseph County Chamber of Commerce definition, the Indiana counties included in Michiana are Elkhart, Kosciusko, La Porte, Marshall, St. Joseph, and Starke, and the Michigan counties included are Berrien and Cass.

2. For example, weather reports from the ABC news station in 2015 included Berrien, Cass, and St. Joseph counties in Michigan, and Elkhart, Fulton, Koscuisko, LaGrange, La Port, Pulaski, Stark, and St. Joseph counties in Indiana.

3. One obstacle in pursuing such information comes from the fact that the national census no longer collects information on religious affiliation, as law prohibits any religious question be mandatory; some religious organizations are counted as businesses, yet this provides little detail on individual practitioners (United States Census Bureau, n.d.). Furthermore, a main source of data regarding churches and church membership, the Association of Statisticians of American Religious Bodies (ASARB), relies only on the religious bodies who were found and contacted and chose to provide information for their surveys. Nevertheless, the state- and county-level figures provided by ASARB offer a basis for grasping some of the broad religious trends in northern Indiana.

4. This analysis is based on population penetration maps provided by the ASARB (Association of Statisticians of American Religious Bodies 2012).

5. The book was written cooperatively by members of the community and the *Goshen News* staff, and the content of many chapters is based upon a series of local newspaper articles that looked back on the history of Goshen at the time of the nation's bicentennial in 1976. The book was then published in 1981 as part of the town's sesquicentennial celebration.

6. The preceding historical summary was constructed primarily from information included on signs posted within the Old Bag Factory building in 2013.

7. Further information on this kiln design can be found on Marvin Bartel's website at http://www.bartelart.com/firing/ecokiln.html or in his article in *Ceramics Monthly* (Bartel 1990).

8. This fact gained substantial media attention after Goshen was named as a former "sundown town," a term designating towns that, through various formal or informal means, excluded African Americans from residing in or even staying in town overnight (Loewen 2005). In March of 2015, the city acknowledged this aspect of its past, issuing a public apology and formally stating that such discrimination is no longer condoned nor permitted; Loewen himself has praised this approach and recommended it as a model for other former sundown towns (Loewen 2015).

9. The 2010 census supports this conclusion; most notably, the black or African American population had nearly doubled since the 2000 census, and the Hispanic or

Latino population had grown by around 50 percent, while the white population saw very little growth (United States Census Bureau 2010)

10. *Seconds* refers to pots that Justin likely would not otherwise put up for sale.

11. The YouTube video, also found at https://youtu.be/hhDQ J9WNUDs, is linked on the AMACO website: American Art Clay Co, Inc. "(PC) Potter's Choice Glazes." Accessed February 13, 2016. http://www.amaco.com/t/glazes-and-underglazes/high-fire/potters-choice.

12. The cups are used to demonstrate the extent of this line of colors that are available on the AMACO website: American Art Clay Co, Inc. "(LM) Low Fire Matt." Accessed February 13, 2016. http://www.amaco.com/t/glazes-and-underglazes/low-fire/low-fire-matt.

SIX

THE POTTER'S WORK:
CONCLUSIONS

As we study art, we may also study the culture and values of the person who created that artwork. With wood-fired pottery as an entry point into the culture of clay in the Michiana region, we can learn so much about the potters who live and work there today. When they speak of their values, in life and in their work with clay, so many say "it's about community." There is no value in work without the support of others and no satisfaction without that work being of value to others. Clay is more than a profession for those who are production potters in Michiana today; pottery represents a passion for a creative and productive life and a deep connection to the people who share that passion.

The world is always changing for artists: families grow, new friendships develop or old friends move away, health challenges arise, business opportunities change, politics shift. Potters must remain relevant just as much as anyone, always reacting to new situations and shifting their work as necessary to continue their business into the future. Along with the broad range of social connections at play in the Michiana potters' lives, there are a wide range of career challenges that can arise throughout a potter's lifetime. While a sense of looking to impending changes may be epitomized in the wood-firing process, it is also quite present in the everyday life of every potter; keeping an eye to the future and preparing for the road ahead is a constant consideration. Continually, a balance must be found between planning for what is next and enjoying the present, between business and pleasure, collaborative work and individual control, maintaining old styles while seeking new inspirations, as many examples in my fieldwork have illustrated. Furthermore, new trials arise at different points in one's career; the start-up challenges faced by a new potter are not the same as midcareer worries, nor are later-life concerns always the same as those one has been through in the past.

I must acknowledge that I have not featured some of Michiana's newest or youngest artists in this text as much as I could, because I have been looking more centrally in this complex social network; those who are well established and thus well connected can speak in depth about the sense of community that they feel and have helped to develop. Yet a steady stream of students, assistants, and interns has been crucial for keeping the Michiana tradition alive and growing at the schools, the guild, the production potteries, and the growing Michiana Pottery Tour, which has featured many of these new faces.[1] I have often imagined a different ethnographic project that could focus on *their* stories—why they come to Michiana, why they choose short-term or long-term opportunities, what they learn here, how their early careers in ceramics are developing in this place, and why, sometimes, they choose to leave. The perspectives of these junior potters are crucial to this place, as they are the ones who can carry this tradition forward, should they choose to.

Furthermore, their concerns are different from those of mid- or late-career artists, and I also acknowledge that some of those considerations have not been foregrounded in my writing as much as they could be. For example, some young potters (such as Mark Goertzen's assistant Irina Gladun, fig. 6.1) speak of the challenge of balancing work and school responsibilities and time commitments, even when they are excited to assist a more experienced artist as an intern or apprentice. Many say it is difficult to work in someone else's studio, either because it entails making pots that are a better fit with the owner's aesthetic than their own or because of the repetitive nature of production pottery, which can be particularly challenging at a stage when a younger artist has enthusiasm for experimenting and wants to give time and energy toward developing their own identifiable style in clay. Furthermore, others struggle to decide whether an artistic career is the right path, sometimes feeling a pull toward other professions with more financial certainty or considering whether they want to give some portion of their time to teaching. When I spoke with Irina in 2015, for example, she was attending Goshen College

Fig. 6.1. Irina confidently stokes Mark's kiln during her second day on shift at a firing in August 2015. *(Photo by author)*

on a music scholarship and had not yet decided what career path would be the best fit for her, whether it involves music, art, or something entirely different. Moshe Hodges, who worked for Mark Goertzen at the Old Bag Factory for many years, provides another example, as he eventually gave up his job there in favor of pursuing very different work in computing.

Madeline Gerig is another of the younger potters working in Goshen. She was just finishing high school when I first met her at a firing of Justin Rothshank's kiln in 2013; she attended Bethany Christian High School, where she learned about pottery from Eric Kauffman. She then went on to study with Merrill Krabill at Goshen College, and she interned with Justin Rothshank for part of 2015. Her aunt and mentor, Jane Graber, is also a ceramic artist; Jane focuses on making miniatures, and her work is often exhibited in the Found Gallery in downtown Goshen. Madeline also makes miniatures, but her work has ranged through many styles in the years since I first met her. An excerpt from the artist statement posted on her website in 2016 illustrated how well her personal outlook on art fit with the rest of the Michiana group, particularly this statement: "My goal is to make simple, beautiful and accessible art that benefits my community" (Gerig 2016). When I spoke with her at her booth at Moey Hart's location of the Michiana Pottery Tour in 2015, Maddie was slated to teach a course at Goshen Youth Arts (the facility started by Zach Tate and Leah Schroeder) in the fall, and she was also planning to rent studio space there. Whether or not she will work in Goshen long-term remains to be seen, but at that time she was expecting to graduate from Goshen College within a year or two and to pursue a career as an artist.

Brandon "Fuzzy" Schwartz is another emerging potter whom I've encountered on many occasions at the Michiana Pottery Tours. In 2013, he spent the first day of the tour as a visitor, going to the many different stops, and then on the second day, Sunday, he helped Dick Lehman with his sales (that year, Dick was exhibiting at Mark Goertzen's location). It was there that I met Fuzzy for the first time and learned that he was also a potter and that he has an online blog where he sometimes writes about his experiences with pottery. Then, at later tours, Fuzzy had his own booth at Moey Hart's location. I spoke with him at his booth in 2015, and he explained that although he has an art education degree and is currently teaching, he would still like to consider the possibility of working full-time in clay someday.

The 2015 tour was, in fact, full of younger potters hosted by those with established stops—a trend that continued in the following years as well. For example, I mentioned previously that Justin hosted Stephanie Galli and two other potters. Garrett DeLooze, from Maryland, also had a booth at Moey's location and has interned with both Mark Goertzen and Justin Rothshank. Cindy Gibson, from Louisiana, has also interned with both Mark and Justin, and she was hosted by Mark during the 2015 tour. Both Garrett and Cindy were in Goshen specifically for the artistic opportunities available to them there, but when I spoke with them, neither had definitive plans for their futures. As Madeline, Fuzzy, Garrett, Cindy, and many others (since these are by no means the only aspiring potters in Michiana, simply the ones I had an opportunity to chat with at length in 2015) continue their work, they will likely have many opportunities and thus many choices: at the very least they, like others before them, will have to decide whether they wish to stay in Michiana and thus be part of this occupational group or whether their needs and values will take them elsewhere, to pursue clay in a different region with a different set of supportive factors that may be, for some, a better fit.

Dick Lehman has spoken to this kind of choice and his own sense of commitment to Michiana when discussing a point in his own career when he and his family were tempted to move away. Ultimately, he says, "Instead of moving somewhere that had all that we imagined, we decided to commit ourselves to making our location one that was equally attractive. It was a small shift, but one with huge implications. Instead of investing energy in trying to find ways to leave this location, we invested in making our town, region, and local arts communities vibrant in their own ways" (Hartenberger 2013).

This navigation between new opportunities and established commitments is a lifelong one, which is reflected in the balance all production potters must find between continuing a predictable production line and expressing new ideas in unique, individual pieces, and between fulfilling their clients' desires and pursing their own preferred aesthetics. In comparison to emerging artists, midcareer potters are particularly attuned to these kinds of challenges; while they may have established an identifiable style and a relatively stable list of clients, they must work hard to keep those clients engaged with their work, striking a balance between work that fits within the established aesthetic of their studio and work that is fresh enough to garner new interest in their pottery. Furthermore, while they might enjoy the stability of an established business (in contrast with the challenge of starting and building a new business), staying in the studio and keeping up a high rate of production and sales can be physically taxing and mentally exhausting, and it can be difficult to find time for a vacation when running a studio alone; often partners or spouses are crucial in providing support, whether it is help running the studio, assistance with sales, moral support, or financial stability. Still, keeping up a steady rate of production is almost always necessary for the potter to satisfy their clientele, maintain a steady income, and save for the future.

At many points in life, new benefits are balanced with new difficulties to overcome. After a lifetime of hard work in ceramics, some older potters have expressed feeling a new sense of creative freedom as they near or enter retirement (and I should note that I find so-called "retired" potters are often just as active as those who aren't). Those whose long-term careers are well established sometimes begin to feel that they have greater license to experiment with their work, particularly once they have both the assurance of a stable income from established clientele and less pressing concerns with sustaining a long-term business operation. Additionally, they have the pleasure of seeing and continuing to support the successes of those whom they have mentored (fig. 6.2). On the other hand, older potters can face different challenges, sometimes physical or medical, in trying to continue their work. For example, stress on one's hands, wrists, and back is prevalent in this profession and can cause additional difficulties when compounded with common later-life ailments such as arthritis.

One potter I spoke with was pleased to be in good health but expressed his concerns about remaining relevant; he was at a point where he was not being invited to as many exhibits as he had been earlier in his career, and he had recently received more rejections than usual for

Fig. 6.2. Marvin Bartel photographs some of the Michiana potters—including some who were once his students—as they work to unload Mark Goertzen's kiln in July 2013. (*Photo by author*)

articles he had written and exhibitions he had entered. Although he was happy to know that he had built a legacy through the younger potters he had mentored over the years, he also wanted to keep making new and exciting work of his own, and he wasn't sure whether he was satisfied making that work only for his own benefit. "Is it enough to be able to do what I want?" he mused. In other words, while it can be invigorating to have more freedom, the work has little satisfaction without an audience to appreciate it. I suspect his audience was not so deaf to his efforts as he might have imagined in that moment, but his lack of confidence in how to move forward brings to light the notion that even an established artist's life is rarely simple or certain. What is certain is that all the potters in Michiana whom I have met, no matter how old, are determined to keep making art for as long as they are physically able. Pottery is more than a career for them; it is a lifelong passion, and they thrive when they are able to share it with others.

THE STUDY OF ARTISTS AS OCCUPATIONAL GROUPS

"At work, the potter manages the transformation of nature, building culture while fulfilling the self, serving society, and patching the world together with pieces of clay that connect the past with the present, the useful with the beautiful, the material with the spiritual. The one who can do all that does enough. The potter has won the right to confidence" (Glassie 1999b, 116). Glassie's words in *The Potter's Art* were some of the first I ever read that spoke of the *life* of a potter—attending to more than just the artistic products of a potter—and those ideas have guided much of my own approach to studying this art form. This quote is a fitting tribute to the potters who are able to maintain a balance in all of the complex factors in their lives, whose dedication affords them a steady career in clay. In Michiana, we find that most do so through commitment to developing their skill in work along with a devotion to maintaining the social relationships that provide critical sustenance for their work.

Why should we attend to these social relationships between artists? In part because the depth of knowledge and complex network of interpersonal connections that it reveals continues the scholarly work of pushing back against historical conceptions of the naive or anonymous folk artist. But, more importantly, in developing a deeper understanding of tradition and creativity, we need to acknowledge the myriad complex relationships that influence an artist's everyday life; an artist relies upon more than just one or two notable teachers to develop their identity and skill as an artist, and any biography that would imply such simplicity would be woefully incomplete.

It seems clear there has not been enough attention paid to horizontal transmission in the arts—particularly in writing about wood firing, as I addressed in chapter 3—nor to social aspects of everyday life that play a key role in artistic production. In the work of folklorists, I suspect that this trend could be tied to methodology in fieldwork, as I have oft been taught: folklorists are frequently advised to begin with life history while doing fieldwork. I have no argument with this method, and indeed I use it myself, but I will say that it is only a beginning and not a sufficient approach by itself. My own opening question in an interview often falls along the lines of "how did you get started with clay?" because it gives me the opportunity to see how the artist views themself, before proceeding to more intimate details of life.

The life-history approach and attention to tracing chronology is certainly crucial in underdocumented arts and is by no means a detriment to folklore scholarship; however, there is much more to the pursuit of a thorough ethnography than just life history. When we have the opportunity to document artists at work in the present, it is worthwhile to pay attention to not just their processes and products but also the social interactions that are an important part of their everyday lives. Furthermore, this approach is particularly critical when working in a tradition that is not family-oriented, when social influences are not as easily traced as genealogy. Many family members are indeed involved in the Michiana potters' work, but the Michiana tradition is not one that has typically been transmitted from parent to child, as has been the case in some other studies of pottery traditions. Given that it is a relatively new establishment, it is certainly possible that we will one day see second- or third-generation Michiana potters; indeed, many children and other relatives of the Michiana potters have expressed an interest in clay and have dabbled in their own ceramic creations, though they have not become full-time potters themselves. For the present, other modes of transmission are much more prevalent, and discussions of ceramic methods and challenges are primarily with peers or mentors rather than with family members—thus my focus on the development of the occupational group.

As the preceding chapters have demonstrated, there are numerous types of social interactions that can play a key role in the development of a sense of shared identity among artists: time spent developing vocational habitus in shared learning spaces; participating in collaborative production methods and developing empathy through liminal experiences; the collection, exchange, and display of objects as resources for social, professional, and creative development; commitment to living in a particular region with access to the right resources and, more importantly, like-minded people. All of these facets have helped to form the basis of the artistic community in Michiana, and to greater or lesser degrees, each is crucial to the success of every individual within the group.

Furthermore, this study suggests that an investigation into similar aspects of other occupational groups could help scholars working with contemporary artists to better understand the kinds of collaborative environments that facilitate creativity and positive feelings about work. I propose this model as an ethnographic heuristic—a way of approaching the study of a group of artists, a model of the kinds of questions to ask in such a study—but not as a guarantee of results. I do not suggest that all occupational groups of artists will come together through the same kinds of life experiences. However, artist identities are always co-constructed and maintained in dialogue with other people, with place, with objects, and with ideals and philosophies of living. Inquiry into these realms can help to build a more complete picture of a group of regionally-oriented professional artists.

How broadly can we think of the process of learning a vocation? What do we gain by considering not just formal education or specific teachers or mentors, as some might be inclined to do, but also the informal interactions that occur in formal spaces or the ongoing learning that happens when one is no longer called "student"? What can we learn about the shared values and priorities of a group through interrogating the educational spaces that they share? The answers I found in Michiana were not explicitly linked to classrooms and teachers but rather to extensive interpersonal connections and collaborations, experiences of space, materials, and technology, and incorporation of religious and secular values.

In Michiana, wood firing is both an aesthetic and a social choice; it is a choice to participate in a specific environment, to take on particular risks, to engage in physical activity that is challenging and even a bit dangerous. In the study of another occupational group of artists, I would ask, what challenges bring them together? Do they share equipment, and if so, why and how? What special, occasional events are important for the group? What aspect of their work provides them with time and space to bond with one another? What kinds of powerful moments have helped to forge their sense of community? How are new members of the group brought into these experiences? The social dimensions of work are as vital to creativity as the aesthetic ones.

Fig. 6.3. Participating potters look over work that has just been unloaded from Bill Kremer's kiln after a firing in November 2015. (*Left to right*) Brandon "Fuzzy" Schwartz, Troy Bungart, Zach Tate. (*Photo by author*)

In the study of any physical art form, it would be difficult to neglect the art objects themselves; in the study of an occupational group of artists, though, I encourage close consideration of how those objects circulate within the group (fig. 6.3). How do artists interact with their completed artworks? What does the art they keep at home, in their studio, or elsewhere mean to them, and what stories do they tell about it? How do they acquire the objects in their collections, from whom, and under what conditions? What ideals, interests, or relationships do those objects represent? Where are these objects displayed and for whose benefit? Contemporary artist-collectors can provide incredible, personal insights into the work that they keep, and it is here that ethnographers have an opportunity both to help create a more thorough record for the future and to learn about the artists' experiences of their art world through these objects.

Finally, thinking of an occupational group of artists as a network, what are the connections on the periphery that allow the center to be so dense? What or who is close enough to the region to have an effect but far enough away that they are not part of everyday life and thus could be overlooked? Who is working in similar-but-different mediums or on related artistic endeavors in the area? Who are the like-minded individuals who are not part of the occupational group—the family members, friends, colleagues, and acquaintances who are part of the fabric of life that surrounds and sustains members of the occupational group? What regionally oriented values or religious connections might they share? What is specific to this place but not specific to this medium? There is no duplicate of Michiana to be found in the world, but there are without a doubt other groups of artists choosing to stay and work together in a place because it offers the right combination of environment, resources, and people.

SENSE OF COMMUNITY AND THE SIGNIFICANCE OF CHOICE

In researching this book, I have been engaged in tracing social networks in Michiana—connections between artists of varying locales, media, and professional levels, between artists and those who support them, and through objects that act as intermediaries between artists. These connections are concrete, their interactions observable, and yet documentation of a network is not fully representative of the "sense of community" that so many potters in Michiana speak of. In the first chapter, I noted the interrelationship between the notions of art world, network, community, and group. Becker's conception of an art world as a network ([1982] 2008) has been an important guide throughout this study, and Noyes's distinctions between networks, communities, and groups provides clarity to the understanding that a community is not the direct correlative of a network (1995, 452). It is at this theoretical turn that I assert, time and again throughout this text, that *presence matters*. Community, as Noyes says, emerges in performance, in interaction, and networks exist only so long as those connections are continually invoked and revitalized (471–72).

In elucidating the details of social connections in Michiana, I have demonstrated that a sense of vocationally oriented community can be found among professionals who connect both within and outside of their workplaces. While daily interactions—such as sharing resources like materials and equipment while working in the same studio—help in building these connections, there are also certain times throughout the year that are crucial for community building despite occurring less often. When it is time to build and fire kilns together, when striving to learn new skills or to collaborate on making a unique pot, or when working toward the development of a pottery tour that enables every potter in the area to raise their profile and meet more potential clients—in these vital situations, other artists who are present in the same region are the most crucial support system that a potter can have. Their proximity means they can choose to encounter and support one another easily, both professionally and through other shared pastimes. The sense of community they speak of develops out of the fact that they take pleasure in many of the same activities, find frustration in some of the same aspects of their lives, and most notably because they support one another in these endeavors and are in dialogue with one another about these values.

Furthermore, I have shown that these dialogues are not limited to speech and text. Embodied experiences do not need to be discussed to elicit a shared understanding of the experience; pottery often involves

Fig. 6.4. The many potters who participated in firing Mark Goertzen's kiln in summer 2013 pose in front of the kiln, each holding one of their recently finished pots. Top row *(left to right)*: Royce Hildebrand, Todd Pletcher, Mark Goertzen, Scott Lehman, Anna Corona. Bottom row *(left to right)*: Todd Leech, Stephanie Craig, Dick Lehman, Bill Hunt. *(Photo by author)*

hard, physical labor, and having physical knowledge of the craft means understanding the challenges that other craftspeople endure. While wood firing necessitates much verbal communication about the technical considerations of the process, stepping up to the fire and feeding the flames provides a sensual knowledge of the labor and danger entailed, and it is an intuitive leap to know that others who stoke the kiln feel the same rush of heat. Furthermore, the emotional states that are shared during the liminal experience of firing go beyond what might be verbally communicated. Meanwhile, the sharing of objects—through communal making and through exchange—contributes to a shared aesthetic, both visually and tactilely. While pottery is a constant source of conversation, feeling the clay, holding a pot, and experiencing the use of a functional object all entail tactile knowledge that cannot be completely communicated through words. The *feeling* of these physical experiences is just as important as the teacher who says "this is good work" and discusses verbally the successful qualities of weight, balance, form, texture, and more.

In the introduction, I posed the following: given that a single artist can achieve tremendous recognition and artistic success as an individual, what can that person achieve through a myriad of connections with other artists, particularly those working in the same region and medium? Among the Michiana potters, it is clear that the answer lies in the satisfaction they find in teaching, serving their community, working collaboratively, and in their ability to pursue wood-fired aesthetics that would be challenging to achieve without the help of others (fig. 6.4). Together they find individual artistic success, and they are also able to work with one another to develop recognition for the arts in their region, which provides a place and lifestyle they appreciate as well as an expanded customer base. Furthermore, they experience great satisfaction in knowing they are surrounded by others who understand and appreciate the values that they hold.

I began this book speaking of serendipity in my own life, and I know that many similarly fortuitous connections have played roles in the lives of all the Michiana potters, bringing them into contact with the right people and the right opportunities at the right moments for all to fall into place. Yet I would not presume to call the development of the Michiana Aesthetic nor the pottery community there the result of accident or serendipity. It is the clear result of conscious choices made by a group of professionals who are happy to benefit from working near and with one another. They have chosen to stay within or move to a region that fits their needs, both with physical resources and like-minded people, and they have chosen to do all they can to help that place live up to the potential they see in it. They have chosen to take part in educational opportunities that fit with their own established values, and they have also chosen to provide education to others, expressing that which they feel is best within themselves. They have chosen to work collaboratively—coming together in their studios, on single projects, or at wood firings—appreciating the aesthetic values they hold in common and striving together to bring those ideals into reality. They have chosen to exchange gifts, to collect one another's work, and to hold dear those objects that evoke the most meaningful memories of the people and experiences that inspire them. It is through these choices that such a strong sense of community among potters in Michiana has developed, and it will be through the choices of others who join them that this tradition will continue to grow into the future.

NOTE

1. See Appendix I for lists of tour participants. Furthermore, many of the assistants and interns at the Old Bag Factory and Justin Rothshank's studio, listed in Appendix II, have been working to establish themselves as ceramic artists.

EPILOGUE:
CONSTANT CHANGE

If you will indulge me for a moment, pretend nothing has changed in the world since 2016. That is how this book was written; it is based on fieldwork that took place primarily between 2012 and 2016, and I am all too cognizant of the fact that the Michiana community has continued to change in ways that I cannot fully understand when I cannot be present. It is difficult to publish a book about what *was* when I know that what *is now* (as you read) will be different; this book will become a static representation of a place, and it will have its own life in the future representing the Michiana pottery tradition, even as Michiana and its potters continue to change. Change is inevitable, and it is already reflected in these pages, in the personal histories of Michiana potters and their decisions to move to or remain in Michiana.

One of the great joys of ethnographic fieldwork, for me, has been the privilege of coming to know how various elements of life—social, aesthetic, functional—come together for a community of artists in a particular time and place, as they did in Michiana. But one of the great challenges of fieldwork—or more specifically, in writing about fieldwork-based research—is knowing that you are encountering a particular place in time and that your knowledge is limited by your resources, your observations, and your very nature as an ethnographer—that is, an outsider. This book has come about through constant consultation with my potter colleagues in Michiana; many of them have read earlier versions of this text, and have offered input about my analyses along the way. I am eternally grateful for their input, and I hope this book is a reasonable

Fig. E.1. The potters who exhibited and sold work at Justin Rothshank's stop on the 2018 Michiana Pottery Tour. (*Left to right*) Sadie Misiuk, Paul Eshelman, Todd Pletcher, Justin Rothshank, Kevin Kowalski, Taylor Emery, Keith Hershberger, Layton Rothshank. (*Photo by author*)

representation of their experiences during the early to mid-2010s, even when it cannot reflect the changes that have occurred since that time.

What has changed already, as I finish writing in 2018? Sadly, Dick Lehman's dear friend in Japan, Shiho Kanzaki, passed away in February of this year, and I know his presence, even at a distance, will be missed. Elsewhere, career developments and family changes—more than I could list here—have affected many potters' lives. Marvin Bartel and Bill Kremer both continue to hint at plans for so-called retirement or the possibility of working less. Meanwhile, Troy Bungart began working for the Schaller Gallery in St. Joseph, Michigan. Suzanne Ehst, Mark Goertzen's wife, finished her PhD and continues her work in education at Goshen College. Scott and Hannah Lehman now have two sweet little children, the older of whom is very close in age to my own eldest child. Justin and Brooke Rothshank also welcomed a new addition to their family. Tom Unzicker decided to move from Kansas to Laos with his family, pursuing pottery and service in a new place. And every time I attend the Michiana Pottery Tour, I get to meet and chat with newer or younger potters—Sadie Misiuk, Jennifer Beachy, Alec Hoogland, Jacob Hostetler, Taylor Emery, Garrett DeLooze, Cindy Gibson, Maddie Gerig, Peter Fauver, and others—who are working in the region, learning whether a ceramics career in this place will be the right fit for them (fig. E.1). Sometimes we meet and converse again; sometimes they move on before I have the opportunity to get to know them better. As I noted in the concluding chapter, life is always changing, and potters must constantly plan for or react to new circumstances and opportunities, continually seeking balance between personal and professional considerations.

One substantial change, one that put into mind the necessity of this epilogue, is that Todd Pletcher and his partner, Anna, announced that they were moving to Australia in 2016, soon after I finished the earliest draft of this text. Having relied so heavily on Todd's insights about the Michiana community, I admittedly had a difficult time wrapping my head around this particular change. The move came about because Anna had an exciting career opportunity in Sydney that they decided to pursue; although I have not seen her since they left, it sounds as though it has been a good move for her. Todd began making pots at a studio in Sydney and travels back to the United States often to visit friends and family, lead workshops, and participate on the Michiana Pottery Tour.

When I saw Todd at the 2017 tour and asked him about the decision to move to Australia, he talked about it in terms of not missing any opportunities in life—he knew they were in a place in their lives where they could try moving to a new place, and they wanted to see what the experience would be like. He told me about the challenges of trying to immigrate to a new country, how the uncertainty of that process had cast a shadow over his enjoyment of a new place where they had new friends and were trying to make a new home. He spoke of the difficulty of making pottery in the middle of a big city (especially in comparison to Michiana), the lack of resources for pursuing wood firing in such an environment, and the ways his work began changing as a result of new circumstances. He spoke in terms of possibilities rather than certainties; maybe staying in Australia in hopes of permanently immigrating, maybe returning to Goshen, maybe returning to the United States but living in a different region. Maybe he'd find a place to wood fire again, but being part of a different wood-firing group would mean different expectations, different experiences, different results.

Our conversation at that 2017 tour was bittersweet; we reminisced about the fact that when we met at the first Michiana Pottery Tour in 2012, he was just coming to the decision to move back to Goshen, and I was just realizing that I had found an intriguing place and people among whom I wanted to pursue my research. So many projects have been envisioned and completed in that time—for both of us—and much has changed. But new life opportunities arise, and people move on to new places and new endeavors, and Todd and I did so in parallel, both beginning to separate from Michiana in our own ways at the same time—though I don't believe either of us will ever completely disconnect from the community there.

As for me, my research is going in different directions these days, but even these new avenues consistently bring my thoughts back to Michiana. In chapter 6, I encouraged the use of this book as a model for studying other occupational groups, particularly contemporary artists, and I have started to do this myself, engaging with other pottery tours and pottery-oriented groups around the Midwest. Armed with a bevy of questions—about formal and informal education, about shared spaces and collaborative processes, about special occasions and overcoming shared challenges, about exchanging and displaying objects, and about the particularities of place, region, history, and sometimes religion—I am trying to gain an understanding of these other groups. What will I learn about the social relationships and additional connections (with places, objects, experiences, values) that have helped these potters develop their own sense of shared identity and feelings of community? It remains to be seen, but I look forward to discovering both the parallels and the idiosyncrasies. And I am also eager for others to try this approach to research in additional artist communities, eager to see their discoveries and learn about the ways that social connections and local presence matter for other groups of contemporary artists.

As I think about these changes and choices and wonder what the future holds, I hear echoes of Marvin's advice: "Try it and see." The phrase, first recounted to me by Dick Lehman six years ago, feels poignant as I

Fig. E.2. Tea Bowl, cone ten reduction firing. An example of work made by Dick Lehman, a result of many glaze experiments. *(Photo courtesy of Dick Lehman)*

bring one project to a close and embark on new ones. Trying something new may yield results that are positive, or negative, or somewhere in between; the certainty is that we will learn something new in the process. Dick, too, is still experimenting, always trying new ideas, seeing what the possibilities may be. His work, too, has changed since we first reconnected in 2012, because of his relocation to a new studio, changing life circumstances, and, largely, his willingness to continue exploring new possibilities. After testing hundreds of new glaze combinations in recent years, he is developing a stunning new line of work—this time not wood fired but reduction fired in a gas kiln—with brilliant colors and unusual effects adorning the surfaces of his gestural forms (fig. E.2).

So Todd, like other Michiana potters before him, will try life and art in a new place and see what the future holds. I will try new avenues of research and see what new work is possible with the knowledge I've gained from my dear friends from Michiana. Dick, along with many others, will try new experiments in clay and glaze and see what these ever-captivating materials have to offer. We will all keep trying, keep seeing, and undoubtedly we will learn something new about ourselves, our communities, and our art.

APPENDIX I:
MICHIANA POTTERY
TOUR MAPS

The maps on the following pages show the locations and artists featured in the first five years of the Michiana Pottery Tour, 2012 through 2016. It is possible that some maps may not reflect minimal last-minute changes to the lineup at each location; in any case, these are the maps that were provided to visitors via the Michiana Pottery Tour website and sometimes also in printed form at locations around the tour.

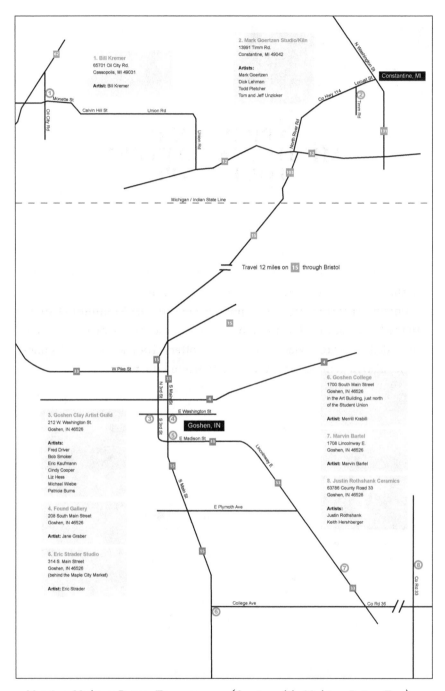

Map A1.1. Michiana Pottery Tour map, 2012. (*Courtesy of the Michiana Pottery Tour*)

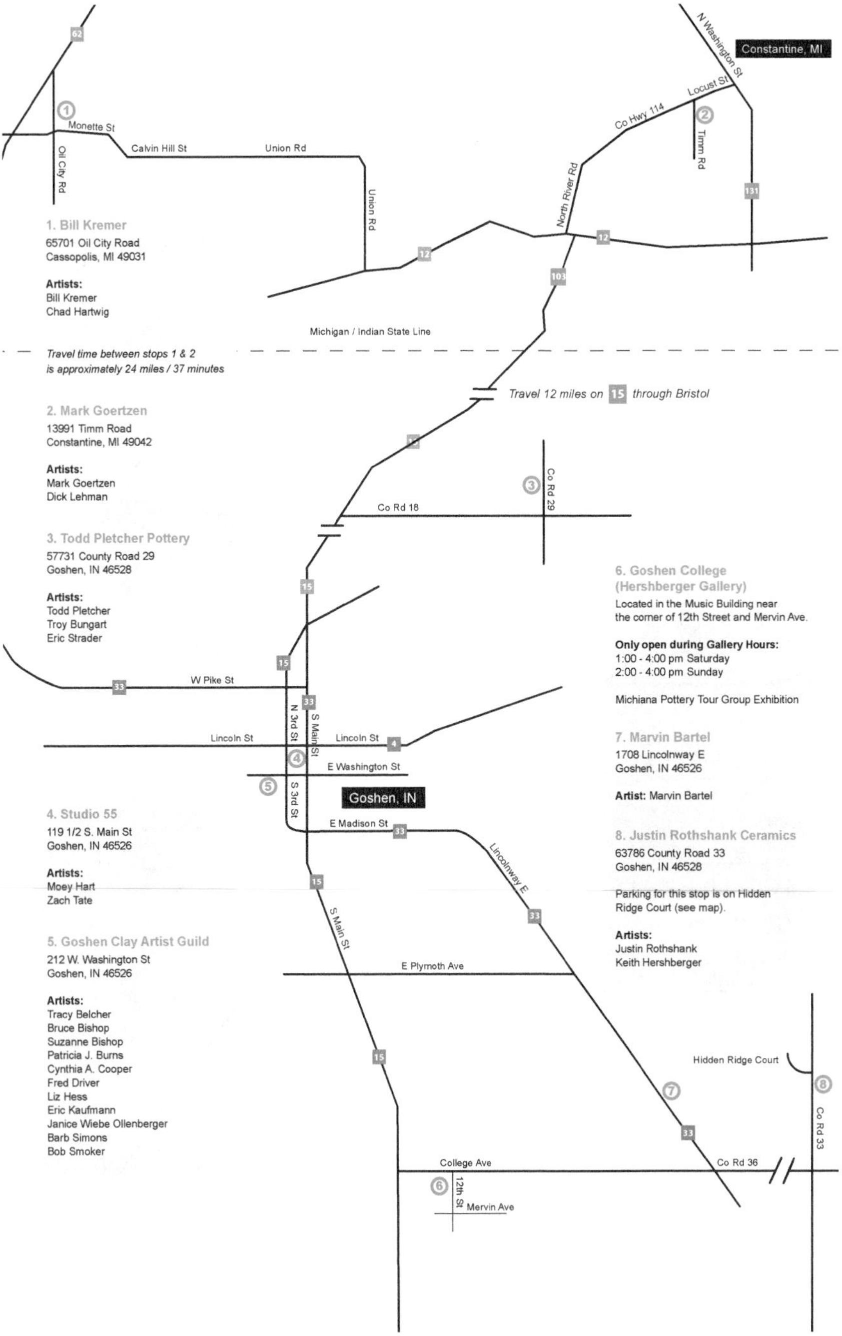
62
Monette St
Oil City Rd
Calvin Hill St
Union Rd
Union Rd
N Washington St
Constantine, MI
Locust St
Co Hwy 114
Timm Rd
North River Rd
131
12
12
103
1. Bill Kremer
65701 Oil City Road
Cassopolis, MI 49031
Artists:
Bill Kremer
Chad Hartwig
Michigan / Indian State Line
Travel time between stops 1 & 2
is approximately 24 miles / 37 minutes
Travel 12 miles on 15 through Bristol
2. Mark Goertzen
13991 Timm Road
Constantine, MI 49042
Artists:
Mark Goertzen
Dick Lehman
Co Rd 29
Co Rd 18
3. Todd Pletcher Pottery
57731 County Road 29
Goshen, IN 46528
Artists:
Todd Pletcher
Troy Bungart
Eric Strader
6. Goshen College
(Hershberger Gallery)
Located in the Music Building near
the corner of 12th Street and Mervin Ave.
Only open during Gallery Hours:
1:00 - 4:00 pm Saturday
2:00 - 4:00 pm Sunday
Michiana Pottery Tour Group Exhibition
15
15
33
W Pike St
33
N 3rd St
S Main St
Lincoln St
Lincoln St
4
E Washington St
S 3rd St
Goshen, IN
E Madison St
33
7. Marvin Bartel
1708 Lincolnway E
Goshen, IN 46526
Artist: Marvin Bartel
4. Studio 55
119 1/2 S. Main St
Goshen, IN 46526
Artists:
Moey Hart
Zach Tate
8. Justin Rothshank Ceramics
63786 County Road 33
Goshen, IN 46528
Parking for this stop is on Hidden
Ridge Court (see map).
Artists:
Justin Rothshank
Keith Hershberger
Lincolnway E
15
S Main St
33
E Plymoth Ave
5. Goshen Clay Artist Guild
212 W. Washington St
Goshen, IN 46526
Artists:
Tracy Belcher
Bruce Bishop
Suzanne Bishop
Patricia J. Burns
Cynthia A. Cooper
Fred Driver
Liz Hess
Eric Kaufmann
Janice Wiebe Ollenberger
Barb Simons
Bob Smoker
15
Hidden Ridge Court
Co Rd 33
33
College Ave
Co Rd 36
12th St
Mervin Ave

Map A1.2. Michiana Pottery Tour map, 2013. *(Courtesy of the Michiana Pottery Tour)*

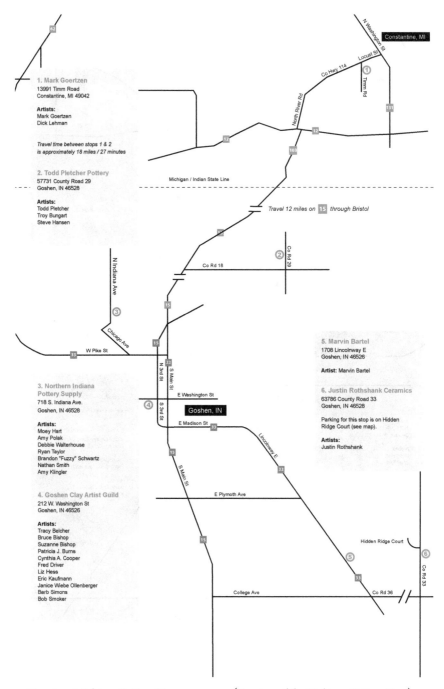

1. **Mark Goertzen**
13991 Timm Road
Constantine, MI 49042

Artists:
Mark Goertzen
Dick Lehman

*Travel time between stops 1 & 2
is approximately 18 miles / 27 minutes*

2. **Todd Pletcher Pottery**
57731 County Road 29
Goshen, IN 46528

Artists:
Todd Pletcher
Troy Bungart
Steve Hansen

Michigan / Indian State Line

Travel 12 miles on 15 through Bristol

Co Rd 18

3. **Northern Indiana
Pottery Supply**
718 S. Indiana Ave.
Goshen, IN 46528

Artists:
Moey Hart
Amy Polak
Debbie Walterhouse
Ryan Taylor
Brandon "Fuzzy" Schwartz
Nathan Smith
Amy Klingler

4. **Goshen Clay Artist Guild**
212 W. Washington St
Goshen, IN 46526

Artists:
Tracy Belcher
Bruce Bishop
Suzanne Bishop
Patricia J. Burns
Cynthia A. Cooper
Fred Driver
Liz Hess
Eric Kaufmann
Janice Wiebe Ollenberger
Barb Simons
Bob Smoker

5. **Marvin Bartel**
1708 Lincolnway E
Goshen, IN 46526

Artist: Marvin Bartel

6. **Justin Rothshank Ceramics**
63786 County Road 33
Goshen, IN 46528

Parking for this stop is on Hidden
Ridge Court (see map).

Artists:
Justin Rothshank

Constantine, MI

Goshen, IN

Map A1.3. Michiana Pottery Tour map, 2014. (*Courtesy of the Michiana Pottery Tour*)

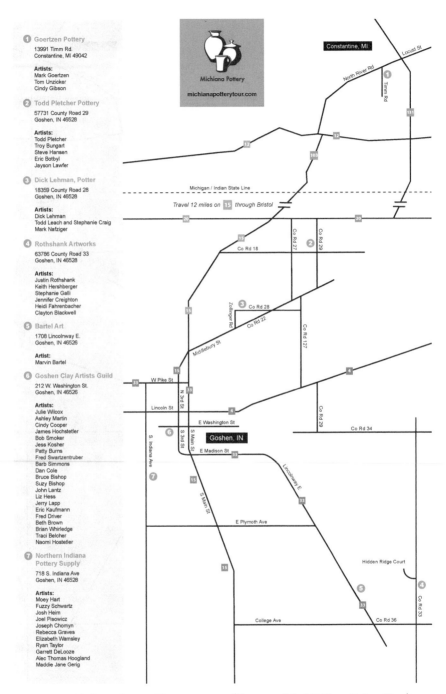

1 Goertzen Pottery

13991 Timm Rd.
Constantine, MI 49042

Artists:
Mark Goertzen
Tom Unzicker
Cindy Gibson

2 Todd Pletcher Pottery

57731 County Road 29
Goshen, IN 46528

Artists:
Todd Pletcher
Troy Bungart
Steve Hansen
Eric Botbyl
Jayson Lawfer

3 Dick Lehman, Potter

18359 County Road 28
Goshen, IN 46528

Artists:
Dick Lehman
Todd Leach and Stephanie Craig
Mark Nafziger

4 Rothshank Artworks

63786 County Road 33
Goshen, IN 46528

Artists:
Justin Rothshank
Keith Hershberger
Stephanie Galli
Jennifer Creighton
Heidi Fahrenbacher
Clayton Blackwell

5 Bartel Art

1708 Lincolnway E.
Goshen, IN 46526

Artist:
Marvin Bartel

6 Goshen Clay Artists Guild

212 W. Washington St.
Goshen, IN 46526

Artists:
Julie Wilcox
Ashley Martin
Cindy Cooper
James Hochstetler
Bob Smoker
Jess Kosher
Patty Burns
Fred Swartzentruber
Barb Simmons
Dan Cole
Bruce Bishop
Suzy Bishop
John Lantz
Liz Hess
Jerry Lapp
Eric Kaufmann
Fred Driver
Beth Brown
Brian Whirledge
Traci Belcher
Naomi Hostetler

7 Northern Indiana Pottery Supply

718 S. Indiana Ave
Goshen, IN 46528

Artists:
Moey Hart
Fuzzy Schwartz
Josh Heim
Joel Pisowicz
Joseph Chomyn
Rebecca Graves
Elizabeth Wamsley
Ryan Taylor
Garrett DeLooze
Alec Thomas Hoogland
Maddie Jane Gerig

Map A1.4. Michiana Pottery Tour map, 2015. *(Courtesy of the Michiana Pottery Tour)*

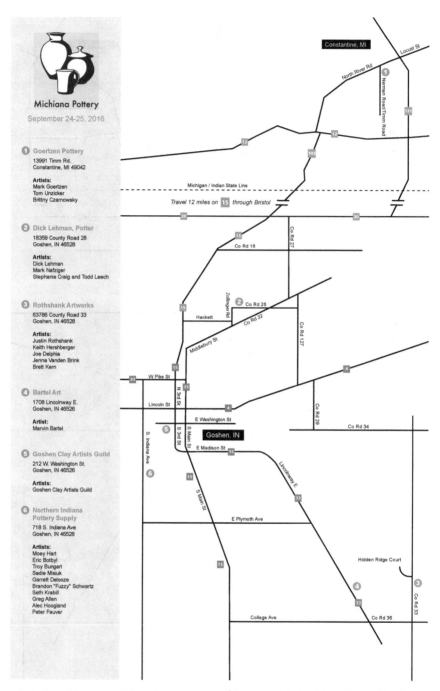

Map A1.5. Michiana Pottery Tour map, 2016. (*Courtesy of the Michiana Pottery Tour*)

APPENDIX II:
APPRENTICES, ASSISTANTS, AND/OR INTERNS

David Gamber	Tom Unzicker
Norma Wysong	Jeff Unzicker
Mark Goertzen	Eric Strader
Greg Stahly	Peter Olsen
Todd Pletcher	Lane Kaufmann
Barry Carpenter	Moshe Hodges

Moshe Hodges	Royce Hilderbrand
Faith Day	Cindy Gibson
Irina Gladun	

Note: the above lists, provided by Dick and Mark, are limited to those who worked for significant periods of time at the studio and who have stayed in the field of ceramics. Paul Roten, Loren Beidler, and Levi Kropf were also employed for a notable amount of time but went on to careers in other fields.

JUSTIN ROTHSHANK'S INTERNS/RESIDENT ARTISTS (2010–2016)

2016:	Sadie Misiuk
	Garrett DeLooze
	Parker Hunt
2016:	Cindy Gibson
	Caleb Longenecker
	Maddie Gerig
2014:	Jamie Morrow
	Mark Tarabula
2013:	Rebecca Krofcheck
2012:	Meghan Borland
2011:	Ryan Taylor
2010:	Craig Hartenberger
	Zach Tate

Note: most residents have worked with Justin between three months and one year. The internships he offers are typically unpaid, and interns often find part-time jobs elsewhere in town while they work with Justin. Further information about the opportunities he provides can be found on his website: https://rothshank.com/contact/internships/.

WORKS CITED

Association of Statisticians of American Religious Bodies. 1995. "Appendix—Churches and Church Membership." In *Hoosier Faiths: A History of Indiana's Churches and Religious Groups*, by L. C. Rudolph, 680–98. Bloomington: Indiana University Press.

———. 2012. "Maps and Charts for 2010." U.S. Religion Census 1952 to 2010. Accessed December 21, 2015. http://www.rcms2010.org/maps2010.php.

Baker, Ronald L., and Marvin Carmony. 1975. *Indiana Place Names*. Bloomington: Indiana University Press.

Bartel, Marvin. 1990. "A Revolutionary Kiln Design: Nearly 100% Fuel Efficiency." *Ceramics Monthly*, September 1990.

———. 2012. "The Art of Motivation and Critique in Self-Directed Learning." In *The Learner-Directed Classroom*, edited by Diane B. Jaquith and Nan E. Hathaway, 131–42. New York: Teachers College.

Becker, Howard S. [1982] 2008. *Art Worlds*. Berkeley: University of California Press.

Ben-Amos, Dan. 1971. "Toward a Definition of Folklore in Context." *The Journal of American Folklore* 84, no. 331 (1971): 3–15. https://doi.org/10.2307/539729.

Bourdieu, Pierre. 1990. *The Logic of Practice*. Stanford: Stanford University Press.

———. [1972] 1997. *Outline of a Theory of Practice*. New York: Cambridge University Press.

Burns, Sarah. 1996. *Inventing the Modern Artist: Art and Culture in Gilded Age America*. New Haven: Yale University Press.

Burrison, John A. 2008. *Brothers in Clay: The Story of Georgia Folk Pottery*. Athens: University of Georgia Press.

———. 2010. *From Mud to Jug: The Folk Potters and Pottery of Northeast Georgia*. Athens: University of Georgia Press, in collaboration with The Folk Pottery Museum of Northeast Georgia.

Byington, Robert H. 1978. "Strategies for Collecting Occupational Folklife in Contemporary Urban/Industrial Contexts." *Western Folklore* 37 (3): 185–98.

Cashman, Ray, Tom Mould, and Pravina Shukla, eds. 2011. *The Individual and Tradition: Folkloristic Perspectives*. Bloomington: Indiana University Press.

Ceramics Monthly. 2001. *Wood Firing Journeys and Techniques*. Westerville, OH: American Ceramic Society.

Chittenden, Varick A. 1995. *Vietnam Remembered: The Folk Art of Marine Combat Veteran Michael D. Cousino, Sr.* Jackson: University Press of Mississippi.

Colley, Helen, David James, Kim Diment, and Michael Tedder. 2003. "Learning as Becoming in Vocational Education and Training: Class, Gender and the Role of Vocational Habitus." *Journal of Vocational Education and Training* 55 (4): 471–98.

Conrad, Robert W., ed. 1981. *Goshen: The First 150 years.* Goshen, IN: News Printing Company.

Cort, Louise Allison. 2001. *Shigaraki: Potters' Valley.* Bangkok: Orchid.

Deetz, James. 1996. *In Small Things Forgotten: An Archaeology of Early American Life.* New York: Anchor.

Dewhurst, C. Kurt. 1984. "The Arts of Working: Manipulating the Urban Work Environment." *Western Folklore* 43, no. 3 (July): 189–90, 192–202. https://doi.org/10.2307/1499900.

———. 1986. *Grand Ledge Folk Pottery: Traditions at Work.* Ann Arbor: UMI Research Press.

Dewhurst, C. Kurt, and Marsha MacDowell. 1987. "The Pottery and the People: A Community Experience." In *Michigan Folklife Reader,* edited by C. Kurt Dewhurst and Yvonne Lockwood, 245–62. East Lansing, MI: Michigan State University Press.

Duffy, Karen. 2011. "Bringing Them Back: Wanda Aragon and the Revival of Historic Pottery Designs at Acoma." In *The Individual and Tradition: Folkloristic Perspectives,* edited by Ray Cashman, Tom Mould, and Pravina Shukla, 195–218. Bloomington: Indiana University Press.

Dundes, Alan. 1965. "What Is Folklore?" In *The Study of Folklore,* edited by Alan Dundes, 1–3. Englewood Cliffs, NJ: Prentice-Hall.

Durkheim, Émile. [1912] 1995. *The Elementary Forms of the Religious Life.* Translated by Karen E. Fields. New York: Free Press.

Elkhart County Convention & Visitors Bureau. 2015a. *Official Amish Country Travel Guide.* Accessed November 9, 2015. http://www.amishcountry.org.

———. 2015b. "The RV Capital, Elkhart County, Indiana: RV Manufacturers." Accessed September 2, 2015. http://www.amishcountry.org/rv-travel/manufacturers.

Evans, Timothy H. 1998. *King of the Western Saddle: The Sheridan Saddle and the Art of Don King.* Jackson: University Press of Mississippi.

Findlen, Paula. 2004. "The Museum: Its Classical Etymology and Renaissance Genealogy." In *Grasping the World: The Idea of the Museum,* edited by Donald Preziosi and Claire Farago, 159–91. Burlington: Ashgate.

Fischer, Ronald, Dimitris Xygalatas, Panagiotis Mitkidis, Paul Reddish, Penny Tok, Ivana Konvalinka, and Joseph Bulbulia. 2014. "The Fire-Walker's High: Affect and Physiological Responses in an Extreme Collective Ritual." Public Library of Science (PLOS ONE). http://journals.plos.org/plosone/article?id=10.1371/journal.pone.0088355.

Fitchen, John. 2001. *The New World Dutch Barn: The Evolution, Forms, and Structure of a Disappearing Icon.* Syracuse: Syracuse University Press.

Galloway, Julia. 2015. "Chapter 2: Post Graduation > Apprenticeships." Field Guide for Ceramic Artisans. Accessed September 15, 2015. http://juliagalloway.com/field-guide/chapter-2/apprenticeships.

Georges, Robert. 1984. "You Often Eat What Others Think You Are: Food as an Index of Others' Conceptions of Who One Is." *Western Folklore* 43 (4): 249–56.

Gerig, Madeline. 2016. "Madeline Gerig Ceramics and Sculpture." Accessed August 1, 2016. http://www.madelinegerig.com.

Glassie, Henry. 1995a. *The Spirit of Folk Art: The Girard Collection at the Museum of International Folk Art*. New York: Harry N. Abrams, Inc., in association with the Museum of New Mexico, Santa Fe.

———. 1995b. "Tradition." *The Journal of American Folklore* 108, no. 430 (Autumn): 395–412.

———. 1999a. *Material Culture*. Bloomington: Indiana University Press.

———. 1999b. *The Potter's Art*. Bloomington: Indiana University Press.

———. 2010. *Prince Twins Seven-Seven: His Art, His Life in Nigeria, His Exile in America*. Bloomington: Indiana University Press.

Green, Archie. 1978. "Industrial Lore: A Bibliographic-Semantic Query." *Western Folklore* 37 (3): 213–44.

Hartenberger, Craig. 2013. "Work, Play, and People: A Conversation with Dick Lehman." *Studio Potter* (Summer/Fall): 85–94.

Herman, Bernard. 2016. *Fever Within: The Art of Ronald Lockett*. Chapel Hill: The University of North Carolina Press.

Hewitt, Mark. 2011. "A Few of My Favorite Things about North Carolina Pottery." In *The Individual and Tradition: Folkloristic Perspectives*, edited by Ray Cashman, Tom Mould, and Pravina Shukla, 455–70. Bloomington: Indiana University Press.

Hewitt, Mark, and Nancy Sweezy. 2005. *The Potter's Eye: Art and Tradition in North Carolina Pottery*. Chapel Hill: University of North Carolina Press.

Hunt, Marjorie. 1999. *The Stone Carvers: Master Craftsmen of Washington National Cathedral*. Washington, DC: Smithsonian Books.

Hymes, Dell. 1974. *Foundations in Sociolinguistics: An Ethnographic Approach*. Philadelphia: University of Pennsylvania Press.

Institute of International Education. 2014. "Open Doors Data." Institute of International Education. Accessed February 2, 2016. https://www.iie.org/en/Why-IIE/Announcements/2014/11/2014-11-17-Open-Doors-Data.

Jones, Michael Owen. 1989. *Craftsman of the Cumberlands: Tradition and Creativity*. Lexington: University Press of Kentucky.

Kilar, Jeremy W. 1993. "The Great Lakes Industrial Region." In *Encyclopedia of American Social History, Vol. 2*, edited by Mary Kupiec Cayton, Elliot J. Gorn, and Peter W. Williams, 973–86. New York: Charles Scribner's Sons.

Kim, Sojin. 1995. *Chicano Graffiti and Murals: The Neighborhood Art of Peter Quezada*. Jackson: University Press of Mississippi.

Kirshenblatt-Gimblett, Barbara. 1989. "Objects of Memory: Material Culture as Life Review." In *Folk Groups and Folklore Genres: A Reader*, edited by Elliott Oring, 329–38. Logan: Utah State University Press.

Kitchener, Amy V. 1994. *The Holiday Yards of Florencio Morales: "El Hombre De Las Banderas."* Jackson: University Press of Mississippi.

Koch, Gertraud. 2012. "Work and Professions." In *A Companion to Folklore*, edited by Regina F. Bendix and Galit Hasan-Rokem, 154–68. West Sussex, UK: Wiley-Blackwell.

Lave, Jean. 2011. *Apprenticeship in Critical Ethnographic Practice*. Chicago: The University of Chicago Press.

Lave, Jean, and Etienne Wenger. [1991] 2011. *Situated Learning: Legitimate Peripheral Participation*. New York: Cambridge University Press.

Leach, Bernard. (1972) 2013. "Introduction." In *The Unknown Craftsman: A Japanese Insight into Beauty*, by Soetsu Yanagi, 87–100. New York: Kodansha USA, Inc.

Lehman, Dick. 1993. "The Mug That Changed My Life." The Studio Potter Network Newsletter. Accessed February 10, 2016. http://www.dicklehman.com/html/writing/writing_mug.html.

———. 1996. "Side Firing: Where the Life Is." *Ceramics Monthly*, April 1996.

———. 1999. "An Approach to Long Woodfire." *Ceramics Technical*, December 1999.

———. 2004. "Toward a Vocabulary for Wood Firing Effects." *Ceramics Monthly*, March 2004.

———. 2008. "The Thursday Night Challenge: Stagnation, Deepening and Stoking the Fire Within." *Ceramics Monthly*, June/July/August 2008.

———. 2014a. "Itinerant Wood Firer." *Ceramics Monthly*, September 2014.

———. 2014b. "LARGE JAR: WOOD-FIRED FOR 15 DAYS . . . ALL-NATURAL-ASH SURFACE, #3247." DickLehman.com Ceramics for Sale. Accessed November 16, 2014. http://dicklehman.com/html/ceramics.for.sale/detail.php?pottery_id=1742#.

———. 2014c. "The Michiana Aesthetic?" *Email to Meredith McGriff*. February 5, 2014.

Loewen, James W. 2005. *Sundown Towns: A Hidden Dimension of American Racism*. New York: New Press.

———. 2015. "Sundown Towns: A Hidden Dimension of American Racism by James W. Loewen." Accessed November 9, 2015. http://sundown.afro.illinois.edu/sundowntowns.php.

MacCannell, Dean. 1976. *The Tourist: A New Theory of the Leisure Class*. New York: Schocken Books.

Mauss, Marcel. [1954] 2000. *The Gift: The Form and Reason for Exchange in Archaic Societies*. Translated by W. D. Halls. New York: W. W. Norton & Company.

McCarl Jr., Robert S. 1978. "Occupational Folklife: A Theoretical Hypothesis." *Western Folklore* 37 (3): 145–60.

McGurk, Nick. 2011. "One Man Helps Change the Face of Goshen." Accessed November 9, 2015. http://www.wndu.com/home/headlines/How_one_man_helped_change_the_face_of_Goshen_113485199.html.

McKimmie, Kathy M. 2009. *Clay Times Three: The Tale of Three Nashville, Indiana Potteries*. Bloomington: Quarry Books, Indiana University Press.

Mecham, Denny Hubbard, ed. 2009. *The Living Tradition: North Carolina Potters Speak*. Conover, NC: Published for the North Carolina Pottery Center by Goosepen Studio & Press.

Metcalf, Eugene W. 1983. "Black Art, Folk Art, and Social Control." *Winterthur Portfolio* 18, no. 4 (Winter): 271–89.

Michiana Area Council of Governments. n.d. "Michiana Area Council of Governments." Accessed September 2, 2015. http://www.macog.com/.

Miller, Daniel. 2001. *The Dialectics of Shopping*. Chicago: The University of Chicago Press.

Minogue, Coll, and Robert Sanderson. 2000. *Wood-fired Ceramics: Contemporary Practices*. Philadelphia: University of Pennsylvania Press.

Moeran, Brian D. 1981. "Yanagi Muneyoshi and the Japanese Folk Craft Movement." *Asian Folklore Studies* 40(1): 87–99.

NAFSA: Association of International Educators. 2012. "Public Opinion Supports International Education." Accessed February 2, 2016. https://www.nafsa.org/policy-and -advocacy/policy-resources/public-opinion-supports-international-education.

Noyes, Dorothy. 1995. "Group." *The Journal of American Folklore* 108, no. 430 (Autumn): 449–78.

———. 2003. *Fire in the Plaça: Catalan Festival Politics After Franco*. Philadelphia: University of Pennsylvania Press.

O'Hara, Delia. 2015. "Fertile Ground: Goshen, Indiana." American Craft Council. Accessed September 15, 2015. http://craftcouncil.org/magazine/article/fertile-ground -goshen-indiana.

The Old Bag Factory. 2011. "Chase Bag Factory 1910–1982." The Old Bag Factory—History. Accessed October 6, 2015. http://www.oldbagfactory.com/our_history.html.

Olsen, Frederick L. 2011. *The Kiln Book*. Philadelphia: University of Pennsylvania Press.

The Onion. 2001. "Lone Smart Aleck Ruins RV Hall of Fame for Serious Visitors." The Onion—Local News. Accessed July 28, 2018. https://local.theonion.com/lone-smart -aleck-ruins-rv-hall-of-fame-for-serious-visi-1819566227.

Petry, Ashley. 2012. "Artists Find a Home in Goshen." *Indy Star*. Last modified July 25, 2012. http://www.indystar.com/story/life/2015/07/25/travel-goshen/30663241/.

Pomian, Krzysztof. 1994. "The Collection: Between the Visible and the Invisible." In *Interpreting Objects and Collections*, edited by Susan M. Pearce, 160–74. London: Routledge.

Purdue University Libraries, Archives and Special Collections. 2012. "Fry, Laura A. (1857–1943)." Accessed September 15, 2015. http://www4.lib.purdue.edu/archon /?p=creators/creator&id=209.

Redekop, Calvin, Stephen C. Ainlay, and Robert Siemens. 1995. *Mennonite Entrepreneurs*. Baltimore: The Johns Hopkins University Press.

Roberts, Warren E. 1996. *Log Buildings of Southern Indiana*. Bloomington: Trickster.

Rogers, Phil. 2003. *Ash Glazes*. Philadelphia: University of Pennsylvania Press.

Rothshank, Justin. 2012. "Trading Experiences." *Ceramics Monthly*, April 2012.

———. 2014. "Studio Visit: Justin Rothshank, Goshen, Indiana." *Ceramics Monthly*, May 2014.

Rothshank, Justin, and Brad Stephenson. 2007. "Union Project." *Ceramics Monthly*, May 2007.

Rudolph, L. C. 1995. *Hoosier Faiths: A History of Indiana's Churches and Religious Groups*. Bloomington: Indiana University Press.

Schwartz, Brandon. 2015. "Michiana Pottery Tour Info?" *Email to Meredith McGriff*. October 1, 2015.

Shukla, Pravina. 2008. *The Grace of Four Moons: Dress, Adornment, and the Art of the Body in Modern India*. Bloomington: Indiana University Press.

Sklar, Deidre. 1994. "Can Bodylore be Brought to Its Senses?" *The Journal of American Folklore* 107 (423): 9–22.

Smith, Melanie. 2009. *Issues in Cultural Tourism Studies*. New York: Routledge.

St. Joseph County Chamber of Commerce. n.d. "Communities in St. Joseph County." Accessed September 2, 2015. http://www.sjchamber.org/live/communities-in -st.-joseph-coounty/.

Sweezy, Nancy. 1994. *Raised in Clay: The Southern Pottery Tradition*. Chapel Hill: University of North Carolina Press.

Tangherlini, Timothy C. 1998. *Talking Trauma: Paramedics and Their Stories*. Jackson: University Press of Mississippi.

Traditional Arts Indiana. n.d. "What Is Traditional Arts Indiana?" Accessed August 31, 2015. http://www.traditionalartsindiana.org/about/what-is-traditional-arts-indiana/.

Trimble, Stanley W. 2010. "Recognizing Nature's Bequest." In *The Making of the American Landscape*, edited by Michael P. Conzen, 11–31. New York: Routledge.

Troy, Jack. 1995. *Wood-Fired Stoneware and Porcelain*. Radnor, PA: Chilton Book Company.

Turner, Victor. [1969] 1997. *The Ritual Process: Structure and Anti-Structure*. Chicago: Aldine.

United States Census Bureau. 2010. "Profile of General Population and Housing Characteristics." Accessed August 26, 2015. http://factfinder.census.gov/.

———. 2013. "Children Characteristics: 2009–2013 American Community Survey 5-Year Estimates." Accessed August 26, 2015. http://factfinder.census.gov/.

———. n.d. "Does the Census Bureau Have Data for Religion?" Accessed November 5, 2015. https://ask.census.gov/faq.php?id=5000&faqId=29.

United States Department of Agriculture. n.d. "National Agriculture Statistics Service: 2014 State Agricultural Overview, Indiana." Accessed September 2, 2015. http://www.nass.usda.gov/Quick_Stats/Ag_Overview/stateOverview.php?state=INDIANA.

van Gennep, Arnold. [1909] 1960. *The Rites of Passage*. Translated by Monika B. Vizedom and Gabrielle L. Caffee. Chicago: University of Chicago Press.

Vlatch, John Michael. 1992. *Charleston Blacksmith: The Work of Philip Simmons*. Columbia: University of South Carolina Press.

Watson, Carolisa. 2016. "Viki Graber—Willow Basketmaker." In *Indiana Folk Arts: 200 Years of Tradition and Innovation*, edited by Jon Kay, 50–51. Bloomington, IN: Traditional Arts Indiana.

Wilson, William A. 2006. "Herder, Folklore, and Romantic Nationalism." In *The Marrow of Human Experience: Essays on Folklore by William A. Wilson*, edited by Jill Terry Rudy and Diane Call. Logan, UT: University Press of Colorado.

Worster, Donald. 1993. "The Natural Environment: The North." In *Encyclopedia of American Social History, Vol. 2*, edited by Mary Kupiec Cayton, Elliot J. Gorn, and Peter W. Williams, 1145–52. New York: Charles Scribner's Sons.

Xygalatas, Dimitris. 2014. "Trial by Fire: From Fire-walking to the Ice-bucket Challenge, Ritual Pain and Suffering Forge Intense Social Bonds." *Aeon*. Accessed January 15, 2016. https://aeon.co/essays/how-extreme-rituals-forge-intense-social-bonds.

Yanagi, Sōetsu. [1972] 2013. *The Unknown Craftsman: A Japanese Insight into Beauty*. Adapted by Bernard Leach. New York: Kodansha USA.

Zug, Charles G. 1986. *Turners and Burners: The Folk Potters of North Carolina*. Chapel Hill: University of North Carolina Press.

INDEX

workshops (educational events), 57, 81, 93,
107, 214, 220, 221; attending, 87, 92, 108;
teaching, 72, 74, 76, 84, 93, 95n17, 205,
209, 244
workshops (work spaces), 122, 209. *See also*
ateliers *and specific potters and studios*

Yanagi Soetsu, 105, 106–7, 180

Zug, Charles, 13, 105–6, 172–73

MEREDITH A. E. McGRIFF is Membership Director of the American Folklore Society and cofounder of Hoosier Films.